CEOE
Field 04
OSAT
Chemistry
Teacher Certification Exam

By: Sharon Wynne, M.S
Southern Connecticut State University

XAMonline, INC.
Boston

Copyright © 2007 XAMonline, Inc.
All rights reserved. No part of the material protected by this copyright notice may be reproduced or utilized in any form or by any means, electronic or mechanical, including photocopying, recording or by any information storage and retrievable system, without written permission from the copyright holder.

To obtain permission(s) to use the material from this work for any purpose including workshops or seminars, please submit a written request to:

> XAMonline, Inc.
> 21 Orient Ave.
> Melrose, MA 02176
> Toll Free 1-800-301-4647
> Email: info@xamonline.com
> Web www.xamonline.com
> Fax: 1-781-662-9268

Library of Congress Cataloging-in-Publication Data

Wynne, Sharon A.
  OSAT Chemistry Field 04: Teacher Certification / Sharon A. Wynne. -2nd ed.
  ISBN 978-1-58197-776-9
    1. OSAT Chemistry Field 04.   2. Study Guides.   3. CEOE
    4. Teachers' Certification & Licensure.   5. Careers

Disclaimer:
The opinions expressed in this publication are the sole works of XAMonline and were created independently from the National Education Association, Educational Testing Service, or any State Department of Education, National Evaluation Systems or other testing affiliates.

Between the time of publication and printing, state specific standards as well as testing formats and website information may change that is not included in part or in whole within this product. Sample test questions are developed by XAMonline and reflect similar content as on real tests; however, they are not former tests. XAMonline assembles content that aligns with state standards but makes no claims nor guarantees teacher candidates a passing score. Numerical scores are determined by testing companies such as NES or ETS and then are compared with individual state standards. A passing score varies from state to state.

Printed in the United States of America

CEOE: OSAT Chemistry Field 04
ISBN: 978-1-58197-776-9

TEACHER CERTIFICATION EXAM

ABOUT THE OSAT CHEMISTRY TEST (FIELD CODE 04)

The Oklahoma Subject Area Test (OSAT™) in Chemistry (field code 04) is designed to assess subject matter knowledge and skills required of entry-level Chemistry teachers in Oklahoma. It is a component of the Certification Examinations for Oklahoma Educators (CEOE™) program, the purpose of which is to help the state meet its goal of ensuring that all candidates seeking certification in Oklahoma have the general education knowledge, professional knowledge, and subject matter knowledge necessary to perform the job of an entry-level educator in Oklahoma schools. In addition to the OSAT, individuals seeking an initial Oklahoma license must also pass the Oklahoma General Education Test (OGET™) and the appropriate Oklahoma Professional Teaching Examination (OPTE™). For more information on which tests are required, see the current version of the CEOE Registration Bulletin.

All OSATs are criterion referenced; that is, each test is designed to measure an examinee's knowledge in relation to an established standard of competence (criterion) rather than in relation to the performance of other examinees on the test. The minimum passing score for each OSAT is based on the professional judgments and recommendations of Oklahoma educators and is established by the Oklahoma Commission for Teacher Preparation.

Test competencies are organized into groups known as subareas. The subareas define the major content areas of the test. **A list of subareas and competencies are found in the Table of Contents for this guide.** The number of competencies within each subarea typically reflects the emphasis given to that subarea on the test. In general, subareas with greater numbers of competencies will receive more coverage on the test.

Each test includes a section of selected-response (multiple-choice) questions. Each selected-response question has four response options. For these sections, you will indicate answers on an electronically scored answer sheet. Your score on the selected-response question section is based on the total number of selected-response questions you answer correctly.

The Chemistry OSAT also includes one constructed-response assignment, which requires an extended written response. In your response to the assignment, you are expected to demonstrate the depth of your understanding of Chemistry through your ability to apply your knowledge and skills rather than merely to recite factual information. **The constructed-response assignment will be based specifically on the competencies in Subarea I–Foundations of Scientific Inquiry.**

CHEMISTRY

TEACHER CERTIFICATION EXAM

Each test session is four hours in length. All examinees will be provided with a scientific calculator with functions that include the following: addition, subtraction, multiplication, division, square root, percent, sine, cosine, tangent, exponents, and logarithms. Please see the current CEOE Registration Bulletin for information regarding the brand and model of calculator that will be supplied. **You may not bring your own calculator to the test.**

CHEMISTRY

TEACHER CERTIFICATION EXAM

Table of Contents

Study and Testing Tips vi

Periodic Table of the Elements x

SUBAREA I—FOUNDATIONS OF SCIENTIFIC INQUIRY 1

Competency 0001: Understand the relationships and common themes that connect mathematics, science, and technology... 1

Competency 0002: Understand the historical and contemporary contexts of the study of chemistry... 2

Competency 0003: Understand the process of scientific inquiry and the role of observation and experimentation in explaining natural phenomena 9

Competency 0004: Understand principles of measurement and the process of gathering, organizing, reporting, and interpreting scientific data 14

Competency 0005: Understand equipment, materials, and chemicals used in chemistry investigations; and apply procedures for their proper, safe, and legal use 25

SUBAREA II—MATTER AND ATOMIC STRUCTURE 44

Competency 0006: Understand the concept of matter, and analyze chemical and physical properties of and changes in matter.. 44

Competency 0007: Understand the various models of atomic structure, the principles of quantum theory, and the properties and interactions of subatomic particles 49

Competency 0008: Understand the organization of the periodic table................ 57

Competency 0009: Understand the kinetic molecular theory, the nature of phase changes, and the gas laws 61

Competency 0010: Understand the process of nuclear transformation 65

Competency 0011: Understand the principles of thermodynamics and calorimetry. 69

Competency 0012: Understand energy relationships in chemical bonding and chemical reactions 79

CHEMISTRY

Competency 0013: Understand the types of bonds between atoms (including ionic, covalent, and metallic bonds), the formation of these bonds, and properties of substances containing the different bonds 81

Competency 0014: Understand types and characteristics of molecular interaction and properties of substances containing different types of interactive forces between molecules. 95

Competency 0015: Understand the nomenclature and structure of organic compounds 98

SUBAREA IV—CHEMICAL REACTIONS 113

Competency 0016: Understand factors that affect reaction rates and methods of measuring reaction rates 113

Competency 0017: Understand the principles of chemical equilibrium 121

Competency 0018: Understand the theories, principles, and applications of acid-base chemistry 125

Competency 0019: Understand redox reactions and electrochemistry 135

Competency 0020: Understand the nature of organic reactions 138

SUBAREA V—QUANTITATIVE RELATIONSHIPS 141

Competency 0021: Understand the mole concept 141

Competency 0022: Understand the relationship between the mole concept and chemical formulas 142

Competency 0023: Understand the quantitative relationships expressed in chemical equations 145

Competency 0024: Understand the properties of solutions and colloidal suspensions, and analyze factors that affect solubility 149

SUBAREA VI—INTERACTIONS OF CHEMISTRY AND THE ENVIRONMENT 154

Competency 0025: Understand industrial and household chemistry 154

Competency 0026: Understand the uses and hazards of nuclear reactions 156

CHEMISTRY

TEACHER CERTIFICATION EXAM

Competency 0027: Understand factors and processes related to the release of chemicals into the environment 158

Sample Selected-Response Questions 160
Answer Key 185
Answers with Solutions 186
Sample Constructed-Response Question 252
Sample Constructed-Response Answer 253

TEACHER CERTIFICATION EXAM

Great Study and Testing Tips!

What to study in order to prepare for the subject assessments is the focus of this study guide but equally important is *how* you study.

You can increase your chances of truly mastering the information by taking some simple, but effective steps.

Study Tips:

1. Some foods aid the learning process. Foods such as milk, nuts, seeds, rice, and oats help your study efforts by releasing natural memory enhancers called CCKs (*cholecystokinin*) composed of *tryptophan*, *choline*, and *phenylalanine*. All of these chemicals enhance the neurotransmitters associated with memory. Before studying, try a light, protein-rich meal of eggs, turkey, and fish. All of these foods release the memory enhancing chemicals. The better the connections, the more you comprehend.

Likewise, before you take a test, stick to a light snack of energy boosting and relaxing foods. A glass of milk, a piece of fruit, or some peanuts all release various memory-boosting chemicals and help you to relax and focus on the subject at hand.

2. Learn to take great notes. A by-product of our modern culture is that we have grown accustomed to getting our information in short doses (i.e. TV news sound bites or USA Today style newspaper articles.)

Consequently, we've subconsciously trained ourselves to assimilate information better in neat little packages. If your notes are scrawled all over the paper, it fragments the flow of the information. Strive for clarity. Newspapers use a standard format to achieve clarity. Your notes can be much clearer through use of proper formatting. A very effective format is called the *"Cornell Method."*

> Take a sheet of loose-leaf lined notebook paper and draw a line all the way down the paper about 1-2" from the left-hand edge.
>
> Draw another line across the width of the paper about 1-2" up from the bottom. Repeat this process on the reverse side of the page.

Look at the highly effective result. You have ample room for notes, a left hand margin for special emphasis items or inserting supplementary data from the textbook, a large area at the bottom for a brief summary, and a little rectangular space for just about anything you want.

3. Get the concept then the details. Too often we focus on the details and don't gather an understanding of the concept. However, if you simply memorize only dates, places, or names, you may well miss the whole point of the subject.

A key way to understand things is to put them in your own words. If you are working from a textbook, automatically summarize each paragraph in your mind. If you are outlining text, don't simply copy the author's words.

Rephrase them in your own words. You remember your own thoughts and words much better than someone else's, and subconsciously tend to associate the important details to the core concepts.

4. Ask Why? Pull apart written material paragraph by paragraph and don't forget the captions under the illustrations.

Example: If the heading is "Stream Erosion", flip it around to read "Why do streams erode?" Then answer the questions.

If you train your mind to think in a series of questions and answers, not only will you learn more, but it also helps to lessen the test anxiety because you are used to answering questions.

5. Read for reinforcement and future needs. Even if you only have 10 minutes, put your notes or a book in your hand. Your mind is similar to a computer; you have to input data in order to have it processed. *By reading, you are creating the neural connections for future retrieval.* The more times you read something, the more you reinforce the learning of ideas.

Even if you don't fully understand something on the first pass, *your mind stores much of the material for later recall.*

6. Relax to learn so go into exile. Our bodies respond to an inner clock called biorhythms. Burning the midnight oil works well for some people, but not everyone.

If possible, set aside a particular place to study that is free of distractions. Shut off the television, cell phone, pager and exile your friends and family during your study period.

If you really are bothered by silence, try background music. Light classical music at a low volume has been shown to aid in concentration over other types. Music that evokes pleasant emotions without lyrics are highly suggested. Try just about anything by Mozart. It relaxes you.

CHEMISTRY

7. Use arrows not highlighters. At best, it's difficult to read a page full of yellow, pink, blue, and green streaks. Try staring at a neon sign for a while and you'll soon see that the horde of colors obscure the message.

A quick note, a brief dash of color, an underline, and an arrow pointing to a particular passage is much clearer than a horde of highlighted words.

8. Budget your study time. Although you shouldn't ignore any of the material, *allocate your available study time in the same ratio that topics may appear on the test.*

TEACHER CERTIFICATION EXAM

Testing Tips:

1. **Get smart, play dumb.** **Don't read anything into the question.** Don't make an assumption that the test writer is looking for something else than what is asked. Stick to the question as written and don't read extra things into it.

2. **Read the question and all the choices *twice* before answering the question.** You may miss something by not carefully reading, and then re-reading both the question and the answers.

If you really don't have a clue as to the right answer, leave it blank on the first time through. Go on to the other questions, as they may provide a clue as to how to answer the skipped questions.

If later on, you still can't answer the skipped ones . . . ***Guess.*** The only penalty for guessing is that you *might* get it wrong. Only one thing is certain; if you don't put anything down, you will get it wrong!

3. **Turn the question into a statement.** Look at the way the questions are worded. The syntax of the question usually provides a clue. Does it seem more familiar as a statement rather than as a question? Does it sound strange?

By turning a question into a statement, you may be able to spot if an answer sounds right, and it may also trigger memories of material you have read.

4. **Look for hidden clues.** It's actually very difficult to compose multiple-foil (choice) questions without giving away part of the answer in the options presented.

In most multiple-choice questions you can often readily eliminate one or two of the potential answers. This leaves you with only two real possibilities and automatically your odds go to Fifty-Fifty for very little work.

5. **Trust your instincts.** For every fact that you have read, you subconsciously retain something of that knowledge. On questions that you aren't really certain about, go with your basic instincts. **Your first impression on how to answer a question is usually correct.**

6. **Mark your answers directly on the test booklet.** Don't bother trying to fill in the optical scan sheet on the first pass through the test.
Just be very careful not to mis-mark your answers when you eventually transcribe them to the scan sheet.

7. **Watch the clock!** You have a set amount of time to answer the questions. Don't get bogged down trying to answer a single question at the expense of 10 questions you can more readily answer.

Periodic Table of the Elements

Group	1 IA	2 IIA	3 IIIB	4 IVB	5 VB	6 VIB	7 VIIB	8 VIIIB	9 VIIIB	10 VIIIB	11 IB	12 IIB	13 IIIA	14 IVA	15 VA	16 VIA	17 VIIA	18 VIIIA
Period 1	hydrogen 1 **H** 1.0079																	helium 2 **He** 4.002
2	lithium 3 **Li** 6.941	beryllium 4 **Be** 9.0122											boron 5 **B** 10.811	carbon 6 **C** 12.011	nitrogen 7 **N** 14.007	oxygen 8 **O** 15.999	fluorine 9 **F** 18.998	neon 10 **Ne** 20.18
3	sodium 11 **Na** 22.990	magnesium 12 **Mg** 24.305											aluminum 13 **Al** 26.982	silicon 14 **Si** 28.086	phosphorus 15 **P** 30.974	sulfur 16 **S** 32.065	chlorine 17 **Cl** 35.453	argon 18 **Ar** 39.94
4	potassium 19 **K** 39.098	calcium 20 **Ca** 40.078	scandium 21 **Sc** 44.956	titanium 22 **Ti** 47.867	vanadium 23 **V** 50.942	chromium 24 **Cr** 51.996	manganese 25 **Mn** 54.938	iron 26 **Fe** 55.845	cobalt 27 **Co** 58.933	nickel 28 **Ni** 58.693	copper 29 **Cu** 63.546	zinc 30 **Zn** 65.409	gallium 31 **Ga** 69.723	germanium 32 **Ge** 72.64	arsenic 33 **As** 74.922	selenium 34 **Se** 78.96	bromine 35 **Br** 79.904	krypton 36 **Kr** 83.79
5	rubidium 37 **Rb** 85.468	strontium 38 **Sr** 87.62	yttrium 39 **Y** 88.906	zirconium 40 **Zr** 91.224	niobium 41 **Nb** 92.906	molybdenum 42 **Mo** 95.94	technetium 43 **Tc** [98]	ruthenium 44 **Ru** 101.07	rhodium 45 **Rh** 102.91	palladium 46 **Pd** 106.42	silver 47 **Ag** 107.87	cadmium 48 **Cd** 112.41	indium 49 **In** 114.82	tin 50 **Sn** 118.71	antimony 51 **Sb** 121.76	tellurium 52 **Te** 127.60	iodine 53 **I** 126.90	xenon 54 **Xe** 131.29
6	cesium 55 **Cs** 132.91	barium 56 **Ba** 137.33	57-71 *	hafnium 72 **Hf** 178.49	tantalum 73 **Ta** 180.95	tungsten 74 **W** 183.84	rhenium 75 **Re** 186.21	osmium 76 **Os** 190.23	iridium 77 **Ir** 192.22	platinum 78 **Pt** 195.08	gold 79 **Au** 196.97	mercury 80 **Hg** 200.59	thallium 81 **Tl** 204.38	lead 82 **Pb** 207.2	bismuth 83 **Bi** 208.98	polonium 84 **Po** [209]	astatine 85 **At** [210]	radon 86 **Rn** [222]
7	francium 87 **Fr** [223]	radium 88 **Ra** [226]	89-103 **	rutherfordium 104 **Rf** [261]	dubnium 105 **Db** [262]	seaborgium 106 **Sg** [266]	bohrium 107 **Bh** [264]	hassium 108 **Hs** [277]	meitnerium 109 **Mt** [268]	darmstadtium 110 **Ds** [271]	roentgenium 111 **Rg** [272]							

*Lanthanoids

| lanthanum 57 **La** 138.91 | cerium 58 **Ce** 140.12 | praseodymium 59 **Pr** 140.91 | neodymium 60 **Nd** 144.24 | promethium 61 **Pm** [145] | samarium 62 **Sm** 150.36 | europium 63 **Eu** 151.96 | gadolinium 64 **Gd** 157.25 | terbium 65 **Tb** 158.93 | dysprosium 66 **Dy** 162.50 | holmium 67 **Ho** 164.93 | erbium 68 **Er** 167.26 | thulium 69 **Tm** 168.93 | ytterbium 70 **Yb** 173.04 | lutetium 71 **Lu** 174.97 |

**Actinoids

| actinium 89 **Ac** [227] | thorium 90 **Th** 232.04 | protactinium 91 **Pa** 231.04 | uranium 92 **U** 238.03 | neptunium 93 **Np** [244] | plutonium 94 **Pu** [244] | americium 95 **Am** [243] | curium 96 **Cm** [247] | berkelium 97 **Bk** [247] | californium 98 **Cf** [251] | einsteinium 99 **Es** [252] | fermium 100 **Fm** [257] | mendelevium 101 **Md** [258] | nobelium 102 **No** [259] | lawrencium 103 **Lr** [262] |

Atomic mass values from IUPAC review (2001): http://www.iupac.org/reports/periodic_table/

TEACHER CERTIFICATION EXAM

SUBAREA I - FOUNDATIONS OF SCIENTIFIC INQUIRY

Competency 0001: Understand the relationships and common themes that connect mathematics, science, and technology.

The union of science, technology, and mathematics has shaped the world we live in today. Science describes the world. It attempts to explain how nature works; from our own bodies to the tiny particles making up the world, from the entire earth to the worlds beyond. Science lets us know in advance what will happen when a cell splits or when two chemicals react. Science is ever-changing. Throughout history, people have developed and validated many different ideas about the flow of the universe. Changing explanations as technology develops allows for new information to emerge.

Technology is the use of scientific knowledge to solve problems. For example, science studies the flow of electrons but technology takes the flow of electrons to create a supercomputer. Mathematics, in turn provides the language to allow this knowledge to be communicated. It creates models for science to use to explain natural phenomena.

The economy is dependent upon the existence of technology. The job market changes as new technologies develop. For example, with the advent of computer technologies, many trained workers are needed, moving our economy from the post-war production line economy to a knowledge-economy based on information technology. This economy is driven by start-ups and entrepreneurs looking for innovation but not radical breakthroughs. It relies on sources of capitol from venture capitalists, IPOs and investors. It is also forcing a new kind of research to occur. Industrial labs are being redefined or eliminated, creating a convergence between scientific disciplines and engineering, providing for new entrepreneur opportunities.

At the same time, advances in scientific knowledge and technology often present ethical dilemmas for society. Industrialization brought the consumption of great amounts of energy, for example. This in turned creates environmental problems, leads to wars, and a depletion of natural resources. Scientific knowledge tells us there is oil is shale that we have not accessed yet. Technology developments will allow us to reach the oil and power our economy. At the same time, new technologies will emerge providing for alternative power supplies like wind farms or soy fuels. New types of skills will be needed to support these new technologies and the job market; education and our society will shift in response.

The need for technology development drives science, and discoveries in science drive society. Arguably, the first personal computers were mass-marketed by IBM and Apple in the late 1970's. The IBM 5100 had 16K of memory, a five inch screen, and cost nearly $11,000 in 1975! A mere twenty-five years later, computers are everywhere and used for everything.

They have gigabytes of memory and monitors larger than some televisions! Why did computers develop so quickly? The interconnection between science, mathematics, technology, and society.

Competency 0002: Understand the historical and contemporary contexts of the study of chemistry.

Development of Modern Chemistry

Chemistry emerged from two ancient roots: craft traditions and philosophy. The oldest ceramic crafts (i.e., pottery) known are from roughly 10000 BC in Japan. Metallurgical crafts in Eurasia and Africa began to develop by trial and error around 4000-2500 BC resulting in the production of copper, bronze, iron, and steel tools. Other craft traditions in brewing, tanning, and dyeing led to many useful empirical ways to manipulate matter.

Ancient philosophers in Greece, India, China, and Japan speculated that all matter was composed of four or five elements. The Greeks thought that these were: fire, air, earth, and water. Indian philosophers and the Greek Aristotle also thought a fifth element—"aether" or "quintessence"—filled all of empty space. The Greek philosopher Democritus thought that matter was composed of indivisible and indestructible atoms. These concepts are now known as classical elements and classical atomic theory.

Before the emergence of the scientific method, attempts to understand matter relied on alchemy: a mixture of mysticism, best guesses, and supernatural explanations. Goals of alchemy were the transmutation of other metals into gold and the synthesis of an elixir to cure all diseases. Ancient Egyptian alchemists developed cement and glass. Chinese alchemists developed gunpowder in the 800s AD.

During the height of European alchemy in the 1300s, the philosopher William of Occam proposed the idea that when trying to explain a process or develop a theory, the simplest explanation with the fewest variables is best. This is known as Occam's Razor. European alchemy slowly developed into modern chemistry during the 1600s and 1700s. This began to occur after Francis Bacon and René Descartes described the scientific method in the early 1600s.

Robert Boyle was educated in alchemy in the mid-1600s, but he published a book called *The Skeptical Chemist* that attacked alchemy and advocated using the scientific method. He is sometimes called the founder of modern chemistry because of his emphasis on proving a theory before accepting it, but the birth of modern chemistry is usually attributed to Lavoisier. Boyle rejected the 4 classical elements and proposed the modern definition of an element. Boyle's law states that gas volume is proportional to the reciprocal of pressure.

Blaise Pascal in the mid-1600s determined the relationship between pressure and the height of a liquid in a barometer. He also helped to establish the scientific method. The SI unit of pressure is named after him.

Isaac Newton studied the nature of light, the laws of gravity, and the laws of motion around 1700. The SI unit of force is named after him.

Daniel Bernoulli proposed the kinetic molecular theory for gases in the early 1700s to explain the nature of heat and Boyle's Law. At that time, heat was thought to be related to the release of a substance called *phlogiston* from combustible material.

James Watt created an efficient steam engine in the 1760s-1780s. Later chemists and physicists would develop the theory behind this empirical engineering accomplishment. The SI unit of power is named after him.

Joseph Priestley studied various gases in the 1770s. He was the first to produce and drink carbonated water, and he was the first to isolate oxygen from air. Priestley thought oxygen was air with its normal phlogiston removed so it could burn more fuel and accept more phlogiston than natural air.

Antoine Lavoisier is called the father of modern chemistry because he performed quantitative, controlled experiments. He carefully weighed material before and after combustion to determine that burning objects gain weight. Lavoisier formulated the rule that chemical reactions do not alter total mass after finding that reactions in a closed container do not change weight. This disproved the plogiston theory, and he named Priestley's substance oxygen. He demonstrated that air and water were not elements. He defined an element as a substance that could not be broken down further. He published the first modern chemistry textbook, *Elementary Treatise of Chemistry*. Lavoisier was executed in the Reign of Terror at the height of the French Revolution.

Additional Gas Laws in the 1700s and 1800s
These contributions built on the foundation developed by Boyle in the 1600s.

Jacque Charles developed Charles's law in the late 1700s. This states that gas volume is proportional to absolute temperature.

William Henry developed the law stating that gas solubility in a liquid is proportional to the pressure of gas over the liquid. This is known as Henry's Law

Joseph Louis Gay-Lussac developed the gas law stating that gas pressure is directly proportional to absolute temperature. He also determined that 2 volumes of hydrogen react with one of oxygen to produce water and that other reactions occurred with similar simple ratios. These observations led him to develop the Law of Combining Volumes.

CHEMISTRY

Amedeo Avogadro developed the hypothesis that equal volumes of different gases contain an equal numbers of molecules if the gases are at the same temperature and pressure. The proportionality between volume and number of moles is called Avagadro's Law, and the number of molecules in a mole is called Avagadro's Number. Both were posthumously named in his honor.

Thomas Graham developed Graham's Law of effusion and diffusion in the 1830s. He is called the father of colloid chemistry.

Electricity and Magnetism in the 1700s and 1800s
Benjamin Franklin studied electricity in the mid-1700s. He developed the concept of positive and negative electrical charges. His most famous experiment showed that lightning is an electrical process.

Luigi Galvani discovered bioelectricity. In the late 1700s, he noticed that the legs of dead frogs twitched when they came into contact with an electrical source.

In the late 1700s, Charles Augustin Coulomb derived mathematical equations for attraction **and repulsion** between electrically charged objects.

Alessandro **Volta** built the first **battery** in 1800 permitting future research and applications to have a source of continuous electrical current available. The SI unit of electric potential difference is named after him.

André-Marie **Ampère** created a mathematical theory in the 1820s for magnetic fields and electric currents. The SI unit of electrical current is named after him.

Michael **Faraday** is best known for work in the 1820s and 1830s establishing that a moving magnetic field induces an electric potential. He built the first **dynamo** for electricity generation. He also discovered benzene, invented oxidation numbers, and popularized the terms *electrode*, *anode*, and *cathode*. The SI unit of electrical capacitance is named in his honor.

James Clerk **Maxwell** derived the **Maxwell Equations** in 1864. These expressions completely describe **electric and magnetic fields** and their interaction with matter. Also see Ludwig Boltzmann below for Maxwell's contribution to thermodynamics.

Nineteenth Century Chemistry: Caloric Theory and Thermodynamics
Lavoisier proposed in the late 18th century that the heat generated by combustion was due to a weightless material substance called **caloric** that flowed from one place to another and was never destroyed.

CHEMISTRY

In 1798, **Benjamin Thomson**, also known as **Count Rumford** measured the heat produced when cannon were bored underwater and concluded that caloric was not a conserved substance because heat could continue to be generated indefinitely by this process.

Sadi **Carnot** in the 1820s used caloric theory in developing theories for the **heat engine** to explain the engine already developed by Watt. Heat engines perform mechanical work by expanding and contracting a piston at two different temperatures.

In the 1820s, Robert **Brown** observed dust particles and particles in pollen grains moving in a random motion. This was later called **Brownian motion**.

Germain Henri **Hess** developed **Hess's Law** in 1840 after studying the heat required or emitted from reactions composed of several steps.

James Prescott **Joule** determined the equivalence of heat energy to mechanical work in the 1840s by carefully measuring the heat produced by friction. Joule attacked the caloric theory and played a major role in the acceptance of **kinetic molecular theory**. The SI unit of energy is named after him.

William Thomson, 1st Baron of Kelvin also called **Lord Kelvin** recognized the existence of **absolute temperature** in the 1840s and proposed the temperature scale named after him. He failed in an attempt to reconcile caloric theory with Joule's discovery and caloric theory began to fall out of favor.

Hermann von **Helmholtz** in the 1840s proposed that **energy is conserved** during physical and chemical processes, not heat as proposed in caloric theory

Rudolf **Clausius** in the 1860s introduced the concept of **entropy**.

In the 1870s, Ludwig **Boltzmann** generalized earlier work by Maxwell solving the **velocity or energy distribution among gas molecules**. The final diagram in shows the Maxwell-Boltzmann distribution for kinetic energy at two temperatures. Maxwell's contribution to electromagnetism is described above.

Johannes **van der Waals** in the 1870s was the first to consider **intermolecular attractive forces** in modeling the behavior of liquids and non-ideal gases.

Francois Marie **Raoult** studied colligative properties in the 1870s. He developed **Raoult's Law** relating solute and solvent mole fraction to vapor pressure lowering.

Jacobus **van't Hoff** was the first to fully describe **stereoisomerism** in the 1870s. He later studied **colligative properties** and the impact of temperature on equilibria.

Josiah Willard **Gibbs** studied thermodynamics and statistical mechanics in the 1870s. He formulated the concept now called **Gibbs free energy** that will determine whether or not a chemical process at constant pressure will spontaneously occur.

Henri Louis **Le Chatelier** described chemical **equilibrium** in the 1880s using **Le Chatelier's Principle**.

In the 1880s, Svante **Arrhenius** developed the idea of **activation energy.** He also described the dissociation of salts—including **acids and bases**—into ions. Before then, salts in solution were thought to exist as intact molecules and ions were mostly thought to exist as electrolysis products. Arrhenius also predicted that CO_2 emissions would lead to global warming .

In 1905, **Albert Einstein** created a **mathematical model of Brownian motion** based on the impact of water molecules on suspended particles. Kinetic molecular theory could now be observed under the microscope. Einstein's more famous later work in physics on **relativity** may be applied to chemistry by correlating the energy change of a chemical reaction with extremely small changes in the total mass of reactants and products.

Nineteenth and Twentieth Century: Atomic Theory
See Competency 0007 for the contributions to atomic theory of John **Dalton**, J. J. **Thomson,** Max **Planck,** Ernest **Rutherford,** Niels **Bohr,** Louis **de Broglie,** Werner **Heisenberg, and** Erwin **Schrödinger.**

Wolfgang **Pauli** helped to develop quantum mechanics in the 1920s by forming the concept of spin and the **exclusion principle**.

Friedrich **Hund** determined a set of **rules to determine the ground state** of a multi-electron atom in the 1920s. One particular rule is called **Hund's Rule** in introductory chemistry courses.

Discovery and Synthesis: Nineteenth Century:
Humphry **Davy** used Volta's battery in the early 1800s for **electrolysis of salt solutions**. He synthesized several pure elements using electrolysis to generate non-spontaneous reactions.

Jöns Jakob **Berzelius** isolated several elements, but he is best known for inventing modern **chemical notation** by using one or two letters to represent elements in the early 1800s.

Friedrich **Wöhler** isolated several elements, but he is best known for the chemical **synthesis of an organic compound** in 1828 using the carbon in silver cyanide. Before Wöhler, many had believed that a transcendent "life-force" was needed to make the molecules of life.

CHEMISTRY

Justus **von Liebig** studied the chemicals involved in agriculture in the 1840s. He has been called the **father of agricultural chemistry**.

Louis **Pasteur** studied **chirality** in the 1840s by separating a mixture of two chiral molecules. His greater contribution was in biology for discovering the germ theory of disease.

Henry **Bessemer** in the 1850s developed the **Bessemer Process** for mass producing steel by blowing air through molten iron to oxidize impurities.

Friedrich August **Kekulé** von Stradonitz studied the chemistry of carbon in the 1850s and 1860s. He proposed the **ring structure of benzene** and that carbon was tetravalent.

Anders Jonas **Ångström** was one of the founders of the science of spectroscopy. In the 1860s, he found hydrogen and other **elements in the spectrum of the sun**. A non-SI unit of length equal to 0.1 nm is named for him.

Alfred **Nobel** invented the explosive **dynamite** in the 1860s and continued to develop other explosives. In his will he used his fortune to establish the **Nobel Prizes**.

Dmitri **Mendeleev** developed the first modern **periodic table** in 1869.

Discovery and Synthesis: Turn of the 20th Century
William **Ramsay** and Lord **Rayleigh** (John William Strutt) isolated the **noble gases**.

Wilhelm Konrad **Röntgen** discovered **X-rays**.

Antoine Henri **Becquerel discovered radioactivity** using uranium salts.

Marie **Curie** named the property radioactivity and determined that it was **a property of atoms** that did not depend on which molecule contained the element.

Pierre and Marie **Curie** utilized the properties of radioactivity to **isolate radium** and other radioactive elements. Marie Curie was the first woman to receive a Nobel Prize and the first person to receive two. Her story continues to inspire. See http://nobelprize.org/physics/articles/curie/index.html for a biography.

Frederick **Soddy** and William **Ramsay** discovered that **radioactive decay can produce helium** (alpha particles).

Fritz **Haber** developed the **Haber Process** for synthesizing ammonia from hydrogen and nitrogen using an iron **catalyst**. Ammonia is still produced by this method to make fertilizers, textiles, and other products.

Robert Andrew **Millikan** determined the **charge of an electron** using an oil-drop experiment.

Discovery and Synthesis: 20th Century
Gilbert Newton **Lewis** described **covalent bonds** as sharing electrons in the 1910s and the **electron pair donor/acceptor theory of acids and bases** in the 1920s. Lewis dot structures and Lewis acids are named after him.

Johannes Nicolaus **Brønsted** and Thomas Martin **Lowry** simultaneously developed the **proton donor/acceptor theory of acids and bases** in the 1920s.

Irving **Langmuir** in the 1920s developed the science of **surface chemistry** to describe interactions at the interface of two phases. This field is important to heterogeneous catalysis .

Fritz **London** studied the electrical nature of chemical bonding in the 1920s. The weak intermolecular **London dispersion forces** are named after him.

Hans Wilhelm **Geiger** developed the **Geiger counter** for measuring ionizing radiation in the 1930s.

Wallace **Carothers** and his team first synthesized **organic polymers** (including neoprene, polyester and nylon) in the 1930s.

In the 1930s, Linus **Pauling** published his results on **the nature of the covalent bond.** Pauling electronegativity is named after him. In the 1950s, Pauling determined the α-helical structure of proteins.

Lise **Meitner** and Otto **Hahn** discovered **nuclear fission** in the 1930s.
Glenn Theodore **Seaborg** created and isolated several **elements larger than uranium** in the 1940s. Seaborg reorganized the periodic table to its current form.

James **Watson** and Francis **Crick** determined the double helix structure of DNA in the 1950s.

Neil **Bartlett** produced **compounds containing noble gases** in the 1960s, proving that they are not completely chemically inert.

Harold Kroto, Richard Smalley, and Robert Curl discovered the **buckyball C_{60}** in the 1980s.

CHEMISTRY

Competency 0003: Understand the process of scientific inquiry and the role of observation and experimentation in explaining natural phenomena.

Modern science began around the late 16th century with a new way of thinking about the world. Few scientists will disagree with Carl Sagan's assertion that "science is a way of thinking much more than it is a body of knowledge" (Broca's Brain, 1979). Thus science is a process of inquiry and investigation. It is a way of thinking and acting, not just a body of knowledge to be acquired by memorizing facts and principles. This way of thinking, the scientific method, is based on the idea that scientists begin their investigations with observations. From these observations they develop a hypothesis, which is extended in the form of a predication, and challenge the hypothesis through experimentation and thus further observations. Science has progressed in its understanding of nature through careful observation, a lively imagination, and increasing sophisticated instrumentation. Science is distinguished from other fields of study in that it provides guidelines or methods for conducting research, and the research findings must be reproducible by other scientists for those findings to be valid. It is important to recognize that scientific practice is not always this systematic. Discoveries have been made that are serendipitous and others have not started with the observation of data. Einstein's theory of relativity started not with the observation of data but with a kind of intellectual puzzle.

The Scientific method is just a logical set of steps that a scientist goes through to solve a problem. There are as many different scientific methods as there are scientists experimenting. However, there seems to be some pattern to their work.

While an inquiry may start at any point in this method and may not involve all of the steps here is the pattern:

Observations
Scientific questions result from observations of events in nature or events observed in the laboratory. An **observation** is not just a look at what happens. It also includes measurements and careful records of the event. Records could include photos, drawings, or written descriptions. The observations and data collection lead to a question. In chemistry, observations almost always deal with the behavior of matter. Having arrived at a question, a scientist usually researches the scientific literature to see what is known about the question. Maybe the question has already been answered. The scientist then may want to test the answer found in the literature. Or, maybe the research will lead to a new question.

Sometimes the same observations are made over and over again and are always the same. For example, you can observe that daylight lasts longer in summer than in winter. This observation never varies.

Such observations are called **laws** of nature. Probably the most important law in chemistry was discovered in the late 1700s. Chemists observed that no mass was ever lost or gained in chemical reactions. This law became known as the law of conservation of mass. Explaining this law was a major topic of chemistry in the early 19th century.

Hypothesis
If the question has not been answered, the scientist may prepare for an experiment by making a hypothesis. A **hypothesis** is a statement of a possible answer to the question. It is a tentative explanation for a set of facts and can be tested by experiments. Although hypotheses are usually based on observations, they may also be based on a sudden idea or intuition.

Experiment
An **experiment** tests the hypothesis to determine whether it may be a correct answer to the question or a solution to the problem. Some experiments may test the effect of one thing on another under controlled conditions. Such experiments have two variables. The experimenter controls one variable, callred the *independent variable*. The other variable, the *dependent variable*, is the change caused by changing the independent variable.

For example, suppose a researcher wanted to test the effect of vitamin A on the ability of rats to see in dim light. The independent variable would be the dose of Vitamin A added to the rats' diet. The dependent variable would be the intensity of light that causes the rats to react. All other factors, such as time, temperature, age, water given to the rats, the other nutrients given to the rats, and similar factors, are held constant. Chemists sometimes do short experiments "just to see what happens" or to see what products a certain reaction produces. Often, these are not formal experiments. Rather they are ways of making additional observations about the behavior of matter.

In most experiments, scientists collect quantitative data, which is data that can be measured with instruments. They also collect qualitative data, descriptive information from observations other than measurements. Interpreting data and analyzing observations are important. If data is not organized in a logical manner, wrong conclusions can be drawn. Also, other scientists may not be able to follow your work or repeat your results.

Conclusion
Finally, a scientist must draw conclusions from the experiment. A conclusion must address the hypothesis on which the experiment was based.

The conclusion states whether or not the data supports the hypothesis. If it does not, the conclusion should state what the experiment *did* show. If the hypothesis is not supported, the scientist uses the observations from the experiment to make a new or revised hypothesis., Then, new experiments are planned.

Theory
When a hypothesis survives many experimental tests to determine its validity, the hypothesis may evolve into a **theory**. A theory explains a body of facts and laws that are based on the facts. A theory also reliably predicts the outcome of related events in nature. For example, the law of conservation of matter and many other experimental observations led to a theory proposed early in the 19th century. This theory explained the conservation law by proposing that all matter is made up of atoms which are never created or destroyed in chemical reactions, only rearranged. This atomic theory also successfully predicted the behavior of matter in chemical reactions that had not been studied at the time. As a result, the atomic theory has stood for 200 years with only small modifications.

A theory also serves as a scientific **model**. A model can be a physical model made of wood or plastic, a computer program that simulates events in nature, or simply a mental picture of an idea. A model illustrates a theory and explains nature. In your chemistry course, you will develop a mental (and maybe a physical) model of the atom and its behavior. Outside of science, the word theory is often used to describe someone's unproven notion about something. In science, theory means much more. It is a thoroughly tested explanation of things and events observed in nature.

A theory can never be proven true, but it can be proven untrue. All it takes to prove a theory untrue is to show an exception to the theory. The test of the hypothesis may be observations of phenomena or a model may be built to examine its behavior under certain circumstances.

Steps of a Scientific Method

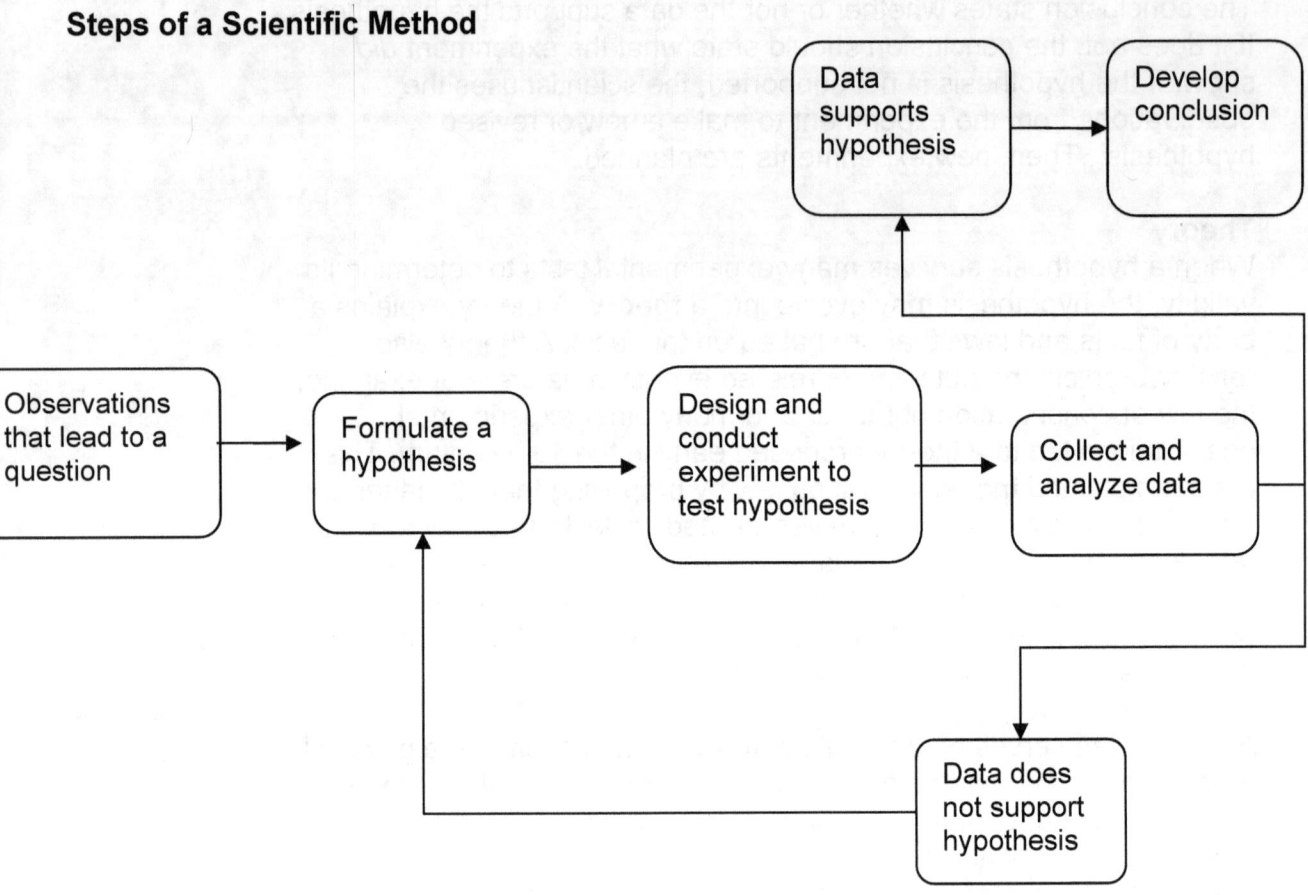

The design of chemical experiments must include every step to obtain the desired data. In other words, the design must be **complete** and it must include all required **controls**.

Complete design
Familiarity with individual experiments and equipment will help you evaluate if anything is missing from the design. For data requiring a difference between two values, the experiment **must determine both values**. For data utilizing the ideal gas law, the experiment **must determine three values of *P*, *V*, *n*, or *T*** in order to determine the fourth or one value and a ratio of the other two in order to determine the fourth.

Example: In a mercury manometer, the level of mercury in contact with a reaction vessel is 70.0 mm lower than the level exposed to the atmosphere. Use the following conversion factors:
$$760 \text{ mm Hg} = 1 \text{ atm} = 101.325 \text{ kPa}.$$
What additional information is required to determine the pressure in the vessel in kPa?

Solution: The barometric pressure is needed to determine vessel pressure from an open-ended manometer. A manometer reading is always a **difference** between two pressures. One standard atmosphere is 760 mm mercury, but on a given day at a given location, the actual ambient pressure may vary. If the barometric pressure on the day of the experiment is 104 kPa, the pressure of the vessel is:
$$104 \text{ kPa} + 70.0 \text{ mm Hg} \times \frac{101.325 \text{ kPa}}{760 \text{ mm Hg}} = 113 \text{ kPa}.$$

Controls

Experimental **controls** prevent factors other than those under study from impacting the outcome of the experiment. An **experimental sample** in a controlled experiment is the unknown to be compared against one or more **control samples**. These should be nearly identical to the experimental sample except for the one aspect whose effect is being tested.

A **negative control** is a control sample that is known to lack the effect. A **positive control** is known to contain the effect. Positive controls of varying strengths are often used to generate a **calibration curve** (also called a **standard curve**).

When determining the concentration of a component in a mixture, an **internal standard** is a known concentration of a different substance that is added to the experimental sample. An **external standard** is a known concentration of the substance of interest. External standards are more commonly used. They are not added to the experimental sample; they are analyzed separately.

Replicate samples decrease the impact of random error. A mean is taken of the results from replicate samples to obtain a best value. If one replicate is obviously inconsistent with the results from other samples, it may be discarded as an **outlier** and not counted as an observation when determining the mean. Discarding an outlier is equivalent to assuming the presence of a systematic error for that particular observation. In research, this must be done with great caution because some real-world behavior generates sporadically unusual results.

Example: A pure chemical in aqueous solution is known to absorb light at 615 nm. What controls would best be used with a spectrophotometer to determine the concentration of this chemical when it is present in a mixture with other solutes in an aqueous solution?

Solution: The other solutes may also absorb light at 615 nm. The best negative control would be an identical mixture with the chemical of interest entirely absent. Known concentrations of the chemical could then be added to the negative control to create positive controls (external standards) and develop a calibration curve of the spectrophotometer absorbance reading at 615 nm as a function of concentration. Replicate samples of each standard and of the unknown should be read.

Example: Ethanol is separated from a mixture of organic compounds by gas chromatography. The concentration of each component is proportional to its peak area. However, the chromatograph detector has a variable sensitivity from one run to the next. Is an internal standard required to determine the concentration of ethanol?

Solution: Yes. The variable detector sensitivity may only be accounted for by adding a known concentration of a chemical not found in the mixture as an internal standard to the experimental sample and control samples. The variable sensitivity of the detector will be accounted for by determining the ratio of the peak area for ethanol to the peak area of the added internal standard.

Competency 0004: Understand principles of measurement and the process of gathering, organizing, reporting, and interpreting scientific data.

Units are a part of every measurement. Without the units, the numbers could mean many things. For example, the distance 10 could mean 10 cm or 10 m or 10 km. The units are an important part of every measurement. The units will even help solve mathematical problems.

For example: The density of gold is 19.3 g/cm^3. How many grams of gold would be found in 55 cm^3?

Using dimensional analysis, some unit must cancel. The answer needs to be grams so the cm^3 needs to cancel out. Multiply or divide the units so that the cm^3 cancel. In this case

$$g/cm^3 \times cm^3 = g$$ so that is how to solve the problem.

19.3 g/cm^3 × 55 cm^3 = 1060 g of gold.

SI is an abbreviation of the French *Système International d'Unités* or the **International System of Units**. It is the most widely used system of units in the world and is the system used in science. The use of many SI units in the United States is increasing outside of science and technology. There are two types of SI units: **base units** and **derived units**. The base units are:

Quantity	Unit name	Symbol
Length	meter	m
Mass	kilogram	kg
Amount of substance	mole	mol
Time	second	s
Temperature	kelvin	K
Electric current	ampere	A
Luminous intensity	candela	cd

Amperes and candelas are rarely used in chemistry. The name "kilogram" occurs for the SI base unit of mass for historical reasons. Derived units are formed from the kilogram, but appropriate decimal prefixes are attached to the word "gram."

Derived units measure a quantity that may be **expressed in terms of other units**. The derived units important for chemistry are:

Derived quantity	Unit name	Expression in terms of other units	Symbol
Area	square meter	m^2	
Volume	cubic meter	m^3	
	liter	$dm^3 = 10^{-3}\ m^3$	L or l
Mass	unified atomic mass unit	$(6.022 \times 10^{23})^{-1}$ g	u or Da
Time	minute	60 s	min
	hour	60 min = 3600 s	h
	day	24 h = 86400 s	d
Speed	meter per second	m/s	
Acceleration	meter per second squared	m/s^2	
Temperature*	degree Celsius	K	°C
Mass density	gram per liter	$g/L = 1\ kg/m^3$	
Amount-of-substance concentration (molarity†)	molar	mol/L	M
Molality‡	molal	mol/kg	m
Chemical reaction rate	molar per second†	$M/s = mol/(L \cdot s)$	
Force	newton	$m \cdot kg/s^2$	N
Pressure	pascal	$N/m^2 = kg/(m \cdot s^2)$	Pa
	standard atmosphere§	101325 Pa	atm
Energy, Work, Heat	joule	$N \cdot m = m^3 \cdot Pa = m^2 \cdot kg/s^2$	J
	nutritional calorie§	4184 J	Cal
Heat (molar)	joule per mole	J/mol	
Heat capacity, entropy	joule per kelvin	J/K	
Heat capacity (molar), entropy (molar)	joule per mole kelvin	$J/(mol \cdot K)$	
Specific heat	joule per kilogram kelvin	$J/(kg \cdot K)$	
Power	watt	J/s	W
Electric charge	coulomb	$s \cdot A$	C
Electric potential, electromotive force	volt	W/A	V
Viscosity	pascal second	$Pa \cdot s$	
Surface tension	newton per meter	N/m	

*Temperature differences in kelvin are the same as those differences in degrees Celsius. To obtain degrees Celsius from Kelvin, subtract 273.15.
†Molarity is considered to be an obsolete unit by some physicists.
‡Molality, m, is often considered obsolete. Differentiate m and meters (m) by context.
§These are commonly used non-SI units.

CHEMISTRY

Decimal multiples of SI units are formed by attaching a **prefix** directly before the unit and a symbol prefix directly before the unit symbol. SI prefixes range from 10^{-24} to 10^{24}. Only the prefixes you are likely to encounter in chemistry are shown below:

Factor	Prefix	Symbol	Factor	Prefix	Symbol
10^9	giga—	G	10^{-1}	deci—	d
10^6	mega—	M	10^{-2}	centi—	c
10^3	kilo—	k	10^{-3}	milli—	m
10^2	hecto—	h	10^{-6}	micro—	µ
10^1	deca—	da	10^{-9}	nano—	n
			10^{-12}	pico—	p

Example: 0.0000004355 meters is 4.355×10^{-7} m or 435.5×10^{-9} m. This length is also 435.5 nm or 435.5 nanometers.

Example: Find a unit to express the volume of a cubic crystal that is 0.2 mm on each side so that the number before the unit is between 1 and 1000.

Solution: Volume is length X width X height, so this volume is $(0.0002 \text{ m})^3$ or 8×10^{-12} m^3. Conversions of volumes and areas using powers of units of length must take the power into account. Therefore:
$$1 \text{ m}^3 = 10^3 \text{ dm}^3 = 10^6 \text{ cm}^3 = 10^9 \text{ mm}^3 = 10^{18} \text{ µm}^3,$$
The length 0.0002 m is 2×10^2 µm, so the volume is also 8×10^6 µm^3. This volume could also be expressed as 8×10^{-3} mm^3, but none of these numbers are between 1 and 1000.

Expressing volume in liters is helpful in cases like these. There is no power on the unit of liters, therefore:
$$1 \text{ L} = 10^3 \text{ mL} = 10^6 \text{ µL} = 10^9 \text{ nL}.$$
Converting cubic meters to liters gives
$$8 \times 10^{-12} \text{ m}^3 \times \frac{10^3 \text{ L}}{1 \text{ m}^3} = 8 \times 10^{-9} \text{ L}.$$ The crystal's volume is 8 nanoliters (8 nL).

Example: Determine the ideal gas constant, R, in L•atm/(mol•K) from its SI value of 8.3144 J/(mol•K).

Solution: One joule is identical to one m^3•Pa (see the table on the previous page).
$$8.3144 \frac{\text{m}^3 \cdot \text{Pa}}{\text{mol} \cdot \text{K}} \times \frac{1000 \text{ L}}{1 \text{ m}^3} \times \frac{1 \text{ atm}}{101325 \text{ Pa}} = 0.082057 \frac{\text{L} \cdot \text{atm}}{\text{mol} \cdot \text{K}}$$

TEACHER CERTIFICATION EXAM

A measurement is **precise** when individual measurements of the same quantity **agree with one another**. A measurement is **accurate** when they **agree with the true value** of the quantity being measured. An **accurate** measurement is **valid**. We get the right answer. A **precise** measurement is **reproducible**. We get a similar answer each time. These terms are related to **sources of error** in a measurement.

Precise measurements are near the **arithmetic mean** of the values. The arithmetic mean is the sum of the measurements divided by the number of measurements. The **mean** is commonly called the **average**. It is the **best estimate** of the quantity.

Random error results from **limitations in equipment or techniques**. A larger **random error decreases precision**. Remember that all measurements reported to proper number of significant digits contain an imprecise final digit to reflect random error.

Systematic error results from **imperfect equipment or technique**. A larger **systematic error decreases accuracy**. Instead of a random error with random fluctuations, there is a result that is too large or small.

Example: An environmental engineering company creates a solution of 5.00 ng/L of a toxin and distributes it to four toxicology labs to test their protocols. Each lab tests the material 5 times. Their results are charted as points on the number lines below. Interpret this data in terms of precision, accuracy, and type of error.

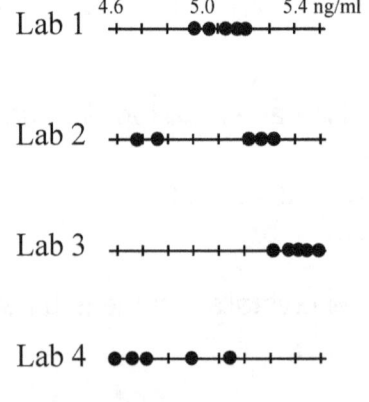

Solution: Results from lab 1 are both accurate and precise when compared to results from the other labs. Results from lab 2 are less precise than those from lab 1. Lab 2 seems to use a protocol that contains a greater random error. However, the mean result from lab 2 is still close to the known value. Lab 3 returned results that were about as precise as lab 1 but inaccurate compared to labs 1 and 2. Lab 3 most likely uses a protocol that yields a systematic error. The data from lab 4 is both imprecise and inaccurate. Systematic and random errors are larger than in lab 1.

Significant figures or **significant digits** are the digits indicating the **precision of a measurement**. There is uncertainty **only** in the last digit.

CHEMISTRY 18

Example: You measure an object with a ruler marked in millimeters. The reading on the ruler is found to be about 2/3 of the way between 12 and 13 mm. What value should be recorded for its length?

Solution: Recording 13 mm does not give all the information that you found.

Recording $12\frac{2}{3}$ mm implies that an exact ratio was determined.

Recording 12.666 mm gives more information than you found. A value of 12.7 mm or 12.6 mm should be recorded because there is uncertainty only in the last digit.

There are five rules for determining the **number of significant digits** in a quantity.

1) All nonzero digits are significant and all zeros between nonzero digits are significant.
    Example: 4.521 kJ and 7002 u both have four significant figures.
2) Zeros to the left of the first nonzero digit are not significant.
    Example: 0.0002 m contains one significant figure.
3) Zeros to the right of the decimal point are significant figures.
    Example: 32.500 g contains five significant figures.
4) The situation for numbers ending in zeros that are not to the right of the decimal point can be unclear, so **this situation should be avoided** by using scientific notation or a different decimal prefix. Sometimes a decimal point is used as a placeholder to indicate the units-digit is significant. A word like "thousand" or "million" may be used in informal contexts to indicate the remaining digits are not significant.
    Example: 12000 Pa would be considered to have five significant digits by many scientists, but in the context, "The pressure rose from 11000 Pa to 12000 Pa," it almost certainly only has two. "12 thousand pascal" only has two significant figures, but 12000. Pa has five because of the decimal point. The value should be represented as 1.2×10^4 Pa (or 1.2000×10^4 Pa). The best alternative would be to use 12 kPa or 12.000 kPa.
5) Exact numbers have no uncertainty and contain an infinite number of significant figures. These relationships are **definitions**. They are not measurements.
    Example: There are exactly 1000 L in one cubic meter.

There are four rules for **rounding off significant figures**.

1) If the leftmost digit to be removed is a four or less, then round down. The last remaining digit stays as it was. Example: Round 43.4 g to 2 significant figures. Answer: 43 g.
2) If the leftmost digit to be removed is a six or more, then round up. The last remaining digit increases by one. Example: Round 6.772 to 2 significant figures. Answer: 6.8 g.

3) If the leftmost digit to be removed is a five that is followed by nonzero digits, then round up. The last remaining digit increases by one. Example: Round 18.502 to 2 significant figures. Answer 19 g.
4) If the leftmost digit to be removed is a five followed by nothing or by only zeros, then force the last remaining digit to be even. If it is odd then round up by increasing it by one. If it is even (including zero) then it stays as it was. Examples: Round 18.50 g and 19.5 g to 2 significant figures. Answers: 18.50 g rounds off to 18 g and 19.5 g rounds off to 20 g.

There are three rules for **calculating with significant figures**.

1) For multiplication or division, the result has the same number of significant figures as the term with the least number of significant figures.
Example: What is the volume of a compartment in the shape of a rectangular prism 1.2 cm long, 2.4 cm high and 0.9 cm deep?
Solution: Volume=length x height x width.
Volume = 1.2 cm × 2.4 cm × 0.9 cm = 2.592 cm (as read on a calculator)
Round to one digit because 0.9 cm has only one significant digit.
Volume = 3 cm^3

2) For addition or subtraction, the result has the same number of digits after the decimal point as the term with the least number of digits after the decimal point.
Example: Volumes of 250.0 mL, 26 µL, and 4.73 mL are added to a flask. What is the total volume in the flask?
Solution: Only identical units may be added to each other, so 26 µL is first converted to 0.026 mL.
Volume = 250.0 mL + 0.026 mL + 4.73 mL = 254.756 mL (calculator value)
Round to one digit after the decimal because 250.0 mL has only one digit after the decimal. Volume = 254.8 mL.

3) For multi-step calculations, maintain all significant figures when using a calculator or computer and round off the final value to the appropriate number of significant figures after the calculation. When calculating by hand or when **writing down an intermediate value** in a multi-step calculation, maintain the first insignificant digit. In this text, insignificant digits in intermediate calculations are shown in italics except in the examples for the two rules above.

Galileo studied the behavior of falling bodies in the 1590's. Almost a century later, Newton followed up on his work and established calculus and physics which governed mechanics for centuries. From that point on, science was on a new pathway. No longer would it merely be the philosophy of the ancient Greeks. It would be a qualitative and quantitative discourse.

CHEMISTRY

TEACHER CERTIFICATION EXAM

Lavoisier made careful measurements in his conservation of mass experiments. Since then, data collection has become a central part of chemical investigations. Data collected, however, takes varied forms depending of the scientific field and complexity of the inquiry.

Data collected is initially organized into tables. Trends or patterns in data can be difficult to identify using tables of numbers. For example, here is a table of carbon dioxide concentrations taken over many years atop Mauna Loa Observatory in Hawaii.

Atmospheric CO_2 concentrations at Mauna Loa

Year	Jan.	Feb.	March	April	May	June	July	Aug.	Sept.	Oct.	Nov.	Dec.	Annual
1958	-99.99	-99.99	315.71	317.45	317.5	-99.99	315.86	314.93	313.19	-99.99	313.34	314.67	-99.99
1959	315.58	316.47	316.65	317.71	318.29	318.16	316.55	314.8	313.84	313.34	314.81	315.59	315.98
1960	316.43	316.97	317.58	319.03	320.03	319.59	318.18	315.91	314.16	313.83	315	316.19	316.91
1961	316.89	317.7	318.54	319.48	320.58	319.78	318.58	316.79	314.99	315.31	316.1	317.01	317.65
1962	317.94	318.56	319.69	320.58	321.01	320.61	319.61	317.4	316.26	315.42	316.69	317.69	318.45
1963	318.74	319.08	319.86	321.39	322.24	321.47	319.74	317.77	316.21	315.99	317.07	318.36	318.99
1964	319.57	-99.99	-99.99	-99.99	322.23	321.89	320.44	318.7	316.7	316.87	317.68	318.71	-99.99
1965	319.44	320.44	320.89	322.13	322.16	321.87	321.21	318.87	317.81	317.3	318.87	319.42	320.03
1966	320.62	321.59	322.39	323.7	324.07	323.75	322.4	320.37	318.64	318.1	319.79	321.03	321.37
1967	322.33	322.5	323.04	324.42	325	324.09	322.55	320.92	319.26	319.39	320.72	321.96	322.18
1968	322.57	323.15	323.89	325.02	325.57	325.36	324.14	322.11	320.33	320.25	321.32	322.9	323.05
1969	324	324.42	325.64	326.66	327.38	326.7	325.89	323.67	322.38	321.78	322.85	324.12	324.62
1970	325.06	325.98	326.93	328.13	328.07	327.66	326.35	324.69	323.1	323.07	324.01	325.13	325.68
1971	326.17	326.68	327.18	327.78	328.92	328.57	327.37	325.43	323.36	323.56	324.8	326.01	326.32
1972	326.77	327.63	327.75	329.72	330.07	329.09	328.05	326.32	324.84	325.2	326.5	327.55	327.46
1973	328.54	329.56	330.3	331.5	332.48	332.07	330.87	329.31	327.51	327.18	328.16	328.64	329.68
1974	329.35	330.71	331.48	332.65	333.09	332.25	331.18	329.4	327.44	327.37	328.46	329.58	330.25
1975	330.4	331.41	332.04	333.31	333.96	333.59	331.91	330.06	328.56	328.34	329.49	330.76	331.15
1976	331.74	332.56	333.5	334.58	334.87	334.34	333.05	330.94	329.3	328.94	330.31	331.68	332.15
1977	332.92	333.42	334.7	336.07	336.74	336.27	334.93	332.75	331.58	331.16	332.4	333.85	333.9
1978	334.97	335.39	336.64	337.76	338.01	337.89	336.54	334.68	332.76	332.54	333.92	334.95	335.5
1979	336.23	336.76	337.96	338.89	339.47	339.29	337.73	336.09	333.91	333.86	335.29	336.73	336.85
1980	338.01	338.36	340.08	340.77	341.46	341.17	339.56	337.6	335.88	336.01	337.1	338.21	338.69
1981	339.23	340.47	341.38	342.51	342.91	342.25	340.49	338.43	336.69	336.85	338.36	339.61	339.93
1982	340.75	341.61	342.7	343.56	344.13	343.35	342.06	339.82	337.97	337.86	339.26	340.49	341.13
1983	341.37	342.52	343.1	344.94	345.75	345.32	343.99	342.39	339.86	339.99	341.16	342.99	342.78
1984	343.7	344.51	345.28	347.08	347.43	346.79	345.4	343.28	341.07	341.35	342.98	344.22	344.42
1985	344.97	346	347.43	348.35	348.93	348.25	346.56	344.69	343.09	342.8	344.24	345.56	345.9
1986	346.29	346.96	347.86	349.55	350.21	349.54	347.94	345.91	344.86	344.17	345.66	346.9	347.15

Year	Jan	Feb	Mar	Apr	May	Jun	Jul	Aug	Sep	Oct	Nov	Dec
1987	348.02	348.47	349.42	350.99	351.84	351.25	349.52	348.1	346.44	346.36	347.81	348.96	348.93
1988	350.43	351.72	352.22	353.59	354.22	353.79	352.39	350.44	348.72	348.88	350.07	351.34	351.48
1989	352.76	353.07	353.68	355.42	355.67	355.13	353.9	351.67	349.8	349.99	351.3	352.53	352.91
1990	353.66	354.7	355.39	356.2	357.16	356.22	354.82	352.91	350.96	351.18	352.83	354.21	354.19
1991	354.72	355.75	357.16	358.6	359.34	358.24	356.17	354.03	352.16	352.21	353.75	354.99	355.59
1992	355.98	356.72	357.81	359.15	359.66	359.25	357.03	355	353.01	353.31	354.16	355.4	356.37
1993	356.7	357.16	358.38	359.46	360.28	359.6	357.57	355.52	353.7	353.98	355.33	356.8	357.04
1994	358.36	358.91	359.97	361.26	361.68	360.95	359.55	357.49	355.84	355.99	357.58	359.04	358.88
1995	359.96	361	361.64	363.45	363.79	363.26	361.9	359.46	358.06	357.75	359.56	360.7	360.88
1996	362.05	363.25	364.03	364.72	365.41	364.97	363.65	361.49	359.46	359.6	360.76	362.33	362.64
1997	363.18	364	364.57	366.35	366.79	365.62	364.47	362.51	360.19	360.77	362.43	364.28	363.76
1998	365.32	366.15	367.31	368.61	369.3	368.87	367.64	365.77	363.9	364.23	365.46	366.97	366.63
1999	368.15	368.86	369.58	371.12	370.97	370.33	369.25	366.91	364.6	365.09	366.63	367.96	368.29
2000	369.08	369.4	370.45	371.59	371.75	371.62	370.04	368.04	366.54	366.63	368.2	369.43	369.4
2001	370.17	371.39	372	372.75	373.88	373.17	371.48	369.42	367.83	367.96	369.55	371.1	370.89
2002	372.29	372.94	373.38	374.71	375.4	375.26	373.87	371.35	370.57	370.1	371.93	373.63	372.95

(Carbon Dioxide Information Analysis Center (CDIAC))

However, more often than not, the data is compiled into graphs. Graphs help scientists visualize and interpret the variation in data. Depending on the nature of the data, there are many types of graphs. Bar graphs, pie charts and line graphs are just a few methods used to pictorially represent numerical data.

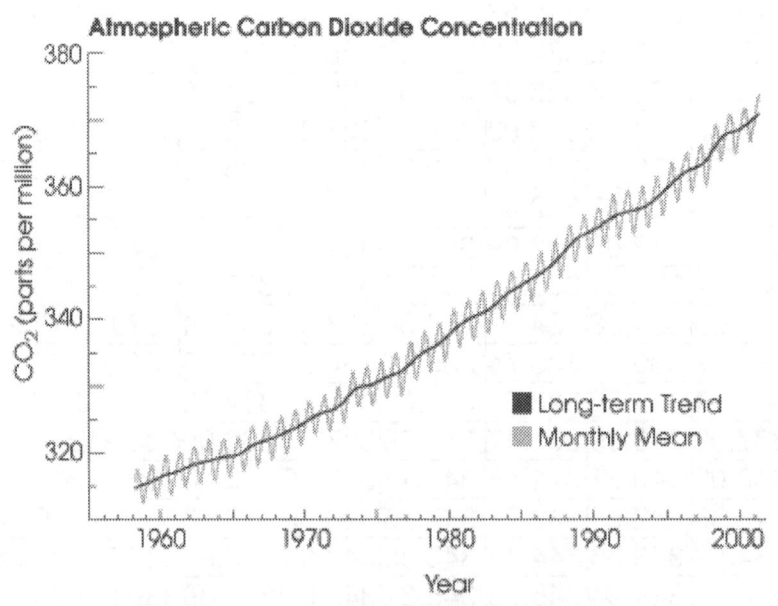

Atmospheric CO_2 measured at Mauna Loa.
This is a famous graph called the Keeling Curve (courtesy NASA).

Interpretation of graphical data shows that on the x-axis is the variable of time in units of years and the y-axis represents the variable of CO_2 concentration in units of parts per million (ppm). The best fit line (solid dark line) shows the trend in CO_2 concentrations during the time period. The steady upward-sloping line indicates a trend of increasing CO_2 concentrations during the time period. However, the light blue line which indicates monthly mean CO_2 levels shows a periodic trend in CO_2 levels during the year. This periodic trend is accounted for by the changes in the seasons. In the spring and summer, deciduous trees and plants undergo increased increased photosynthesis and remove more CO_2 from the atmosphere in the Northern Hemisphere.

The interpretation of data and construction and interpretation of graphs are central practices in science. Graphs are effective visual tools which relay information quickly and reveal trends easily. While there are several different types of graphical displays, extracting information from them can be described in three basic steps.

1. Describe the graph: What does the title say? What is displayed on the x- and y-axis, including the units.
    - Determine the set-up of the graph.
    - Make sure the units used are understood.
      For example, g·cm³ means g/cm³
    - Notice symbols used and check for legend or explanation.

2. Describe the data: Identify the range of data. Are patterns reflected in the data?
3. Interpret the data: How do patterns seen in the graph relate to other things? What conclusions can be drawn from the patterns?

There are seven basic types of graphs.

Column Graphs
Column graphs consist of patterned rectangles displayed along a baseline called the x-category or the horizontal axis. The height of the rectangle represents the amount of data. Column graphs best show:
• changes in data over time (short time series)

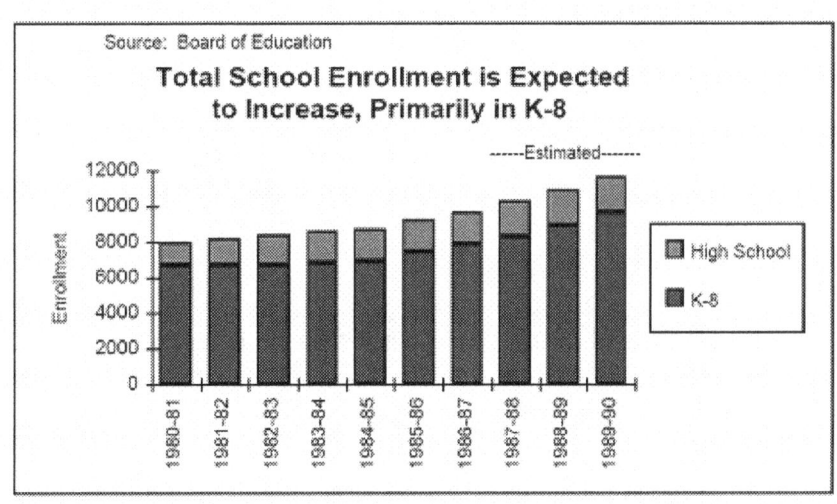

• comparisons of several items (relationship between two series)

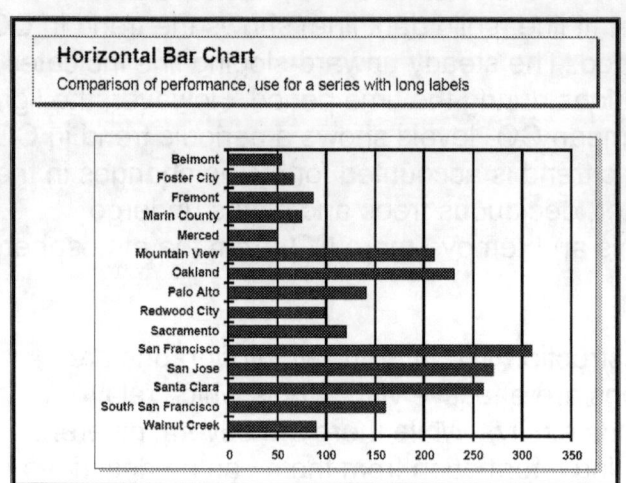

Bar Graphs
Column graphs in which the rectangles are arranged horizontally. The length of each rectangle represents its value. Bar graphs are sometimes referred to as histograms. Bar graphs best show:

• data series with no natural order.

Bar graphs are good for looking at differences amongst similar things. If the data are a time series, a carefully chosen column graph is generally more appropriate but bar graphs can be used to vary a presentation when many column graphs of time series are used. One advantage of bar graphs is that there is greater horizontal space for variable descriptors because the vertical axis is the category axis.

Line Graphs
Line graphs show data points connected by lines; different series are given different line markings (for example, dashed or dotted) or different tick marks. Line graphs are useful when the data points are more important than the transitions between them. They best show:
 • the comparison of long series
 • a general trend is the message.
Line graphs are good for showing trends or changes over time.

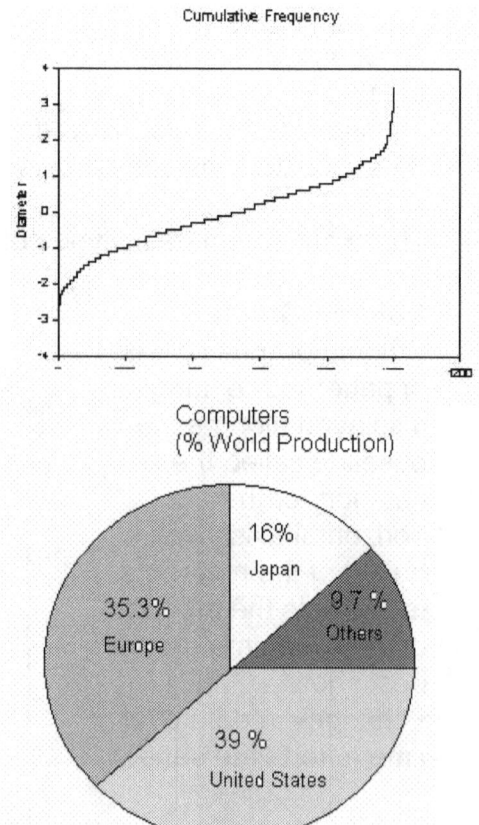

Pie Charts
A pie chart is a circle with radii connecting the center to the edge. The area between two radii is called a slice. Data values are proportionate to the angle between the radii.
Pie charts best show:
 • parts of a whole
Be careful of too many slices since they result in a cluttered graph. Six slices are as many as can be handled on one pie.

CHEMISTRY 24

Area Graphs

Area charts show the relative contributions over time that each data series makes to a whole picture and are "stacked line graphs" in the sense that values are added to the variables below. Unlike line graphs, the space between lines is filled with shadings.

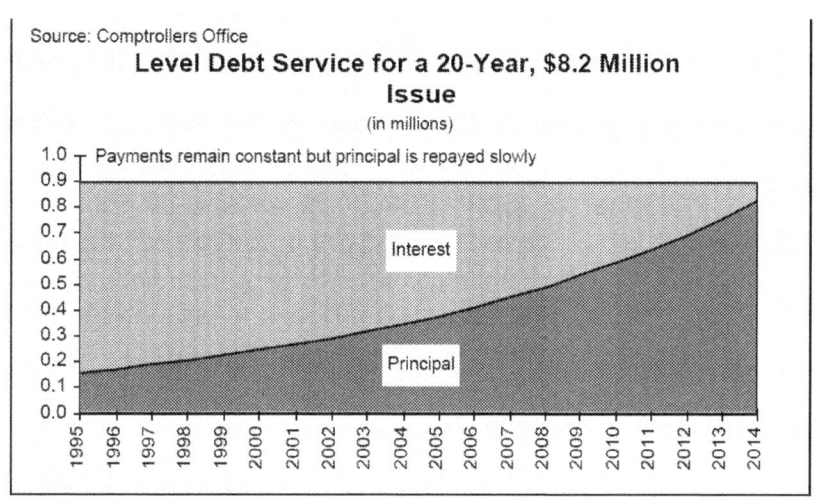

Area graphs are similar to line graphs with the added drama of shading between lines to emphasize variation between whatever the lines represent. They differ from line graphs in that the shaded areas are "added" one on top of the next. Thus, the scale provides accurate measurements only for the lowest part of the graph. This can cause misinterpretation if not fully understood. If reasonable, consider putting the "flattest" graph on the bottom.

Scatter Graphs

A scatter plot is the simplest type of graph. It simply plots the data points against their values, without adding an connecting lines, bars or other stuff. The first variable is measured along the x-axis and the second along the y-axis. Because of this, scatter graphs do not have descriptors in the same sense as other graphs. Scatter graphs best show

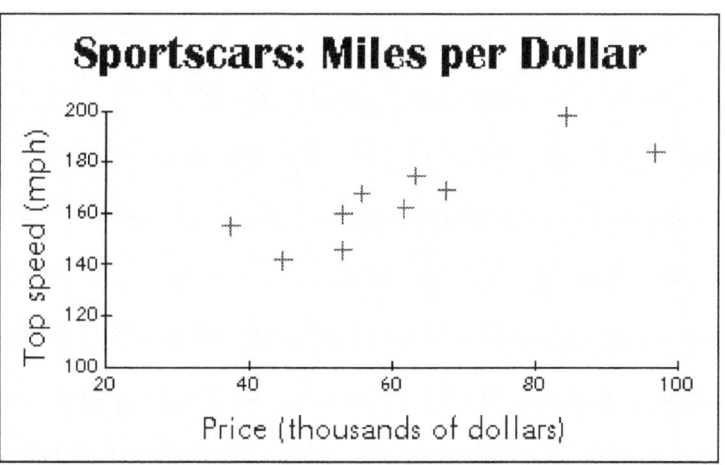

possible relationships between two variables. The purpose of the graph is to try to decide if some partial or indirect relationship—a correlation—exists.

Competency 0005: Understand equipment, materials, and chemicals used in chemistry investigations; and apply procedures for their proper, safe, and legal use.

Chemical purchase, use, and disposal
- Inventory all chemicals on hand at least annually. Keep the list up-to-date as chemicals are consumed and replacement chemicals are received.

- If possible, limit the purchase of chemicals to quantities that will be consumed within one year and that are packaged in small containers suitable for direct use in the lab without transfer to other containers.
- Label all chemicals to be stored with date of receipt or preparation and have labels initialed by the person responsible.
- Generally, bottles of chemicals should not remain:
    - Unused on shelves in the lab for more than one week. Move these chemicals to the storeroom or main stockroom.
    - In the storeroom near the lab unused for more than one month. Move these chemicals to the main stockroom.
    - Check shelf life of chemicals. Properly dispose of any out dated chemicals.
- Ensure that the disposal procedures for waste chemicals conform to environmental protection requirements.
- Do not purchase or store large quantities of flammable liquids. Fire department officials can recommend the maximum quantities that may be kept on hand.
- Never open a chemical container until you understand the label and the relevant portions of the MSDS.

Chemical Storage Plan for Laboratories

- Chemicals should be stored according to hazard class (ex. flammables, oxidizers, health hazards/toxins, corrosives, etc.).
- Store chemicals away from direct sunlight or localized heat.
- All chemical containers should be properly labeled, dated upon receipt, and dated upon opening.
- Store hazardous chemicals below shoulder height of the shortest person working in the lab.
- Shelves should be painted or covered with chemical-resistant paint or chemical-resistant coating.
- Shelves should be secure and strong enough to hold chemicals being stored on them. Do not overload shelves.
- Personnel should be aware of the hazards associated with all hazardous materials.
- Separate solids from liquids.

Below are examples of chemical groups that can be used to categorize storage. Use these groups as examples when separating chemicals for compatibility. Please note: reactive chemicals must be more closely analyzed since they have a greater potential for violent reactions. Contact Laboratory Safety if you have any questions concerning chemical storage.

Acids

- Make sure that all acids are stored by compatibility (ex. separate inorganics from organics).
- Store concentrated acids on lower shelves in chemical-resistant trays or in a corrosives cabinet. This will temporarily contain spills or leaks and protect shelving from residue.
- Separate acids from incompatible materials such as bases, active metals (ex. sodium, magnesium, potassium) and from chemicals which can generate toxic gases when combined (ex. sodium cyanide and iron sulfide).

Bases

- Store bases away from acids.
- Store concentrated bases on lower shelves in chemical-resistant trays or in a corrosives cabinet. This will temporarily contain spills or leaks and protect shelving from residue.

Flammables

- Approved flammable storage cabinets should be used for flammable liquid storage.
- You may store 20 gallons of flammable liquids per 100 sq.ft. in a properly fire separated lab. The maximum allowable quantity for flammable liquid storage in any size lab is not to exceed 120 gallons.
- You may store up to 10 gallons of flammable liquids outside of approved flammable storage cabinets.
- An additional 25 gallons may be stored outside of an approved storage cabinet if it is stored in approved safety cans not to exceed 2 gallons in size.
- Use only explosion-proof or intrinsically safe refrigerators and freezers for storing flammable liquids.

Peroxide-Forming Chemicals

- Peroxide-forming chemicals should be stored in airtight containers in a dark, cool, and dry place.
- Unstable chemicals such as peroxide-formers must always be labeled with date received, date opened, and disposal/expiration date.
- Peroxide-forming chemicals should be properly disposed of before the date of expected peroxide formation (typically 6-12 months after opening).

- Suspicion of peroxide contamination should be immediately investigated. Contact Laboratory Safety for procedures.

Water-Reactive Chemicals

- Water reactive chemicals should be stored in a cool, dry place.
- Do not store water reactive chemicals under sinks or near water baths.
- Class D fire extinguishers for the specific water reactive chemical being stored should be made available.

Oxidizers

- Make sure that all oxidizers are stored by compatibility.
- Store oxidizers away from flammables, combustibles, and reducing agents.

Toxins

- Toxic compounds should be stored according to the nature of the chemical, with appropriate security employed when necessary.
- A "Poison Control Network" telephone number should be posted in the laboratory where toxins are stored. Color coded labeling systems that may be found in your lab:

Hazard	Color Code
Flammables	Red
Health Hazards/Toxins	Blue
Reactives/Oxidizers	Yellow
Contact Hazards	White
General Storage	Gray, Green, Orange

Please Note: Chemicals with labels that are colored and striped may react with other chemicals in the same hazard class. See MSDS for more information. Chemical containers which are not color coded should have hazard information on the label. Read the label carefully and store accordingly.

Schools are regulated by the Environmental Protection Agency, as well as state and local agencies when it comes to disposing of chemical waste. Check with your state science supervisor, local college or university environmental health and safety specialists and the Laboratory Safety Workshop for advice in the disposal of chemical waste. The American Chemical Society publishes an excellent guidebook, *Laboratory Waste Management, A Guidebook* (1994).

The following are merely guidelines for disposing of chemical waste.

You may dispose of hazardous waste as outlined below. It is the responsibility of the generator to ensure hazardous waste does not end up in ground water, soil or the atmosphere through improper disposal.

1. **Sanitary Sewer** - Some chemicals (acids or bases) may be neutralized and disposed to the sanitary sewer. This disposal option must be approved by the local waste water treatment authority prior to disposal. This may not be an option for some small communities that do not have sufficient treatment capacity at the waste water treatment plant for these types of wastes. Hazardous waste may NOT be disposed of in this manner. This includes heavy metals.
2. **Household Hazardous Waste Facility** - Waste chemicals may be disposed through a county household hazardous waste facility (HHW) or through a county contracted household hazardous waste disposal company. Not all counties have a program to accept waste from schools. Verify with your county HHW facility that they can handle your waste prior to making arrangements.
3. **Disposal Through a Contractor** - A contractor may be used for the disposal of the waste chemicals. Remember that you must keep documentation of your hazardous waste disposal for at least three years. This information must include a waste manifest, reclamation agreement or any written record which describes the waste and how much was disposed, where it was disposed and when it was disposed. Waste analysis records must also be kept when making a determination is necessary. **Any unknown chemicals should be considered hazardous!**

The descriptions and diagrams below are included to help you **identify** the proper techniques for conducting specific investigations. They are **not meant as a guide to perform the techniques** in the lab.

Handling liquids

A **beaker** (below left) is a cylindrical cup with a notch at the top. They are often used for making solutions. An **Erlenmeyer** flask (below center) is a conical flask. A liquid in an Erlenmeyer flask will evaporate more slowly than when it is in a beaker and it is easier to swirl about. A **round-bottom flask** (below-right) is also called a Florence flask. It is designed for uniform heating, but it requires a stand to keep it upright.

A **test tube** has a rounded bottom and is designed to hold and to heat small volumes of liquid. A **Pasteur pipet** is a small glass tube with a long thin capillary tip and a latex suction bulb.

A **crucible** is a cup-shaped container made of porcelain or metal for holding chemical compounds when heating them to very high temperatures. A **watch glass** is a concave circular piece of glass that is usually used as surface to evaporate a liquid and observe precipitates or crystallization. A **Dewar flask** is a double walled vacuum flask with a metallic coating to provide good thermal insulation and short term storage of liquid nitrogen.

Fitting and cleaning glassware
If a thermometer or funnel must be threaded through a stopper or a piece of tubing and it won't fit, either **make the hole larger or use a smaller piece of glass**. Use soapy water or glycerol to **lubricate** the glass before inserting it. Hold the glass piece as close as possible to the stopper during insertion. It's also good practice to wrap a towel around the glass and the stopper during this time. **Never apply undue pressure**.

Glassware sometimes contains **tapered ground-glass joints** to allow direct glass-to-glass connections. A thin layer of joint **grease** must be applied when assembling an apparatus with ground-glass joints. Too much grease will contaminate the experiment, and too little will permit the components to be permanently locked together. Disassemble the glassware with a **twisting** motion immediately after the experiment is over.

Cleaning glassware becomes more difficult with time, so it should be cleaned soon after the experiment is completed. Wipe off any lubricant with paper towel moistened in a solvent like hexane before washing the glassware. Use a brush with lab soap and water. Acetone may be used to dissolve most organic residues. Spent solvents should be transferred to a waste container for proper disposal.

Heating
A **hot plate** (shown below) is used to heat Erlenmeyer flasks, beakers and other containers with a flat bottom. Hot plates often have a built-in **magnetic stirrer**. A **heating mantle** has a hemispherical cavity that is used to heat round-bottom flasks. A **Bunsen burner** is designed to burn natural gas. Burners are useful for heating high-boiling point liquids, water, or solutions of non-flammable materials. They are also used for bending glass tubing. Smooth boiling is achieved by adding **boiling stones** to a liquid.

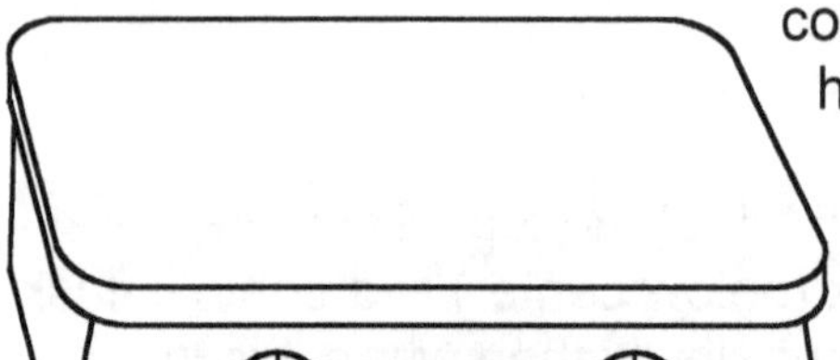

CHEMISTRY

Boiling and melting point determination
Boiling point is determined by heating the liquid along with a boiling stone in a clamped test tube with a clamped thermometer positioned just above the liquid surface and away from the tube walls. The constant highest-value temperature reading after boiling is achieved is the boiling point.

Melting point is determined by placing pulverized solid in a capillary tube and using a rubber band to fasten the capillary to a thermometer so the sample is at the level of the thermometer bulb. The thermometer and sample are inserted into a **Thiele tube** filled with mineral or silicon oil. The Thiele tube has a sidearm that is heated with a Bunsen burner to create a flow of hot oil. This flow maintains an even temperature during heating. The melting point is read when the sample turns into a liquid. Many **electric melting point devices** are also available that heat the sample more slowly to give more accurate results. These are also safer to use than a Thiele tube with a Bunsen burner.

Centrifugation
A **centrifuge** separates two immiscible phases by spinning the mixture (placed in a **centrifuge tube**) at high speeds. A **microfuge** or microcentrifuge is a small centrifuge. The weight of material placed in a centrifuge must be **balanced**, so if one sample is placed in a centrifuge, a tube with roughly an equal mass of water should be placed opposite the sample.

Filtration
The goal of **gravity filtration** is to remove solids from a liquid and obtain a liquid without solid particulates. Filter paper is folded, placed in a funnel on top of a flask, and wetted with the solvent to seal it to the funnel. Next the mixture is poured through, and the solid-free liquid is collected from the flask.

The goal of **vacuum filtration** is usually to remove liquids from a solid to obtain a solid that is dry. An **aspirator** or a **vacuum pump** is used to provide suction though a rubber tube to a **filter trap**. The trap is attached to a **filter flask** (show to the right) by a second rubber tube. The filter flask is an Erlenmeyer flask with a thick wall and a hose barb for the vacuum tube. Filter flasks are used to filter material using a **Büchner funnel** (shown to the right) or a smaller **Hirsch funnel**. These porcelain or plastic funnels hold a circular piece of filter paper. A single-hole rubber stopper supports the funnel in the flask while maintaining suction.

Mixing
Heterogeneous reaction mixtures in flasks are often mixed by **swirling**. To use a magnetic stirrer, a bar magnet coated with Teflon called a flea or a **stir bar** is slid into the container, and the container is placed on the stirrer. The container should be moved and the stir speed adjusted for smooth mixing. Mechanical stirring paddles, agitators, vortexers, or rockers are also used for mixing.

Decanting
When a course solid has settled at the bottom of a flask of liquid, **decanting** the solution simply means pouring out the liquid and leaving the solid behind.

Extraction
Compounds in solution are often separated based on their **solubility differences**. During **liquid-liquid extraction** (also called **solvent extraction**), a second solvent immiscible to the first is added to the solution in a **separatory funnel** (shown at right). Usually one solvent is nonpolar and the other is a polar solvent like water. The two solvents are immiscible and separate from each other after the mixture is shaken to allow solute exchange. One layer contains the compound of interest, and the other contains impurities to be discarded. The solutions in the two layers are separated from each other by draining liquid through the stopcock.

Distillation
Liquids in solution are often separated based on their **boiling point differences**. During simple **distillation**, the solution is placed in a round-bottom flask called the **distillation flask** or **still pot**, and boiling stones are added. The apparatus shown below is assembled (note that clamps and stands are not show), and the still pot is heated using a heating mantle. Hot vapor during boiling escapes through the **distillation head**, enters the **condenser**, and is cooled and condensed back to a liquid. The vapor loses its heat to water flowing through the outside of the condenser. The condensate or **distillate** falls into the **receiving flask**. The apparatus is open to the atmosphere through a vent above the receiving flask. The distillate will contain a higher concentration of material with the lower boiling point. The less volatile component will achieve a high concentration in the still pot. Head temperature is monitored during the process. Distillation may also be used to remove a solid from a pure liquid by boiling and condensing the liquid.

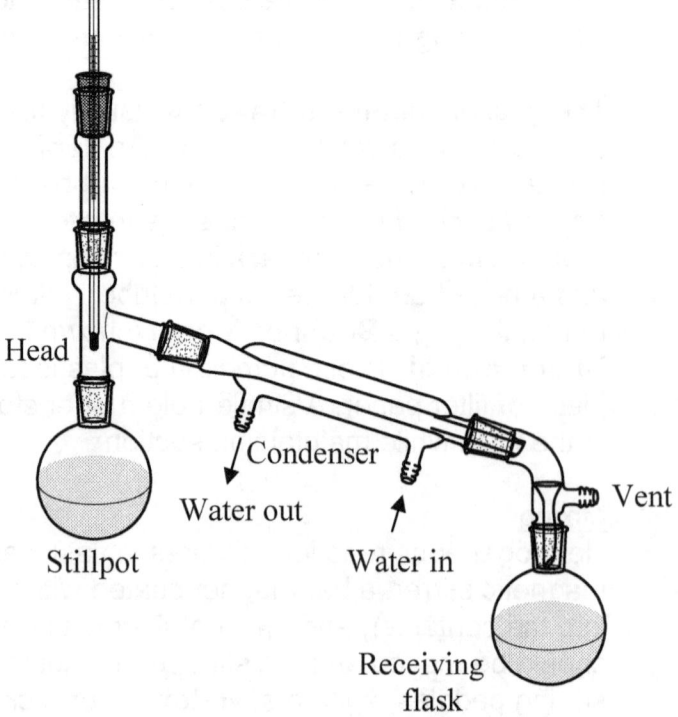

Handling Emergencies

Disclaimer: The information presented below is intended as a starting point for identification purposes only and should not be regarded as a comprehensive guide for safety procedures in the laboratory. It is the responsibility of the readers of this book to consult with professional advisers about safety procedures in their laboratory.

The following list is a summary of the requirements for chemical laboratories:

1) Dousing shower and eye-wash with a floor drain are required where students handle potentially dangerous materials.
2) Accessible fully-charged fire extinguishers of the appropriate type and fire blankets must be present if a fire hazard exists.
3) There must be a master control valve or switch accessible to and within 15 feet of the instructor's station for emergency cut-off of all gas cocks, compressed air valves, water, or electrical services accessible to students. Valves must completely shut-off with a one-quarter turn. This master control is in addition to the regular main gas supply cut-off, and the main supply cut-off must be shut down upon activation of the fire alarm system.
4) A high capacity emergency exhaust system with a source of positive ventilation must be installed, and signs providing instructions must be permanently installed at the emergency exhaust system fan switch.
5) Fume hoods must contain supply fans that automatically shut down when the emergency exhaust fan is turned on.
6) Rooms and/or cabinets for chemical storage must have limited student access and ventilation to the exterior of the building separate from the air-conditioning system. The rooms should be kept at moderate temperature, be well-illuminated, and contain doors lockable from the outside and operable at all times from the inside. Cabinet shelves must have a half-inch lip on the front and be constructed of non-corrosive material.
7) Appropriate caution signs must be placed at hazardous work and storage areas.

Therefore, all chemistry laboratories should be equipped with the following safety equipment. Both teachers and students should be familiar with the operation of this equipment.

Fire extinguisher: Fire extinguishers are rated for the type of fire it will extinguish. Chemical laboratories should have a combination ABC extinguisher along with a type D fire extinguisher. If a type D extinguisher is not available, a bucket of dry sand will do. Make sure you are trained to use the type of extinguisher available in your setting.

- **Class A** fires are ordinary materials like burning paper, lumber, cardboard, plastics etc.
- **Class B** fires involve flammable or combustible liquids such as gasoline, kerosene, and common organic solvents used in the laboratory.
- **Class C** fires involve energized electrical equipment, such as appliances, switches, panel boxes, power tools, hot plates and stirrers. Water is usually a dangerous extinguishing medium for class C fires because of the risk of electrical shock unless a specialized water mist extinguisher is used.
- **Class D** fires involve combustible metals, such as magnesium, titanium, potassium and sodium as well as pyrophoric organometallic reagents such as alkyllithiums, Grignards and diethylzinc. These materials burn at high temperatures and will react violently with water, air, and/or other chemicals. Handle with care!!
- **Class K** fires are kitchen fires. This class was added to the NFPA portable extinguishers Standard 10 in 1998. Kitchen extinguishers installed before June 30, 1998 are "grandfathered" into the standard.

Some fires may be a combination of these! Your fire extinguishers should have ABC ratings on them. These ratings are determined under ANSI/UL Standard 711 and look something like "3-A:40-B:C". Higher numbers mean more firefighting power. In this example, the extinguisher has a good firefighting capacity for Class A, B and C fires. NFPA has a brief description of UL 711 if you want to know more.

Eyewash:

In the event of an eye injury or chemical splash, use the eyewash immediately.

Help the injured person by holding their eyelids open while rinsing.

Rinse copiously and have the eyes checked by a physician afterwards.

Fire Blanket:

A fire blanket can be used to smother a fire. However, use caution when using a fire blanket on a clothing fire. Some fabrics are polymers that melt onto the skin. Stop, Drop and Roll is the best method for extinguishing clothing on fire.

Safety Shower:

Use a safety shower in the event of a chemical spill. Pull the overhead handle and remove clothing that may be contaminated with chemicals, to allow the skin to be rinsed.

Eye protection:

Everyone present must wear eye protection when anyone in the laboratory is performing any of the following activities:
    1) Handling hazardous chemicals
    2) Handling laboratory glassware
    3) Using an open flame.

Safety glasses do not offer protection from splashing liquids. Safety glasses appear similar to ordinary glasses and may be used in an environment that only requires protection from **flying fragments**. Safety glasses with side-shields offer additional protection from **flying fragments approaching from the side**.

Safety goggles offer protection from both flying fragments and splashing liquids. **Only safety goggles** are suitable for eye protection where **hazardous chemicals** are used and handled. Safety goggles with no ventilation (type G) or with indirect ventilation (type H) are both acceptable. Goggles should be marked "Z87" to show they meet federal standards.

Skin protection:
Wear gloves made of a material known to resist penetration by the chemical being handled. Check gloves for holes and the absence of interior contamination. Wash hands and arms and clean under fingernails after working in a laboratory.

Wear a lab coat or apron. Wear footwear that completely covers the feet.

Ventilation:

Using a Fume Hood
A fume hood carries away vapors from reagents or reactions you may be working with. Using a fume hood correctly will reduce your personal exposure to potentially harmful fumes or vapors. When using a fume hood, keep the following in mind.

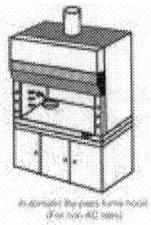

- Place equipment or reactions as far back in the hood as is practical. This will improve the efficiency of fume collection and removal.

- Turn on the light inside the hood using the switch on the outside panel, near the electrical outlets.

- The glass sash of the hood is a safety shield. The sash will fall automatically to the appropriate height for efficient operation and should not be raised above this level, except to move equipment in and out of the hood. Keep the sash between your body and the inside of the hood. If the height of the automatic stop is too high to protect your face and body, lower the sash below this point. Do not stick your head inside a hood or climb inside a hood.

- Wipe up all spills immediately. Clean the glass of your hood, if a splash occurs.

- When you are finished using a hood, lower the sash to the level marked by the sticker on the side.

Work habits
- Never work alone in a laboratory or storage area.
- Never eat, drink, smoke, apply cosmetics, chew gum or tobacco, or store food or beverages in a laboratory environment or storage area.
- Keep containers closed when they are not in use.
- Never pipet by mouth.
- Restrain loose clothing and long hair and remove dangling jewelry.
- Tape all Dewar flasks with fabric-based tape.
- Check all glassware before use. Discard if chips or star cracks are present.
- Never leave heat sources unattended.

- Do not store chemicals and/or apparatus on the lab bench or on the floor or aisles of the lab or storage room.
- Keep lab shelves organized.
- Never place a chemical, not even water, near the edges of a lab bench.
- Use a fume hood that is known to be in operating condition when working with toxic, flammable, and/or volatile substances.
- Never put your head inside a fume hood.
- Never store anything in a fume hood.
- Obtain, read, and be sure you understand the MSDS (see below) for each chemical that is to be used before allowing students to begin an experiment.
- Analyze new lab procedures and student-designed lab procedures in advance to identify any hazardous aspects. Minimize and/or eliminate these components before proceeding. Ask yourself these questions:
  - What are the hazards?
  - What are the worst possible things that could go wrong?
  - How will I deal with them?
  - What are the prudent practices, protective facilities and equipment necessary to minimize the risk of exposure to the hazards?
- Analyze close calls and accidents to eliminate their causes and prevent them from occurring again.
- Identify which chemicals may be disposed of in the drain by consulting the MSDS or the supplier. Clear one chemical down the drain by flushing with water before introducing the next chemical.
- Preplan for emergencies.
  - Keep the fire department informed of your chemical inventory and its location.
  - Consult with a local physician about toxins used in the lab and ensure that your area is prepared in advance to treat victims of toxic exposure.
  - Identify devices that should be shut off if possible in an emergency.
  - Inform your students of the designated escape route and alternate route.

Substitutions
- When feasible, substitute less hazardous chemicals for chemicals with greater hazards in experiments.
- Dilute substances when possible instead of using concentrated solutions.
- Use lesser quantities instead of greater quantities in experiments when possible.
- Use films, videotapes, computer displays, and other methods rather than experiments involving hazardous substances.

Label information
Chemical labels contain safety information in four parts:
1) There will be a signal word. From most to least potentially dangerous, this word will be "Danger!" "Warning!" or "Caution."
2) Statements of hazard (e.g., "Flammable", "May Cause Irritation") follow the signal word. Target organs may be specified.
3) Precautionary measures are listed such as "Keep away from ignition sources" or "Use only with adequate ventilation."
4) First aid information is usually included such as whether to induce vomiting and how to induce vomiting if the chemical is ingested.

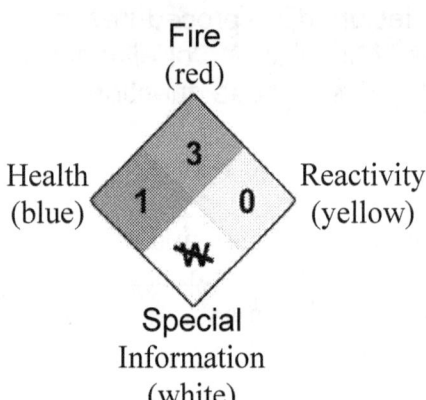

Fire (red)
Health (blue)
Reactivity (yellow)
Special Information (white)

Chemical hazard pictorial
Several different pictorials are used on labels to indicate the level of a chemical hazard. The most common is the **"fire diamond" NFPA (National Fire Prevention Association) pictorial** shown at left. A zero indicates a minimal hazard and a four indicates a severe risk. Special information includes if the chemical reacts with water, **OX** for an oxidizer, **COR ACID** for a corrosive acid, and **COR ALK** for a corrosive base. The "Health" hazard level is for **acute toxicity only**.

Pictorials are designed for **quick reference in emergency situations**, but they are also useful as minimal summaries of safety information for a chemical. They are not required on chemicals you purchase, so it's a good idea to add a label pictorial to every chemical you receive if one is not already present. **The entrance to areas where chemicals are stored should carry a fire diamond label** to represent the materials present.

Procedures for flammable materials: minimize fire risk
The vapors of a flammable liquid **or solid** may travel across the room to an ignition source and cause a fire or explosion.
- Store in an approved safety cabinet for flammable liquids. Store in safety cans if possible.
- Minimize volumes and concentrations used in an experiment with flammables.
- Minimize the time containers are open.
- Minimize ignition sources in the laboratory.
- Ensure that there is good air movement in the laboratory before the experiment.
- Check the fire extinguishers and be certain that you know how to use them.

- Tell the students that the "Stop, Drop, and Roll" technique is best for a clothing fire outside the lab, but in the lab they should walk calmly to the safety shower and use it. Practice this procedure with students in drills.
- A fire blanket should not be used for clothing fires because clothes often contain polymers that melt onto the skin. Pressing these fabrics into the skin with a blanket increases burn damage.
- If a demonstration of an exploding gas or vapor is performed, it should be done behind a safety shield using glass vessels taped with fabric tape.

Procedures for corrosive materials: minimize risk of contact

Corrosive materials **destroy or permanently change living tissue** through chemical action. **Irritants** cause inflammation due to an immune response but not through chemical action. The effect is usually reversible but can be severe and long lasting. **Sensitizers** are irritants that cause no symptoms after the first exposure but may cause irritation during a later exposure.

- Always store corrosives below eye level.
- Only diluted corrosives should be used in pre-high school laboratories and their use at full-strength in high school should be limited.
- Dilute corrosive materials by **adding them to water**. Adding water to a concentrated acid or base can cause rapid boiling and splashing.
- Wear goggles and face shield when handling hazardous corrosives. The face, ears, and neck should be protected.
- Wear gloves known to be impervious to the chemical. Wear sleeve gauntlets and a lab apron made of impervious material if splashing is likely.
- Always wash your hands after handling corrosives.
- Splashes on skin should be flushed with flowing water for 15 minutes while a doctor is called.
- If someone splashes a corrosive material on their clothing:
    - First use the safety shower with clothing on.
    - Have them remove all clothing while under the safety shower including shoes and socks. This is no time for modesty.
    - They should stay under the shower for 15 minutes while a doctor is called.
- Splashes in eyes should be dealt with as follows:
    - Take the victim to the eyewash fountain within 30 seconds.
    - Have them hold their eyelids open with thumb and forefinger and use the eyewash.
    - They must continuously move their eyeballs during 15 minutes of rinsing to cleanse the optic nerve at the back of the eye. A doctor should be called.

Procedures for toxic materials: minimize exposure

Toxic effects are either **chronic** or **acute**. Chronic effects are seen after repeated exposures or after one long exposure. Acute effects occur within a few hours at most.

- Use the smallest amount needed at the lowest concentration for the shortest period of time possible. Weigh the risks against the educational benefits.
- Be aware of the five different routes of exposure
    1) Inhalation-the ability to smell a toxin is not a proper indication of unsafe exposure. Work in the fume hood when using toxins. Minimize dusts and mists by cleaning often, cleaning spills rapidly, and maintaining good ventilation in the lab.
    2) Absorption through intact skin-always wear impervious gloves if the MSDS indicates this route of exposure.
    3) Ingestion
    4) Absorption through other body orifices such as ear canal and eye socket.
    5) Injection by a cut from broken contaminated glassware or other sharp equipment.
- Be aware of the first symptoms of overexposure described by the MSDS. Often these are headache, nausea, and dizziness. Get to fresh air and do not return until the symptoms have passed. If the symptom returns when you come back into the lab, contact a physician and have the space tested.
- Be aware of whether vomiting should be induced in case of ingestion
- Be aware of the recommended procedure in case of unconsciousness.

Procedures for reactive materials: minimize incompatibility

Many chemicals are **self-reactive**. For example, they explode when dried out or when disturbed under certain conditions or they react with components of air. These materials generally **should not be allowed into the high school**. Other precautions must be taken to minimize reactions between **incompatible pairs**.

- Store fuels and oxidizers separately.
- Store reducing agents and oxidizing agents separately.
- Store acids and bases separately.
- Store chemicals that react with fire-fighting materials (i.e., water or carbon dioxide) under conditions that minimize the possibility of a reaction if a fire is being fought in the storage area.
- MSDSs list other incompatible pairs.
- <u>Never</u> store chemicals in alphabetical order by name.
- When incompatible pairs must be supplied to students, do so under direct supervision with very dilute solutions and/or small quantities.

CHEMISTRY

Material Safety Data Sheet (MSDS) information

Many chemicals have a mixture of toxic, corrosive, flammability, and reactivity risks. The **Material Safety Data Sheet** or **MSDS** for a chemical contains detailed safety information that is not presented on the label. This includes acute and chronic health effects, first aid and firefighting measures, what to do in case of a spill, and ecological and disposal considerations.

The MSDS will state whether the chemical is a known or suspected carcinogen, mutagen, or teratogen. A **carcinogen** is a compound that causes cancer (malignant tumors). A **mutagen** alters DNA with the potential effects of causing cancer or birth defects in unconceived children. A **teratogen** produces birth defects and acts during fetal development

There are many parts of an MSDS that are not written for the layperson. Their level of detail and technical content intimidate many people outside the fields of toxicology and industrial safety. According to the American Chemical Society (http://membership.acs.org/c/ccs/pubs/chemical_safety_manual.pdf), an MSDS places "an over-emphasis on the toxic characteristics of the subject chemical."

In a high school chemistry lab, the value of an MSDS is in the words and not in the numerical data it contains, but some knowledge of the numbers is useful for comparing the dangers of one chemical to another. Numerical results of animal toxicity studies are often presented in the form of **LD_{50} values**. These represent the **dose required to kill 50% of animals** tested.

Exposure limits may be presented in three ways:

1) PEL (Permissible Exposure Limit) or TLV-TWA (Threshold Limit Value-Time Weighted Average). This is the maximum permitted concentration of the airborne chemical in volume parts per million (ppm) for a **worker exposed 8 hours daily**.
2) TLV-STEL (Threshold Limit Value-Short Term Exposure Limit). This is the maximum concentration permitted for a 15-minute exposure period.
3) TLV-C (Threshold Limit Value-Ceiling). This is the concentration that should never be exceeded at any moment.

http://hazard.com/msds/index.php contains a large database of MSDSs. http://www.ilpi.com/msds/ref/demystify.html contains a useful "MSDS demystifier." Cut and paste an MSDS into the web page, and hypertext links will appear to a glossary of terms.

TEACHER CERTIFICATION EXAM

Facilities and equipment
- Use separate labeled containers for general trash, broken glass, for each type of hazardous chemical waste—ignitable, corrosive, reactive, and toxic.
- Keep the floor area around safety showers, eyewash fountains, and fire extinguishers clear of all obstructions.
- Never block escape routes.
- Never prop open a fire door.
- Provide safety guards for all moving belts and pulleys.
- Instruct everyone in the lab on the proper use of the safety shower and eyewash fountain (see Corrosive materials above). Most portable eyewash devices cannot maintain the required flow for 15 minutes. A permanent eyewash fountain is preferred.
- If contamination is suspected in the breathing air, arrange for sampling to take place.
- Regularly inspect fire blankets, if present, for rips and holes. Maintain a record of inspection.
- Regularly check safety showers and eyewash fountains for proper rate of flow. Maintain a record of inspection.
- Keep up-to-date emergency phone numbers posted next to the telephone.
- Place fire extinguishers near an escape route.
- Regularly maintain fire extinguishers and maintain a record of inspection. Arrange with the local fire department for training of teachers and administrators in the proper use of extinguishers.
- Regularly check fume hoods for proper airflow. Ensure that fume hood exhaust is not drawn back into the intake for general building ventilation.
- Secure compressed gas cylinders at all times and transport them only while secured on a hand truck.
- Restrict the use and handling of compressed gas to those who have received formal training.
- Install chemical storage shelves with lips. Never use stacked boxes for storage instead of shelves.
- Only use an explosion-proof refrigerator for chemical storage.
- Have appropriate equipment and materials available in advance for spill control and cleanup. Consult the MSDS for each chemical to determine what is required. Replace these materials when they become outdated.
- Provide an appropriate supply of first aid equipment and instruction on its proper use.

Additional comments: Teach safety to students
- Weigh the risks and benefits inherent in lab work, inform students of the hazards and precautions involved in their assignment, and involve students in discussions about safety before every assignment.
- If an incident happens, it can be used to improve lab safety via student participation. Ask the student involved. The student's own words about what occurred should be included in the report.
- Safety information supplied by the manufacturer on a chemical container should be seen by students who actually use the chemical. If you distribute chemicals into smaller containers to be used by students, copy the hazard and precautionary information from the original label onto the labels for the students' containers. Students interested in graphic design may be able to help you perform this task. Labels for many common chemicals may be found here: http://beta.ehs.cornell.edu/labels/cgi-bin/label_selection.pl
- Organize a student safety committee whose task is to conduct one safety inspection and present a report. A different committee may be organized each month or every other month.

Additional comments: General
- Every chemical is hazardous. The way it is used determines the probability of harm.
- Every person is individually and personally responsible for the safe use of chemicals.
- If an accident might happen, it will eventually happen. Proper precautions will ensure the consequences are minimized when it does occur.
- Every accident is predicted by one or more **close calls** where nobody is injured and no property is damaged but something out of the ordinary occurred. Examples might be a student briefly touching a hot surface and saying "Ouch!" with no injury, two students engaged in horseplay, or a student briefly removing safety goggles to read a meniscus level. **Eliminate the cause of a close call and you have stopped a future accident.**

Also see:
http://www.labsafety.org/40steps.htm,
http://www.flinnsci.com/Sections/Safety/safety.asp,
and the American Chemical Society safety publications listed under References.

SUBAREA II - MATTER AND ATOMIC STRUCTURE

Competency 0006: Understand the concept of matter, and analyze chemical and physical properties of and changes in matter.

The word "matter" describes everything that has physical existence, i.e. has mass and takes up space. However, the make up of matter allows it to be separated into categories. The two main classes of matter are **pure substance and mixture.** Each of these classes can also be divided into smaller categories such as element, compound, homogeneous mixture or heterogeneous mixture based on composition.

> **PURE SUBSTANCES:** A pure substance is a form of matter with a definite composition and distinct properties. This type of matter can not be separated by ordinary processes like filtering, centrifuging, boiling or melting.

Pure substances are divided into elements and compounds.

> **Elements:** A single type of matter, called an atom, is present. Elements can not be broken down any farther by ordinary chemical processes. They are the smallest whole part of a substance that still represents that substance.

> **Compounds:** Two or more elements chemically combined are present. A compound may be broken down into its elements by chemical processes such as heating or electric current. Compounds have a uniform composition regardless of the sample size or source of the sample.

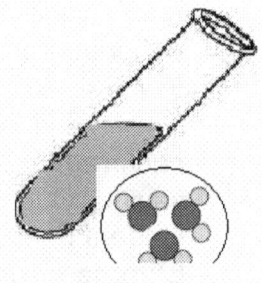

> **MIXTURES:** Two or more pure substances that are not chemically combined are present. Mixtures may be of any proportion and can be physically separated by processes like filtering, centrifuging, boiling or melting.

Mixtures can be classified according to particle size.

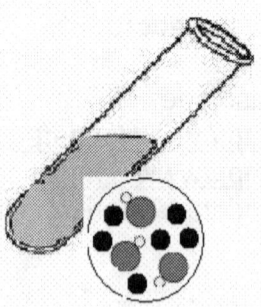

> **Homogeneous Mixtures:** Homogeneous mixtures have the same composition and properties throughout the mixture and are also known as solutions. They have a uniform color and distribution of solute and solvent particles throughout the mixture.

Heterogeneous Mixtures: Heterogeneous mixtures do not have a uniform distribution of particles throughout the mixture. The different components of the mixture can easily be identified and separated.

A **physical change** does not create a new substance. **Atoms are not rearranged into different compounds**. The material has the same chemical composition as it had before the change. Changes of state as described in the previous section are physical changes. Frozen water or gaseous water is still H_2O. Taking a piece of paper and tearing it up is a physical change. You simply have smaller pieces of paper.

A **chemical change** is a chemical reaction. It **converts one substance into another** because atoms are rearranged to form a different compound. Paper undergoes a chemical change when you burn it. You no longer have paper. A chemical change to a pure substance alters its properties.

The identity of an **element** depends on the **number of protons** in the nucleus of the atom. This value is called the **atomic number** and it is sometimes written as a subscript before the symbol for the corresponding element. Atoms and ions of a given element that differ in number of neutrons have a different mass and are called **isotopes**. A nucleus with a specified number of protons and neutrons is called a **nuclide**, and a nuclear particle, either a proton or neutron, may be called a **nucleon**. The total number of nucleons is called the **mass number** and may be written as a superscript before the atomic symbol.

$^{14}_{6}C$ represents an atom of carbon with 6 protons and 8 neutrons.

The **number of neutrons** may be found by **subtracting the atomic number from the mass number**. For example, uranium-235 has 235–92=143 neutrons because it has 235 nucleons and 92 protons.

Different isotopes have different natural abundances and have different nuclear properties, but an atom's chemical properties are almost entirely due to electrons.

Some nuclei are unstable and emit particles and electromagnetic radiation. These emissions from the nucleus are known as **radioactivity**; the unstable isotopes are known as **radioisotopes**; and the nuclear reactions that spontaneously alter them are known as **radioactive decay**.

A pure substance may be an element (such as carbon in diamond) or a compound (such as carbon dioxide, CO_2). **Compounds may be decomposed into two or more different elements. Elements cannot be decomposed into simpler substances.**

Atoms are the smallest possible unit of an element. Carbon atoms may arrange themselves into different pure substances such as graphite and diamond. **Molecules are combinations of tightly bound atoms**. For example, the formula N_2 is a nitrogen molecule, but it is not a compound. It is the element nitrogen. N is a nitrogen atom.

In the kinetic molecular theory of gases, the distinction between atoms and molecules is not very important. Atoms of argon gas obey the ideal gas law in much the same was as molecules of N_2, so the word "molecule" is used less formally in this subfield to include atomic gases.

Molecules have **kinetic energy** (they move around), and they also have **intermolecular attractive forces** (they stick to each other). The relationship between these two determines whether a collection of molecules will be a gas, liquid, or solid.

A **gas** has an indefinite shape and an indefinite volume. The kinetic model for a gas is a collection of widely separated molecules, each moving in a random and free fashion, with negligible attractive or repulsive forces between them. Gases will expand to occupy a larger container so there is more space between the molecules. Gases can also be compressed to fit into a small container so the molecules are less separated.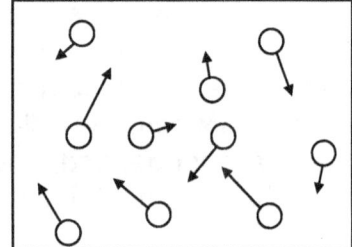
Diffusion occurs when one material spreads into or through another. Gases diffuse rapidly and move from one place to another.

A **liquid** assumes the shape of the portion of any container that it occupies and has a specific volume. The kinetic model for a liquid is a collection of molecules attracted to each other with sufficient strength to keep them close to each other but with insufficient strength to prevent them from moving around randomly. Liquids have a higher density and are much less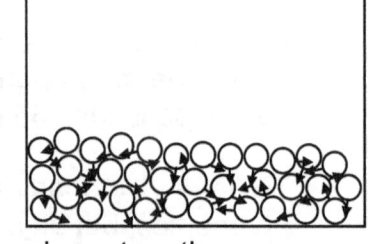
compressible than gases because the molecules in a liquid are closer together. Diffusion occurs more slowly in liquids than in gases because the molecules in a liquid stick to each other and are not completely free to move.

A **solid** has a definite volume and definite shape. The kinetic model for a solid is a collection of molecules attracted to each other with sufficient strength to essentially lock them in place. Each molecule may vibrate, but it has an average position relative to its neighbors. If these positions form an ordered pattern, the solid is called **crystalline**. Otherwise, it is called **amorphous**.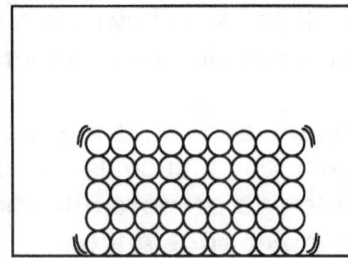

Solids have a high density and are almost incompressible because the molecules are close together. Diffusion occurs extremely slowly because the molecules almost never alter their position.

Phase changes occur when the relative importance of kinetic energy and intermolecular forces is altered sufficiently for a substance to change its state.

The transition from gas to liquid is called **condensation** and from liquid to gas is called **vaporization**. The transition from liquid to solid is called **freezing** and from solid to liquid is called **melting**. The transition from gas to solid is called **deposition** and from solid to gas is called **sublimation**.

Heat removed from a substance during condensation, freezing, or deposition permits new intermolecular bonds to form, and heat added to a substance during vaporization, melting,
or sublimation breaks intermolecular bonds. During these phase transitions, this **latent heat** is removed or added with **no change in the temperature** of the substance because the heat is not being used to alter the speed of the molecules or the kinetic energy when they strike each other or the container walls. Latent heat alters intermolecular bonds.

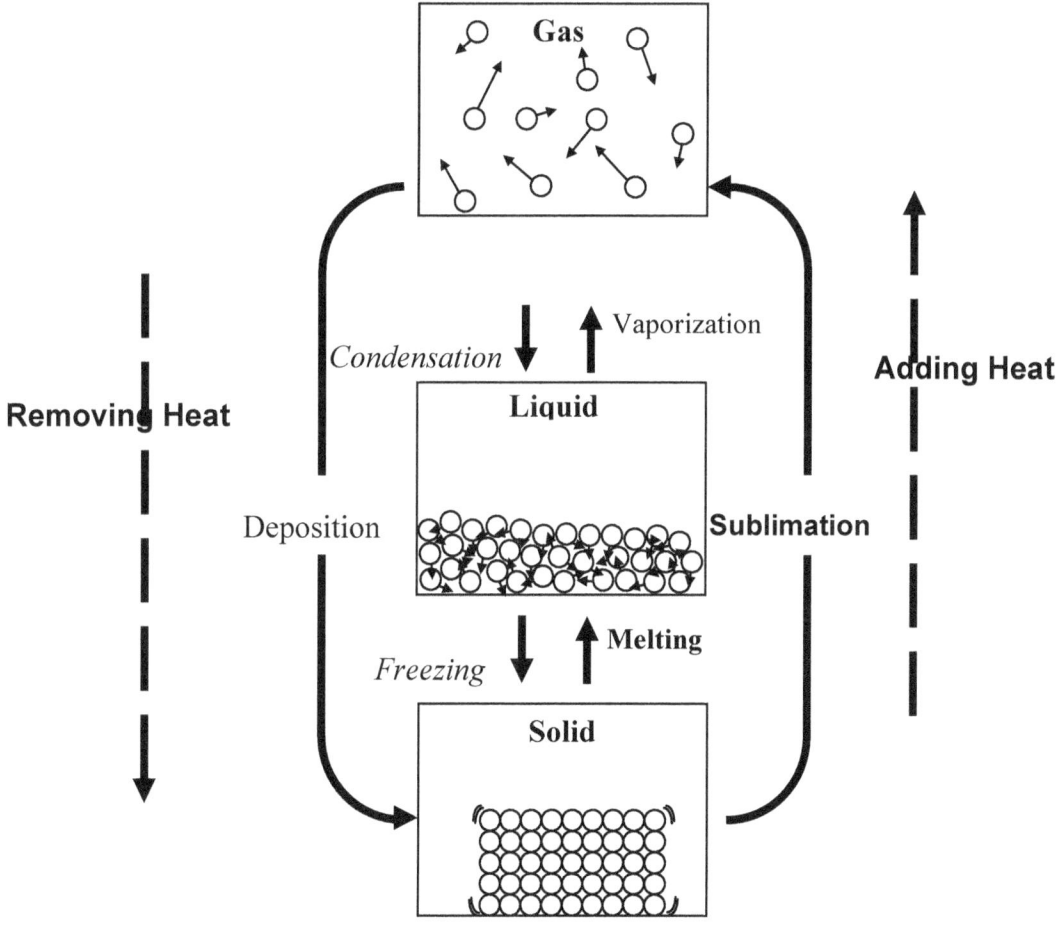

A **physical property** of matter is a property that can be determined without inducing a chemical change. The elemental percent composition of a substance requires that the compound be broken down into its elements, and so it is a chemical property, not a physical one.

The term "structure" in chemistry usually refers to a chemical structure, meaning the spatial arrangement of atoms or its representation in a structural formula. This is a chemical property, not a physical property. All matter has mass and takes up space with an associated size. Matter experiencing gravity has a weight. Most matter we encounter exists in one of three phases.

Melting point refers to the temperature at which a solid becomes a liquid. **Boiling point** refers to the temperature at which a liquid becomes a gas. Melting takes place when there is sufficient energy available to break the intermolecular forces that hold molecules together in a solid. Boiling occurs when there is enough energy available to break the intermolecular forces holding molecules together as a liquid.

Hardness describes how difficult it is to scratch or indent a substance. The hardest natural substance is diamond.

Density measures the mass of a unit volume of material.

Electrical conductivity measures a material's ability to conduct an electric current. The high conductivity of metals is due to the presence of metallic bonds. The high conductivity of electrolyte solutions is due to the presence of ions in solution.

Density is a measure of mass per unit of volume. Units of g/cm^3 are commonly used. SI base units of kg/m^3 are also used. One g/cm^3 is equal to one thousand kg/m^3. Density (ρ) is calculated from mass (m) and volume (V) using the formula:

$$\rho = \frac{m}{V}.$$

The above expression is often manipulated to determine the mass of a substance if its volume and density are known ($m = \rho V$) or the volume of a substance if its mass and density are known ($V = m / \rho$).

The density of water at 4 °C is 1.000 g/cm^3. If an object is denser than the fluid in which it is immersed, it will sink. If it is less dense than the fluid, it will float. Ice floats on water because the solid phase of H_2O at 0 °C is less dense than the liquid phase. The solid phase for most other substances would sink at its melting point because the solid is more dense than the liquid.

Competency 0007: Understand the various models of atomic structure, the principles of quantum theory, and the properties and interactions of subatomic particles.

Dalton
The existence of fundamental units of matter called atoms of different types called elements was proposed by ancient philosophers without any evidence to support the belief. Modern atomic theory is credited to the work of **John Dalton** published in 1803-1807. Observations made by him and others about the composition, properties, and reactions of many compounds led him to develop the following postulates:

1) Each element is composed of small particles called atoms.
2) All atoms of a given element are identical in mass and other properties.
3) Atoms of different elements have different masses and differ in other properties.
4) Atoms of an element are not created, destroyed, or changed into a different type of atom by chemical reactions.
5) Compounds form when atoms of more than one element combine.
6) In a given compound, the relative number and kind of atoms are constant.

Dalton's table of atomic symbols and masses

Dalton determined and published the known relative masses of a number of different atoms. He also formulated the law of partial pressures . Dalton's work focused on the ability of atoms to arrange themselves into molecules and to rearrange themselves via chemical reactions, but he did not investigate the composition of atoms themselves. **Dalton's model of the atom** was a tiny, indivisible, indestructible **particle** of a certain mass, size, and chemical behavior, but Dalton did not deny the possibility that atoms might have a substructure.

Thomson
Joseph John Thomson, often known as **J. J. Thomson**, was the first to examine this substructure. In the mid-1800s, scientists had studied a form of radiation called "cathode rays" or "electrons" that originated from the negative electrode (cathode) when electrical current was forced through an evacuated tube. Thomson determined in 1897 that **electrons have mass**, and because many different cathode materials release electrons, Thomson proposed that the **electron is a subatomic particle**. **Thomson's model of the atom** was a uniformly positive particle with electrons contained in the interior.

This has been called the "plum-pudding" model of the atom where the pudding represents the uniform sphere of positive electricity and the bits of plum represent electrons. For more on Thomson, see http://www.aip.org/history/electron/jjhome.htm.

Planck
Max Planck determined in 1900 that **energy is transferred by radiation in exact multiples of a discrete unit of energy called a quantum**. Quanta of energy are extremely small, and may be found from the frequency of the radiation, v, using the equation:

$$\Delta E = hv, 2hv, 3hv, \ldots$$

where h is Planck's constant and hv is a quantum of energy.

Rutherford
Ernest Rutherford studied atomic structure in 1910-1911 by firing a beam of alpha particles at thin layers of gold leaf. According to Thomson's model, the path of an alpha particle should be deflected only slightly if it struck an atom, but Rutherford observed some alpha particles bouncing almost backwards, suggesting that **nearly all the mass of an atom is contained in a small positively charged nucleus**. **Rutherford's model of the atom** was an analogy to the sun and the planets. A small positively charged nucleus is surrounded by circling electrons and mostly by empty space. Rutherford's experiment is explained in greater detail in this flash animation: http://www.mhhe.com/physsci/chemistry/essentialchemistry/flash/ruther14.swf.

De Broglie
Depending on the experiment, radiation appears to have wave-like or particle-like traits. In 1923-1924, Louis de Broglie applied this **wave/particle duality to all matter with momentum**. The discrete distances from the nucleus described by Bohr corresponded to permissible distances where standing waves could exist. **De Broglie's model of the atom** described electrons as **matter waves in standing wave orbits** around the nucleus. The first three standing waves corresponding to the first three discrete distances are shown in the figure. An applet of de Broglie's model may be found here: http://artsci-ccwin.concordia.ca/facstaff/a-c/bird/c241/D1-part2.html.

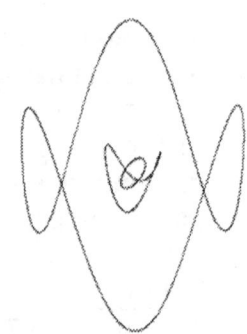

Bohr
Niels Bohr incorporated Planck's quantum concept into Rutherford's model of the atom in 1913 to explain the **discrete frequencies of radiation emitted and absorbed by atoms with one electron** (H, He^+, and Li^{2+}). This electron is attracted to the positive nucleus and is closest to the nucleus at the **ground state** of the atom.

When the electron absorbs energy, it moves into an orbit further from the nucleus and the atom is said to be in an electronically **excited state**. If sufficient energy is absorbed, the electron separates from the nucleus entirely, and the atom is ionized:

$$H \rightarrow H^+ + e^-$$

The energy required for ionization from the ground state is called the atom's **ionization energy**. The discrete frequencies of radiation emitted and absorbed by the atom correspond (using Planck's constant) to discrete energies and in turn to discrete distances from the nucleus. **Bohr's model of the atom** was a small positively charged nucleus surrounded mostly by empty space and by electrons orbiting at certain discrete distances ("shells") corresponding to discrete energy levels. Animations utilizing the Bohr model may be found at the following two URLs: http://artsci-ccwin.concordia.ca/facstaff/a-c/bird/c241/D1.html and http://www.mhhe.com/physsci/chemistry/essentialchemistry/flash/linesp16.swf.

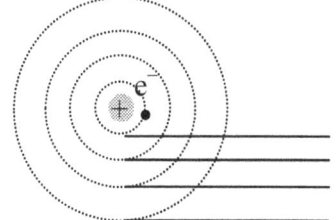

Heisenberg
The realization that both matter and radiation interact as waves led Werner Heisenberg to the conclusion in 1927 that the act of observation and measurement requires the interaction of one wave with another, resulting in an **inherent uncertainty** in the location and momentum of particles. This inability to measure phenomena at the subatomic level is known as the **Heisenberg uncertainty principle**. A discussion of the principle and Heisenberg's other contributions to quantum theory is located at: http://www.aip.org/history/heisenberg/.

Schrödinger
When Erwin Schrödinger studied the atom in 1925, he replaced the idea of precise orbits with regions in space called **orbitals** where electrons were likely to be found. **The Schrödinger equation** describes the **probability** that an electron will be in a given region of space, a quantity known as **electron density** or Ψ^2. The diagrams below are surfaces of constant Ψ^2 found by solving the Schrödinger equation for the hydrogen atom $1s$, $2p_z$ and $3d_0$ orbitals. Additional representations of solutions may be found here: http://library.wolfram.com/webMathematica/Physics/Hydrogen.jsp.

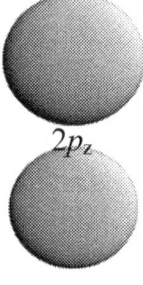
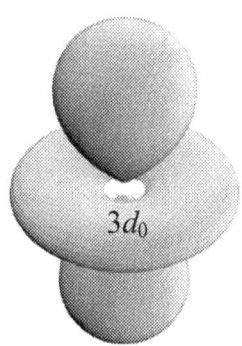

Schrödinger's model of the atom is a mathematical formulation of quantum mechanics that describes the electron density of orbitals. It is the atomic model that has been in use from shortly after it was introduced up to the present.

Protons have a positive charge, **neutrons** have no charge, and **electrons** have a negative charge. Atoms have no net charge and thus have an equal number of protons and electrons. **Anions** are negative ions and contain more electrons than protons. **Cations** are positive ions and contain more protons than electrons. Protons and neutrons are contained in a small volume at the center of the atom called the **nucleus**. Electrons move in the remaining space of the atom and have very little mass—about 1/1800 of the mass of a proton or neutron. Electrons are prevented from flying away from the nucleus by the attraction that exists between opposite electrical charges. This force is known as **electrostatic** or **coulombic** attraction.

Protons and neutrons each contain three **quarks**. A neutron consists of one *up* quark and two down quarks. A proton consists of two up quarks and one *down* quark. Other quarks are named *strange*, *charm*, *bottom*, and *top.*, but these four are not part of atoms. Quarks are a fundamental constituent of matter according to current standard model of particle physics, but individual quarks are not seen. Instead they are always confined within other subatomic particles. There is no need to consider quarks when describing chemical interactions. **Only electrons are involved in chemical reactions**. The position and sizes of these particles in a helium atom is indicated in the

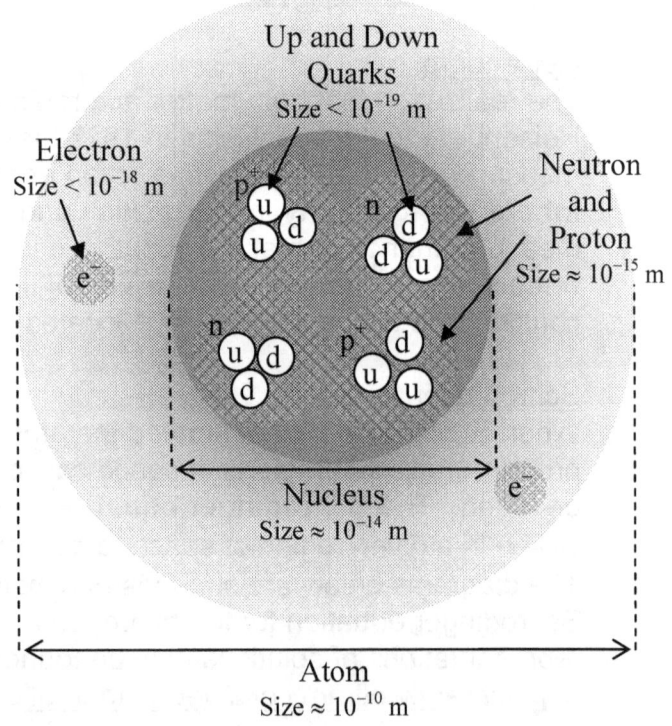

diagram at right. A diagram like this one could never be drawn to scale. If a proton were drawn 1 cm in diameter, the atom's diameter would require a page about 1 km long and a quark's diameter would be less than 1 μm.

The position of an element in the periodic table may be related to its electron configuration, and this configuration in turn results from the quantum theory describing the filling of a shell of electrons.

In this skill, we will take this theory as our starting point. However, it should be remembered that it is the correlation with properties—not with electron arrangements—that have placed the periodic table at the beginning of most chemistry texts.

Quantum numbers

The quantum-mechanical solutions from the Schrödinger Equation utilize three quantum numbers (n, l, and m_l) to describe an orbital and a fourth (m_s) to describe an electron in an orbital. This model is useful for understanding the frequencies of radiation emitted and absorbed by atoms and chemical properties of atoms.

The **principal quantum number n** may have positive integer values (1, 2, 3, …). n is a measure of the **distance** of an orbital from the nucleus, and orbitals with the same value of n are said to be in the same **shell**. This is analogous to the Bohr model of the atom. Each shell may contain up to $2n^2$ electrons.

The **azimuthal quantum number l** may have integer values from 0 to n-1. l describes the angular momentum of an orbital. This determines the orbital's **shape**. Orbitals with the same value of n and l are in the same **subshell**, and each subshell may contain up to $4l + 2$ electrons. Subshells are usually referred to by the principle quantum number followed by a letter corresponding to l as shown in the following table:

Azimuthal quantum number l	0	1	2	3	4
Subshell designation	s	p	d	f	g

The **magnetic quantum number m_l or m** may have integer values from $-l$ to l. m_l is a measure of how an individual orbital responds to an external magnetic field, and it often describes an orbital's **orientation**. A subscript—either the value of m_l or a function of the x-, y-, and z-axes—is used to designate a specific orbital. Each orbital may hold up to two electrons.

The **spin quantum number m_s or s** has one of two possible values: $-1/2$ or $+1/2$. m_s differentiates between the two possible electrons occupying an orbital. Electrons moving through a magnet behave as if they were tiny magnets themselves spinning on their axis in either a clockwise or counterclockwise direction. These two spins may be described as $m_s = -1/2$ and $+1/2$ or as down and up.

The **Pauli exclusion principle** states that **no two electrons in an atom may have the same set of four quantum numbers**.

The following table summarizes the relationship among n, l, and m_l through $n=3$:

n	l	Subshell	m_l	Orbitals in subshell	Maximum number of electrons in subshell
1	0	1s	0	1	2
2	0	2s	0	1	2
	1	2p	−1, 0, 1	3	6
3	0	3s	0	1	2
	1	3p	−1, 0, 1	3	6
	2	3d	−2, −1, 0, 1, 2	5	10

Subshell energy levels
In single-electron atoms (H, He^+, and Li^{2+}) above the ground state, subshells within a shell are all at the same energy level, and an orbital's energy level is only determined by n. However, in all other atoms, multiple electrons repel each other. Electrons in orbitals closer to the nucleus create a screening or **shielding effect** on electrons further away from the nucleus, preventing them from receiving the full attractive force of the nucleus. **In multi-electron atoms, both n and l determine the energy level of an orbital**. In the absence of a magnetic field, **orbitals in the same subshell with different m_l all have the same energy** and are said to be **degenerate orbitals**.

The following list orders subshells by increasing energy level:
1s < 2s < 2p < 3s < 3p < 4s < 3d < 4p < 5s < 4d < 5p < 6s < 4f < 5d < 6p < 7s < 5f < ...

This list may be constructed by arranging the subshells according to n and l and drawing diagonal arrows as shown below:

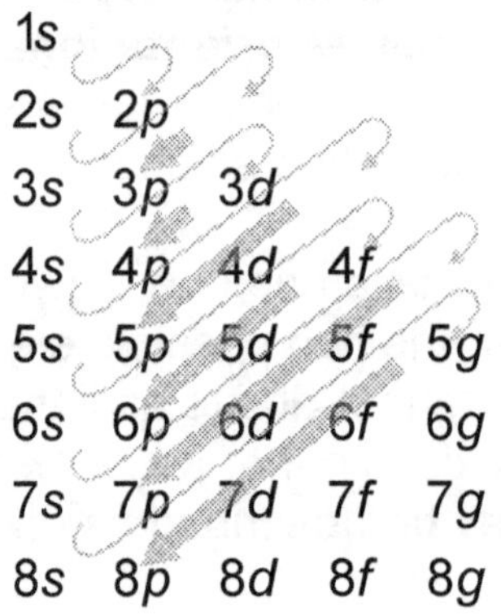

```
1s
2s  2p
3s  3p  3d
4s  4p  4d  4f
5s  5p  5d  5f  5g
6s  6p  6d  6f  6g
7s  7p  7d  7f  7g
8s  8p  8d  8f  8g
```

Drawing electron shell structures
Electron shell structures (also called electron arrangements) in an atom may be represented using three methods: an **electron configuration**, an **orbital diagram**, or an **energy level diagram**.

All three methods require knowledge of the subshells occupied by electrons in a certain atom. The **Aufbau principle** or **building-up rule** states that **electrons at ground state fill orbitals starting at the lowest available energy levels**.

An **electron configuration** is a **list of subshells** with superscripts representing the **number of electrons** in each subshell. For example, an atom of boron has 5 electrons. According to the Aufbau principle, two will fill the $1s$ subshell, two will fill the higher energy $2s$ subshell, and one will occupy the $2p$ subshell which has an even higher energy. The electron configuration of boron is $1s^2 2s^2 2p^1$. Similarly, the electron configuration of a vanadium atom with 23 electrons is:
$$1s^2 2s^2 2p^6 3s^2 3p^6 4s^2 3d^3.$$

Configurations are also written with their principle quantum numbers together:
$$1s^2 2s^2 2p^6 3s^2 3p^6 3d^3 4s^2.$$

Electron configurations are often written to emphasize the outermost electrons. This is done by writing the symbol in brackets for the element with a full p subshell from the previous shell and adding the **outer electron configuration** onto that configuration. The element with the last full p subshell will always be a noble gas from the right-most column of the periodic table. For the vanadium example, the element with the last full p subshell has the configuration $1s^2 2s^2 2p^6 3s^2 3p^6$. This is $_{18}$Ar. The configuration of vanadium may then be written as $[Ar]4s^2 3d^3$ where $4s^2 3d^3$ is the outer electron configuration.

Electron shell structures may also be written by noting the number of electrons in each shell. For vanadium, this would be:
2, 8, 11, 2.

Orbital diagrams assign electrons to individual orbitals so the energy state of individual electrons may be found. This requires knowledge of how electrons occupy orbitals within a subshell. **Hund's rule** states that **before any two electrons occupy the same orbital, other orbitals in that subshell must first contain one electron each with parallel spins**. Electrons with up and down spins are shown by half-arrows, and these are placed in lines of orbitals (represented as boxes or dashes) according to Hund's rule, the Aufbau principle, and the Pauli exclusion principle. Below is the orbital diagram for vanadium:

 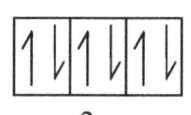   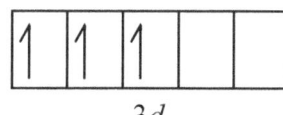
$1s$ $2s$ $2p$ $3s$ $3p$ $4s$ $3d$

An **energy level diagram** is an orbital diagram that shows subshells with higher energy levels higher up on the page. The energy level diagram of vanadium is:

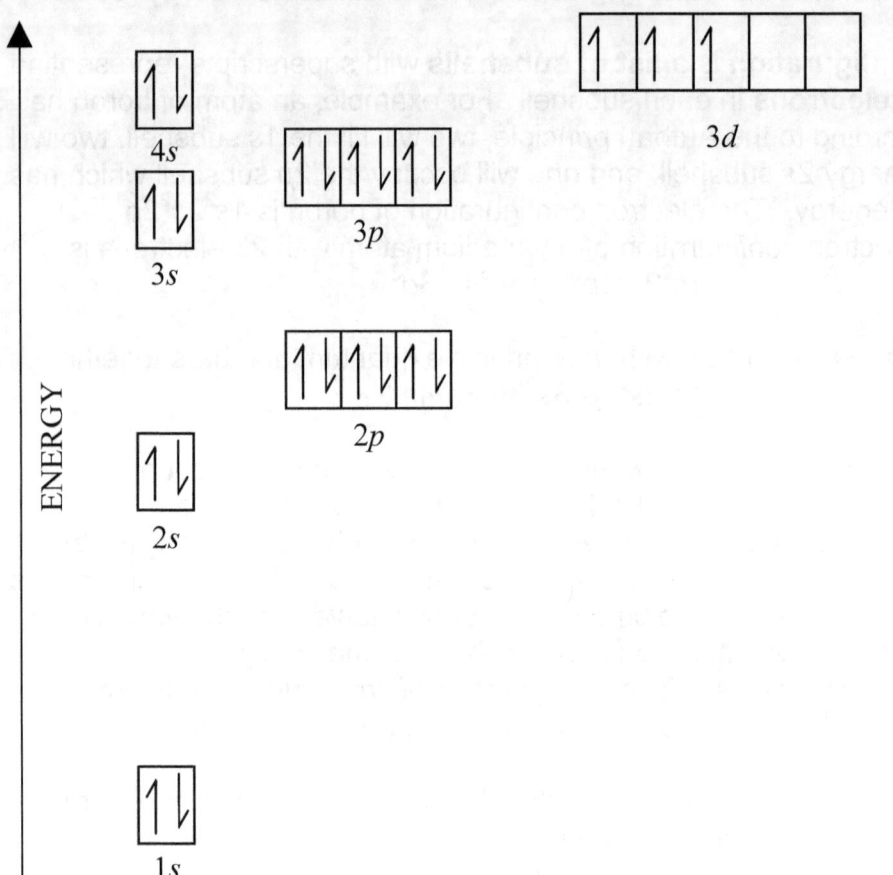

Valence shell electrons and the periodic table
Electrons in the **outermost shell** are called **valence shell electrons**. For example, the electron configuration of Se is $[Ar]4s^2 3d^{10} 4p^4$, and its valence shell electron configuration is $4s^2 4p^4$.

The **periodic table** may be related to the electron shell structure of any element. The table may be divided up into **blocks corresponding to the subshell** designation of the most recent orbital to be filled by the building-up rule.

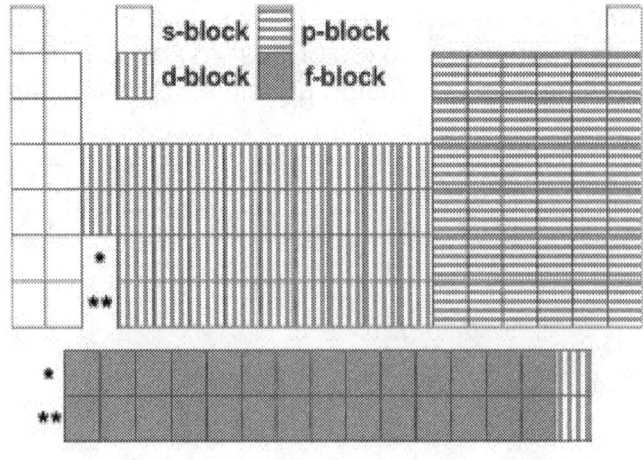

CHEMISTRY 56

Elements in the s- and p-blocks are known as **main-group elements**. The d-block elements are called **transition metals**. The f-block elements are called **inner transition metals**.

The maximum number of electrons in each subshell (2, 6, 10, or 14) determines the number of elements in each block, and the order of energy levels for subshells create the pattern of blocks. These blocks also usually correspond to the value of *l* for the **outermost electron** of the atom. This has important consequences for the physical and chemical properties of the elements. The outermost shell or valence shell principle quantum number (for example, 4 for Se) is also the period number for the element in the table.

Atoms in the d- and f-blocks often have unexpected electron shell structures that cannot be explained using simple rules. Some heavy atoms have unknown electron configurations because the number of different frequencies of radiation emitted and absorbed by these atoms is very large.

http://www.cowtownproductions.com/cowtown/genchem/08_07T1.htm contains a brief tutorial on energy level diagrams.
http://www.colorado.edu/physics/2000/applets/a2.html contains (among other things) energy level diagrams and animations of electron shells and nuclei.
http://intro.chem.okstate.edu/WorkshopFolder/Electronconfnew.html animates the building up of energy level diagrams.

Competency 0008: Understand the organization of the periodic table.

The first periodic table was developed in 1869 by Dmitri Mendeleev. Mendeleev arranged the elements in order of increasing atomic mass into **columns of similar physical and chemical properties**. He then **predicted the existence and the properties of undiscovered elements** to fill the gaps in his table. These interpolations were treated with skepticism until three of Mendeleev's theoretical elements were discovered and were found to have the properties he predicted.

In the modern periodic table, **elements are arranged in numerical order by atomic number**. The elements in a **column are known as a group**, and groups are numbered from 1 to 18. Older numbering styles used roman numerals and letters. **Elements with similar properties are called a family** or a **chemical series**. The modern table, like Mendeleev's, places elements with similar properties into columns. Families are called **group names** when they correspond to a single column. **A row of the periodic table is known as a period**. Periods of the known elements are numbered from 1 to 7.

The periodic table is also organized to correspond to electron configurations within the atom. The table may be divided into blocks corresponding to the subshell of the orbital filled most recently by an electron using the building-up rule. Elements in the same column have similar properties because they have the same valence (outermost) electron configurations. These are the electrons that are most important in determining chemical properties.

Elements in the periodic table are divided into the two categories of **metals** and **nonmetals** with a jagged line separating the two as shown in the figure. Elements near the line exhibit some properties of each and are called **metalloids** or **semimetals**.

The most metallic element is francium at the bottom left of the table, and the most nonmetallic is fluorine. The metallic character of elements within a group

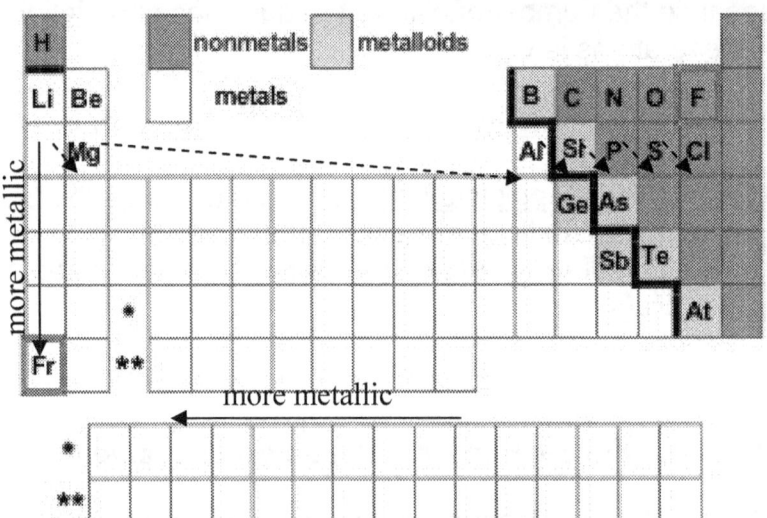

increases with period number. This means that **within a column, the more metallic elements are at the bottom**. The metallic character of elements within a period decreases with group number. Therefore, **within a row, the more metallic elements are on the left**. Among the main group atoms, **elements diagonal to each other** as indicated by the dashed arrows **have similar properties** due to a similar metallic character. The **noble gases** (group 18 elements) are nonmetals and are exceptions to the diagonal rule. Noble gases are **nearly chemically inert**. The heavier noble gases form a number of compounds with oxygen and fluorine such as KrF_2 and XeO_4

Physical properties relating to metallic character are summarized in the following table:

Element	Electrical/thermal conductivity	Malleable/ductile as solids?	Lustrous?	Melting point of oxides, hydrides, and halides
Metals	High	Yes	Yes	High
Metalloids	Intermediate. Altered by dopants (semiconductors)	No (brittle)	Varies	Varies (oxides). Low (hydrides, halides)
Nonmetals	Low (insulators)	No	No	Low

Malleable materials can **be beaten into sheets**. **Ductile** materials can **be pulled into wires**. **Lustrous** materials **have a shine**. Oxides, hydrides, and halides are compounds with O, H, and halogens respectively.

Measures of intermolecular attractions other than melting point are also higher for metal oxides, hydrides, and halides than for the nonmetal compounds. A dopant is a small quantity of an intentionally added impurity. The controlled movement of electrons in doped silicon semiconductors carries digital information in computer circuitry.

Groups 1, 2, 17, and 18 are often identified with the group names shown on the table to the right. Groups 3 through 12 are called the **transition metals**. The lanthanoid series is contained in period 6, and the actinoid series is in period 7. The two series together are called the **inner transition metals**.

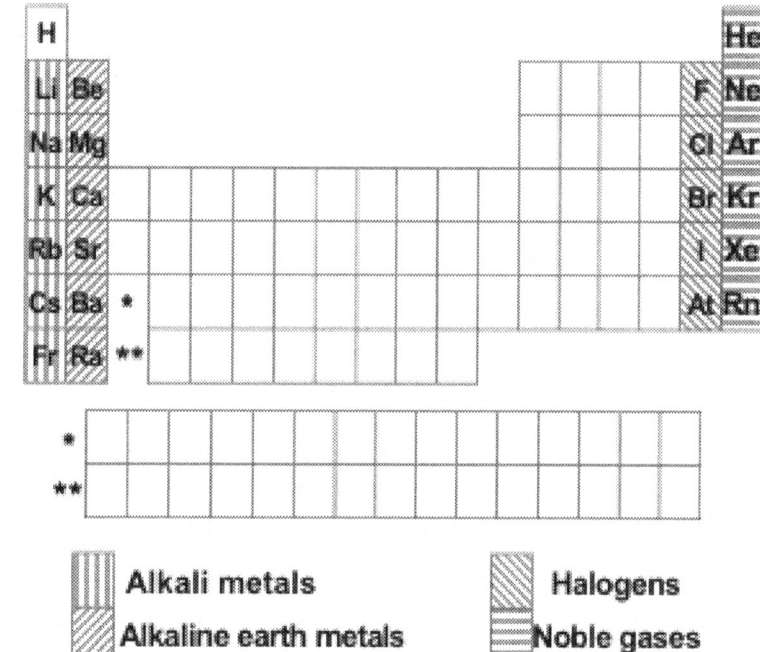

Several elements are found as **diatomic molecules**: (H_2, N_2, O_2, and the halogens: F_2, Cl_2, Br_2, and I_2). Mnemonic devices to remember the diatomic elements are: "$Br_2I_2N_2Cl_2H_2O_2F_2$" (pronounced "Brinklehof") and "**H**ave **N**o **F**ear **O**f **I**ce **C**old **B**eer." These molecules are attracted to one another using **weak London dispersion forces** (see **section 0014**).

Note that **hydrogen** is not an alkali metal. Hydrogen is a colorless gas and is the most abundant element in the universe, but H_2 is very rare in the atmosphere because it is light enough to escape gravity and reach outer space. Hydrogen atoms form more compounds than any other element.

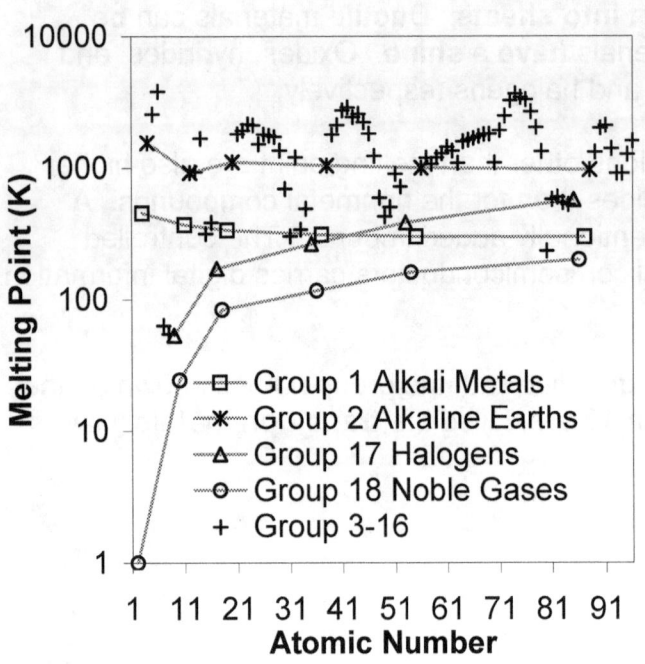

Alkali metals are shiny, soft, metallic solids. They have **low melting points and low densities** compared with other metals because they have a weaker metallic bond (see the square data points in the figures to the left and below). Measures of intermolecular attractions including their **melting points decrease further down the periodic table due to weaker metallic bonds** as the size of atoms increases. Most salts with an alkali metal cation are always soluble

Alkaline earth metals (group 2 elements) are grey, metallic solids. They are harder, denser, and have a higher melting point than the alkali metals (see asterisk data points in the figures), but values for these properties are still low compared to most of the transition metals. Measures of metallic bond strength like melting points for alkaline earths do not follow a simple trend down the periodic table.

When cut by a knife, the exposed surface of an **alkali metal or alkaline earth metal** quickly turns into an oxide. These elements **do not occur in nature as free metals**. Instead, they react with many other elements to form white or grey water-soluble salts. With some exceptions, the oxides of group 1 elements have the formula M_2O, their hydrides are MH, and their halides are MX (for example, NaCl). The oxides of group 2 elements have the formula MO, their hydrides are MH_2, and their halides are MX_2.

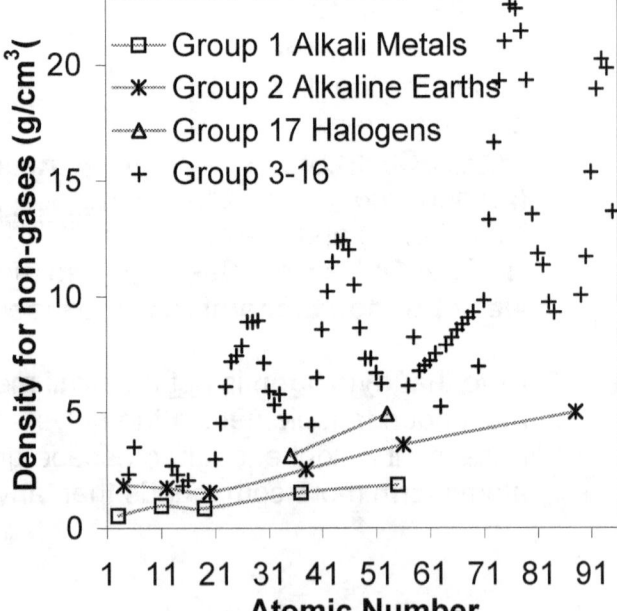

Copper, silver, and gold (group 11) are known as the **noble metals** or **coinage metals** because they are very unreactive.

The most powerful chemical reactions between elements occur between metals and non-metals. This also corresponds to reactions between the most and least electronegative elements. Therefore, **in a reaction with a metal, the most reactive elements are the most nonmetallic elements** or compounds containing those elements. These elements are also the most electronegative. **In a reaction with a nonmetal, the most reactive elements are the most metallic** or least electronegative elements. The reactivity of elements may be described by a **reactivity series**: an ordered list with chemicals that react strongly at one end and nonreactive chemicals at the other. The following reactivity series is for metals reacting with oxygen:

Metal	K	Na	Ca	Mg	Al	Zn	Fe	Pb	Cu	Hg	Ag	Au
Reaction with O_2	Burns violently		Burns rapidly					Oxidizes slowly			No reaction	

There is a **periodicity in oxidation numbers** as shown in the table below for examples of oxides with the maximum oxidation number. Remember that an element may occur in different compounds in several different oxidation states.

Group	1	2	13	14	15	16	17	18
Oxide with maximum oxidation number	Li_2O Na_2O	BeO MgO	B_2O_3 Al_2O_3	CO_2 SiO_2	N_2O_5 P_2O_5	SO_3	Cl_2O_7 Br_2O_7	XeO_4
Oxidation number	+1	+2	+3	+4	+5	+6	+7	+8

They are called "oxidation numbers" because oxygen was the element of choice for reacting with materials when modern chemistry began, and the result was Mendeleev arranging his first table to look similar to this one.

Competency 0009: Understand the kinetic molecular theory, the nature of phase changes, and the gas laws.

The kinetic molecular theory and the nature of phase changes were introduced in **Competency 0006**.

The relationship between **kinetic energy** and **intermolecular forces** determines whether a collection of molecules will be a gas, liquid, or solid. In a gas, the energy of intermolecular forces is much weaker than the kinetic energy of the molecules. Kinetic molecular theory is usually applied for gases and is best applied by imagining ourselves shrinking down to become a molecule and picturing what happens when we bump into other molecules and into container walls.

Gas **pressure** results from molecular collisions with container walls. The **number of molecules** striking an **area** on the walls and the **average kinetic energy** per molecule are the only factors that contribute to pressure. A higher **temperature** increases speed and kinetic energy. There are more collisions at higher temperatures, but the average distance between molecules does not change, and thus density does not change in a sealed container.

Kinetic molecular theory explains why the pressure and temperature of gases behave the way they do by making a few assumptions, namely:

1) The energies of intermolecular attractive and repulsive forces may be neglected.
2) The average kinetic energy of the molecules is proportional to absolute temperature.
3) Energy can be transferred between molecules during collisions and the collisions are elastic, so the average kinetic energy of the molecules doesn't change due to collisions.
4) The volume of all molecules in a gas is negligible compared to the total volume of the container.

Strictly speaking, molecules also contain some kinetic energy by rotating or experiencing other motions. The motion of a molecule from one place to another is called **translation**. Translational kinetic energy is the form that is transferred by collisions, and kinetic molecular theory ignores other forms of kinetic energy because they are not proportional to temperature.

The following table summarizes the application of kinetic molecular theory to an increase in container volume, number of molecules, and temperature:

Effect of an **increase** in one variable with other two constant	Impact on gas: − = decrease, 0 = no change, + = increase						
	Average distance between molecules	Density in a sealed container	Average speed of molecules	Average translational kinetic energy of molecules	Collisions with container walls per second	Collisions per unit area of wall per second	Pressure (P)
Volume of container (V)	+	−	0	0	−	−	−
Number of molecules	−	+	0	0	+	+	+
Temperature (T)	0	0	+	+	+	+	+

Additional details on the kinetic molecular theory may be found at http://hyperphysics.phy-astr.gsu.edu/hbase/kinetic/ktcon.html. An animation of gas particles colliding is located at http://comp.uark.edu/~jgeabana/mol_dyn/.

Boyle's law states that the volume of a fixed amount of gas at constant temperature is inversely proportional to the gas pressure, or:
$$V \propto \frac{1}{P}.$$

Gay-Lussac's law states that the pressure of a fixed amount of gas in a fixed volume is proportional to absolute temperature, or:
$$P \propto T.$$

Charles's law states that the volume of a fixed amount of gas at constant pressure is directly proportional to absolute temperature, or:
$$V \propto T.$$

The **combined gas law** uses the above laws to determine a proportionality expression that is used for a constant quantity of gas:
$$V \propto \frac{T}{P}.$$
The combined gas law is often expressed as an equality between identical amounts of an ideal gas at two different states ($n_1=n_2$):
$$\frac{P_1 V_1}{T_1} = \frac{P_2 V_2}{T_2}.$$

Avogadro's hypothesis states that equal volumes of different gases at the same temperature and pressure contain equal numbers of molecules.
Avogadro's law states that the volume of a gas at constant temperature and pressure is directly proportional to the quantity of gas, or:
$\quad V \propto n$ where n is the number of moles of gas.

Avogadro's law and the combined gas law yield $V \propto \frac{nT}{P}$. The proportionality constant R--the **ideal gas constant**--is used to express this proportionality as the **ideal gas law**:

$PV = nRT$.

The ideal gas law is useful because it contains all the information of Charles's, Avogadro's, Boyle's, and the combined gas laws in a single expression.

Solving ideal gas law problems is a straightforward process of algebraic manipulation. **Errors commonly arise from using improper units**, particularly for the ideal gas constant R. An absolute temperature scale must be used—never °C—and is usually reported using the Kelvin scale, but volume and pressure units often vary from problem to problem.

If pressure is given in atmospheres and volume is given in liters, a value for R of **0.08206 L-atm/(mol-K)** is used. If pressure is given in pascal (newtons/m^2) and volume in m^3, then the SI value for R of **8.314 J/(mol-K)** may be used because a joule is defined as a newton-meter or a pascal-m^3. A value for R of **8.314 Pa-m^3/(mol-K)** is identical to the ideal gas constant using joules.

The ideal gas law may also be rearranged to determine gas molar density in moles per unit volume (molarity):

$$\frac{n}{V} = \frac{P}{RT}.$$

Gas density d in grams per unit volume is found after multiplication by the molecular weight M:

$$d = \frac{nM}{V} = \frac{PM}{RT}.$$

Molecular weight may also be determined from the density of an ideal gas:

$$M = \frac{dV}{n} = \frac{dRT}{P}.$$

Example: Determine the molecular weight of an ideal gas that has a density of 3.24 g/L at 800 K and 3.00 atm.

Solution:
$$M = \frac{dRT}{P} = \frac{\left(3.24 \frac{g}{L}\right)\left(0.08206 \frac{L\text{-atm}}{mol\text{-}K}\right)(800\ K)}{3.00\ atm} = 70.9 \frac{g}{mol}.$$

Tutorials for gas laws may be found online at: http://www.chemistrycoach.com/tutorials-6.htm. A flash animation tutorial for problems involving a piston may be found at http://www.mhhe.com/physsci/chemistry/essentialchemistry/flash/gasesv6.swf.

Many problems are given at "**standard temperature and pressure**" or "**STP.**" Standard conditions are *exactly* **1 atm** (101.325 kPa) and **0 °C (273.15 K)**. At STP, one mole of an ideal gas has a volume of:

$$V = \frac{nRT}{P}$$

$$= \frac{(1\ mole)\left(0.08206 \frac{L\text{-atm}}{mol\text{-}K}\right)(273\ K)}{1\ atm} = 22.4\ L.$$

The value of 22.4 L is known as the **standard molar volume of any gas at STP**.

CHEMISTRY

For mixtures of gases in a container, each gas exerts a **partial pressure** that it would have if it were present in the container alone. **Dalton's law** of partial pressures states that the total pressure of a gas mixture is simply the sum of these partial pressures:

$$P_{total} = P_1 + P_2 + P_3 + \ldots$$

Dalton's law may be applied to the ideal gas law:

$$P_{total}V = (P_1 + P_2 + P_3 + \ldots)V = (n_1 + n_2 + n_3 + \ldots)RT.$$

Effusion occurs when gas escapes through a tiny opening into a vacuum or into a region at lower pressure. **Graham's law** states that the rate of effusion (r) for a gas is inversely proportional to the square root of its molecular weight (M):

$$r \propto \frac{1}{\sqrt{M}}.$$

Graham's law may be used to compare the ratios of effusion rates and molecular weights for two different gases:

$$\frac{r_1}{r_2} = \sqrt{\frac{M_2}{M_1}}.$$

Graham's law uses the same two expressions above to describe the dependence of the **diffusion** rate on molecular weight.

Competency 0010: Understand the process of nuclear transformation.

The energies of nuclear reactions and radioactive decays can only be considered with the aid of **Einstein's equation relating mass and energy**:

$E = mc^2$

where: $E \Rightarrow$ Energy in Joules
$m \Rightarrow$ Mass in kg
$c \Rightarrow$ Speed of light (2.998×10^8 m/s)

A very large amount of energy is associated with small quantities of mass. A more useful equation determines the impact of a change in mass on energy:

$$\Delta E = c^2 \Delta m$$

The mass changes of energetic chemical reactions are too small to measure. It's a safe assumption that mass is conserved for chemical reactions. However, in nuclear reactions, we can obtain values for the masses of reactants and products.

Example: How much energy is released by one gram of Uranium-235 undergoing the fission reaction:

$$^{235}_{92}U + ^{1}_{0}n \rightarrow ^{141}_{56}Ba + ^{92}_{36}Kr + 3^{1}_{0}n\ ?$$

The atomic masses of the components are:
uranium-235 = 235.0439 u, barium-141 = 140.9140 u, krypton-92 = 91.9218 u, and the atomic mass of a neutron is 1.00867 u.

Solution: The total mass of the 2 reacting particles is:
$$235.0439\ u + 1.00867\ u = 236.0526\ u.$$
The total mass of the 5 product particles is:
$$140.9140\ u + 91.9218\ u + 3 \times 1.00867\ u = 235.8618\ u.$$
The change in mass when one atom of ^{235}U experiences this fission is:
$$235.8618\ u - 236.0526\ u = -0.1908\ u$$

The change in mass when one mole of ^{235}U undergoes fission is found by recognizing that the conversion from u to grams and atoms to moles both require Avogadro's number:

$$\frac{-0.1908\ u\ \text{mass change}}{\text{atom of }^{235}_{92}U} \times \frac{6.022 \times 10^{23}\ \text{atoms}}{\text{mol }^{235}_{92}U} \times \frac{1\ g\ \text{mass change}}{6.022 \times 10^{23}\ u\ \text{mass change}}$$

$$= -0.1908\ \frac{g\ \text{mass change}}{\text{mol }^{235}_{92}U}$$

Einstein's equation requires mass change in kg, and we are interested in the fission of one gram of uranium:

$$-0.1908\ \frac{g\ \text{mass change}}{\text{mol }^{235}_{92}U} \times \frac{1\ \text{mol }^{235}_{92}U}{235.0439\ g\ ^{235}_{92}U} \times \frac{1\ kg\ \text{mass change}}{1000\ g\ \text{mass change}}$$

$$= -8.118 \times 10^{-7}\ \frac{kg\ \text{mass change}}{g\ ^{235}_{92}U}$$

This value may be used in Einstein's equation to obtain the number of joules:

$$\Delta E = c^2 \Delta m = \left(2.998 \times 10^8\ \frac{m}{s}\right)^2 \left(-8.118 \times 10^{-7}\ kg\right)$$

$$= 7.296 \times 10^{10}\ J$$

This is a large number for one gram of material. One gram of uranium fission supplies more energy than 500 gallons of gasoline combustion or 10000 kg of exploding TNT.

CHEMISTRY

Types of radiation

Some nuclei are unstable and emit particles and electromagnetic radiation. These emissions from the nucleus are known as **radioactivity**; the unstable isotopes are known as **radioisotopes**; and the nuclear reactions that spontaneously alter them are known as **radioactive decay**. Particles commonly involved in nuclear reactions are listed in the following table:

Particle	Neutron	Proton	Electron	Alpha particle	Beta particle	Gamma rays
Symbol	^1_0n	^1_1p or ^1_1H	$^0_{-1}e$	$^4_2\alpha$ or ^4_2He	$^0_{-1}\beta$ or $^0_{-1}e$	$^0_0\gamma$

Nuclear equations are balanced by equating the sum of mass numbers on both sides of a reaction equation and the sum of atomic numbers on both sides of a reaction equation.

The electron is assigned an atomic number of –1 to account for the conversion during radioactive decay of a neutron to a proton and an emitted electron called a **beta particle**:

$$^1_0n \rightarrow {}^1_1p + {}^0_{-1}e.$$

Sulfur-35 is an isotope that decays by beta emission:

$$^{35}_{16}S \rightarrow {}^{35}_{17}Cl + {}^0_{-1}e.$$

In most cases nuclear reactions result in a **nuclear transmutation** from one element to another. Transmutation was originally connected to the mythical "philosopher's stone" of alchemy that could turn cheaper elements into gold. When Frederick Soddy and Ernest Rutherford first recognized that radioactive decay was changing one element into another, Soddy remembered saying, "Rutherford, this is transmutation!" Rutherford replied, "Soddy, don't call it transmutation. They'll have our heads off as alchemists."

Large isotopes often decay by **alpha particle** emission:

$$^{238}_{92}U \rightarrow {}^{234}_{90}Th + {}^4_2He.$$

Gamma rays are high-energy electromagnetic radiation, and gamma radiation is almost always emitted when other radioactive decay occurs. Gamma rays usually aren't written into nuclear equations because neither the mass number nor the atomic number is altered. One exception is the annihilation of an electron by a positron, an event that only produces gamma radiation:

$$^0_{-1}e + {}^0_1e \rightarrow 2{}^0_0\gamma.$$

When two nuclei collide, they sometimes stick to each other and synthesize a new nucleus. This **nuclear fusion** was first demonstrated by the synthesis of oxygen from nitrogen and alpha particles:

$$^{14}_7N + {}^4_2He \rightarrow {}^{17}_8O + {}^1_1H.$$

CHEMISTRY

Fusion is also used to create new heavy elements, causing periodic tables to grow out of date every few years. In 2004, the name roentgenium was approved (in honor of Wilhelm Roentgen, the discoverer of X-rays) for the element first synthesized in 1994 by the following reaction:

$$^{209}_{83}Bi + ^{64}_{28}Ni \rightarrow ^{272}_{111}Rg + ^{1}_{0}n.$$

A heavy nucleus may also split apart into smaller nuclei by **nuclear fission.**.

Damage to matter caused by radiation
Non-ionizing radiation does not carry enough energy to remove electrons from atoms, and it generally does not cause damage unless it is damage done by heating the material it contacts. Because quantum-events are all-or-nothing, a large amount of non-ionizing radiation is generally harmless, and we can safely live in a world full of lightning flashes and radio waves.

Ionizing radiation carries enough energy to remove an electron, thus turning an atom into an ion. These events can be very damaging to life because they alter the chemistry of important molecules like DNA. Very high exposure can cause radiation poisoning.

Alpha particles are high-energy helium nuclei. They **are the most destructive form of ionizing radiation.** They carry so much energy because of their charge and large mass, but **they can be stopped by a thin sheet of paper**. Alpha emitting radiation is harmful to life if it is inhaled or ingested. Most smoke detectors use alpha-emitting isotopes in a sealed container.

Beta particles are high-energy electrons. They are less harmful to matter than alpha rays because they are less energetic, but they can penetrate further into matter. A thin sheet of aluminum will stop a typical beta particle.

High energy EM radiation (e.g., some ultraviolet, all X-rays, and especially **gamma rays.** is a form of ionizing radiation. Because photons have no mass, gamma rays are less ionizing than alpha or beta particles, but gamma rays can penetrate through matter, so protection against them requires thicker shielding.

The **half-life** of a reaction is the **time required to consume half the reactant**. The rate of radioactive decay for an isotope is usually expressed as a half-life. Solving these problems is straightforward if the given amount of time is an exact multiple of the half-life. For example, the half-life of ^{233}Pa is 27.0 days. This means that of 200 grams of ^{233}Pa will decay according to the following table:

Day	Number of half-lives	^{233}Pa remaining	^{233}Pa decayed since day 0
0	0	200 g	0 g
27.0	1	100 g	100 g
54.0	2	50.0 g	150.0 g
81.0	3	25.0 g	175.0 g
108.0	4	12.5 g	187.5 g

Regardless of whether the given amount of time is an exact multiple of the half-life, the following equation may be used:

$$A_{remaining} = A_{initially} \left(\frac{1}{2}\right)^{\frac{t}{t_{halflife}}}$$

where: $A_{remaining} \Rightarrow$ amount remaining

$A_{initially} \Rightarrow$ amount initially

$t \Rightarrow$ time

$t_{halflife} \Rightarrow$ half-life

Competency 0011: Understand the principles of thermodynamics and calorimetry.

Energy is **the driving force for change**. Energy has units of joules (J). Energy is one of the most fundamental concepts in our world. We use it to move people and things from place to place, to heat and light our homes, to entertain us, to produce food and goods and to communicate with each other. It is not a substance but rather the ability possessed by things.

The principle of conservation of energy states that **energy is neither created nor destroyed**. Any time something happens, energy is being transferred from one place to another or one form to another. None of the energy is lost or gained. Einstein's equation, $E = mc^2$ is viewed by physicists as representing the interconversion of mass and energy, not as the creation of energy from mass.

A few forms of energy are listed below:

Thermal energy is the energy that a substance has due to the **kinetic energy of its molecules** moving about chaotically. The flow of thermal energy from one body to another is called heat.

Chemical energy is the energy that bonds atoms and molecules together.

Nuclear energy is contained in the nucleus of an atom.

Mechanical kinetic energy is the energy of moving objects.

Gravitational potential energy is the energy an object has when it is elevated so it may be released and fall.

Electrical kinetic energy is the energy of electrons in motion along a circuit. The movement of electrons creates an electric current which generates electricity.

Here are some examples of how energy is transformed to do work:

1. Stoves transform the chemical energy of fuel into heat.
2. Hydroelectric plants transform the kinetic energy of falling water into electrical energy
3. A flashlight converts chemical energy stored in batteries to light energy (electromagnetic radiation) and heat.

In every case, **the total amount of energy is not changed by the process**. For example, if 2.0×10^6 J of energy is lost from falling water in a hydroelectric plant that produces 1.5×10^6 J of electrical energy, the remaining 5×10^5 J did not disappear. This energy most likely was converted from the falling water into a **form of energy that is less useful** than electrical energy (such as thermal energy that heats up the equipment).

Heat is a method of transferring energy. Technically, heat is not a form of energy. The type of energy transferred by heat is called **thermal energy, the energy that a substance has due to the kinetic energy of its molecules**. Heat has units of Joules. Heat can not be directly measured. Heat must be calculated.

Heat and temperature are not the same thing. Temperature is a measure of **the average kinetic energy of molecular motion** in a substance. We sense temperature as a measure of "hotness."

A liter of boiling water will transfer more heat than a milliliter of boiling water even though they are both at a temperature of 100 ºC. The liter of water contains more thermal energy because there are more molecules present; the temperatures are identical because the average kinetic energy per molecule is the same. Temperature and density are **intensive properties**, meaning that it does not depend on the amount of material. Volume, mass, and heat content are **extensive properties** because more material will give a higher value for these properties.

When two objects are in thermal contact, **heat flows from a higher to a lower temperature**. In the example to the right, a spoon at room temperature was placed in a hot cup of coffee. Heat will flow from the tea to the spoon (shown by the right diagonal arrow). Heat will also flow from the tea into the air (shown by the small vertical arrows).

In chemistry, we imagine the transfer of heat as a transfer of kinetic energy between atoms, similar to the transfer of kinetic energy between balls on a pool table. When a faster ball strikes a slower one, the fast ball slows down and the slow ball speeds up.

Heat flow from a higher to a lower temperature as analogous to regions where many balls are moving quickly and transferring their kinetic energy to regions where many balls are moving slowly. **Thermal equilibrium** is achieved eventually when the two objects have the same temperature. In the example above, thermal equilibrium will occur when the tea, spoon, and room are all at the same temperature.

An **exothermic** chemical or physical process (such as lighting a match) produces heat and creates a heat flow from the system to its surroundings, raising the temperature of the surrounding environment. An **endothermic** process (such as melting an ice cube in a glass of water) requires heat and creates a heat flow from the surroundings into the system, lowering the temperature of the surrounding environment.

Heat transfer occurs in one of three ways: conduction, convection and radiation.

Conduction is the transfer of heat **directly from one object to another**. Conduction most easily and often occurs in solids but fluids may also transfer energy through conduction. For example, the metal spoon in a hot cup of coffee described in the previous skill will become warm because the hot coffee molecules touch and transfer their thermal energy to the spoon's atoms, warming the spoon's atoms.

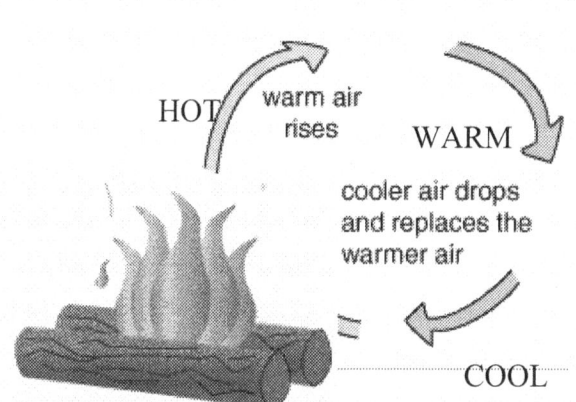

Convection is the transfer of heat through the **movement of gases or liquids called currents**. With a fire, for example, hot air rises, cold air flows into the space vacated by the moving hot air. This cold air is warmed by the fire and rises as well. This creates a continuous pattern of warming air. Convection can also lead to circulation in a liquid, as in the heating of a pot of water over a flame. Heated water expands and becomes more buoyant. Cooler, more dense water near the surface descends and patterns of circulation can be formed, though they will not be as regular as suggested in the drawing. The arrows in these drawing represent the **flow of material** carrying high or low

temperatures. They are not diagrams showing the flow of heat. For the fire and the stove, arrows indicating heat flow would be from the source of the heat upwards.

Radiation is the transfer of energy **via electromagnetic waves** and is the method used by the sun to transport its energy to earth. Light energy can not reach the earth through conduction or convection. Earth and sun are separated by empty space and are not touching so their atoms do not collide and exchange heat. There are no gases or fluids between the sun and earth to transfer energy via convection. Transfer of heat by radiation occurs at the speed of light and travels great distances even in a vacuum.

A warm or hot object gives off **infrared electromagnetic radiation**, which can be absorbed in another object, heating it up. Electric heaters use radiation to heat a room. If a fan is present, they use both radiation and convection.

Internal energy and enthalpy
The **internal energy** of a material is the **sum of the total kinetic energy** of its molecules and the **potential energy** of interactions between those molecules. Total kinetic energy includes the contributions from translational motion and other components of motion such as rotation. The potential energy includes **energy stored in the form of resisting intermolecular attractions** between molecules.

The **enthalpy** (*H*) of a material is the **sum of its internal energy and the mechanical work** it can do by driving a piston. We usually don't deal with mechanical work in high school chemistry, so the differences between internal energy and enthalpy are not important. The key concept is that a change in the **enthalpy** of a substance is the total **energy** change caused by **adding/removing heat** at constant pressure.

When a material is heated and experiences a phase change, **thermal energy is used to break the intermolecular bonds** holding the material together. Similarly, bonds are formed with the release of thermal energy when a material changes its phase during cooling. Therefore, **the energy of a material increases during a phase change that requires heat and decreases during a phase change that releases heat**. For example, the energy of H_2O increases when ice melts and decreases when water freezes.

Heat capacity and specific heat
A substance's molar **heat capacity** is the heat required to **change the temperature of one mole of the substance by one degree**. Heat capacity has units of joules per mol-kelvin or joules per mol-°C. The two units are interchangeable because we are only concerned with differences between one temperature and another. A Kelvin degree and a Celsius are the same size.

The **specific heat** of a substance (also called specific heat capacity) is the heat required to **change the temperature of one gram or kilogram by one degree**. Specific heat has units of joules per mole-gram or joules per mole-kilogram.

CHEMISTRY

These terms are used to solve thermochemistry problems involving a change in temperature by applying the formula:

$q = n \times C \times \Delta T$ where $q \Rightarrow$ heat added (positive) or evolved (negative)

$n \Rightarrow$ amount of material

$C \Rightarrow$ molar heat capacity if n is in moles, specific heat if n is a mass

$\Delta T \Rightarrow$ change in temperature $T_{final} - T_{initial}$

Heats of fusion, vaporization, and sublimation

A substance's **heat of fusion** (ΔH_{fusion}) is the heat required to **change one mole from a solid to a liquid** by freezing. This is also the heat released from the substance when it changes from a liquid to a solid (melts).

A substance's **heat of vaporization** ($\Delta H_{vaporization}$) is the heat required to **change one mole of a substance from a liquid to a gas** or the heat released by condensation.

A substance's heat of sublimation ($\Delta H_{sublimation}$) is the heat required to change one mole directly from a solid to a gas by sublimation or the heat released by deposition.

These three values are also called enthalpies or "latent heats" of fusion, vaporization, and sublimation. They have units of joules per mole, and are negative values when heat is released.

$$\text{Solid} \xrightarrow[\text{melting}]{\Delta H_{fusion}} \text{Liquid} \xrightarrow[\text{vaporization}]{\Delta H_{vaporization}} \text{Gas} \qquad \text{Solid} \xrightarrow[\text{sublimation}]{\Delta H_{sublimation}} \text{Gas}$$

$$\text{Gas} \xrightarrow[\text{condensation}]{-\Delta H_{vaporization}} \text{Liquid} \xrightarrow[\text{freezing}]{-\Delta H_{fusion}} \text{Solid} \qquad \text{Gas} \xrightarrow[\text{deposition}]{-\Delta H_{sublimation}} \text{Solid}$$

These terms are used to solve thermochemistry problems involving a change of phase by applying the formula:

$$q = n \times \Delta H_{change}$$

where $q \Rightarrow$ heat added (positive) or evolved (negative)

$n \Rightarrow$ amount of material

$\Delta H_{change} \Rightarrow$ enthalpy of fusion, vaporization, or sublimation for heat added

$\Rightarrow$ −(enthalpy of fusion, vaporization, or sublimation) for heat evolved

TEACHER CERTIFICATION EXAM

Example: What is the change in energy of 10 g of gold at 25 °C when it is heated beyond its melting point to 1300 °C. You will need the following data for gold:

Solid heat capacity: 28 J/mol-K
Molten heat capacity: 20 J/mol-K
Enthalpy of fusion: 12.6 kJ/mol
Melting point: 1064 °C

Solution: First determine the number of moles used: $10 \text{ g} \times \dfrac{1 \text{ mol}}{197 \text{ g}} = 0.051 \text{ mol}$.

There are then three steps. 1) Heat the solid. 2) Melt the solid. 3) Heat the liquid. All three require energy so they will be positive numbers.

1) Heat the solid:

$$q_1 = n \times C \times \Delta T = 0.051 \text{ mol} \times 28 \dfrac{\text{J}}{\text{mol-K}} \times (1064 \text{ °C} - 25 \text{ °C})$$

$$= 1.48 \times 10^3 \text{ J} = 1.48 \text{ kJ}$$

2) Melt the solid: $q_2 = n \times \Delta H_{fusion} = 0.051 \text{ mol} \times 12.6 \dfrac{\text{kJ}}{\text{mol}}$

$$= 0.64 \text{ kJ}$$

3) Heat the liquid:

$$q_3 = n \times C \times \Delta T = 0.051 \text{ mol} \times 20 \dfrac{\text{J}}{\text{mol-K}} \times (1300 \text{ °C} - 1064 \text{ °C})$$

$$= 2.4 \times 10^2 \text{ J} = 0.24 \text{ kJ}$$

The sum of the three processes is the total change in energy of the gold:

$$q = q_1 + q_2 + q_3 = 1.48 \text{ kJ} + 0.64 \text{ kJ} + 0.24 \text{ kJ} = 2.36 \text{ kJ}$$

$$= 2.4 \text{ kJ}$$

Heat of reaction

When a chemical reaction takes place, the enthalpies of the products will differ from the enthalpies of the reactants. There is an energy change for the reaction ΔH_{rxn}, determined by **the sum of the products minus the sum of the reactants**:

$$\Delta H_{rxn} = H_{product\ 1} + H_{product\ 2} + \ldots - (H_{reactant\ 1} + H_{reactant\ 2} + \ldots).$$

The enthalpy change for a reaction is commonly called the **heat of reaction**.

If the enthalpies of the products are greater than the enthalpies of the reactants then ΔH_{rxn} **is positive** and the reaction is **endothermic**. Endothermic reactions **absorb heat** from their surroundings. The simplest endothermic reactions break chemical bonds.

If the enthalpies of the products are less than the enthalpies of the reactants then ΔH_{rxn} **is negative** and the reaction is **exothermic**. Exothermic reactions **release heat** into their surroundings. The simplest exothermic reactions form new chemical bonds.

The heat absorbed or released by a chemical reaction often has the impact of changing the temperature of the reaction vessel and of the chemicals themselves. The measurement of these heat effects is known as **calorimetry**.

The enthalpy change of a reaction ΔH_{rxn} **is equal in magnitude but has the opposite sign to the enthalpy change for the reverse reaction**. If a series of reactions lead back to the initial reactants then the net energy change for the entire process is zero.

When a reaction is composed of substeps, the **total enthalpy change will be the sum of the changes for each step**. Even if a reaction in reality contains no substeps, we may still write any number of reactions in series that lead from the same reactants to the same products and their sum will be the heat of the reaction of interest. The ability to add together these enthalpies to form ultimate products from initial reactants is known as **Hess's Law**. It is used to determine one heat of reaction from others:

$$\Delta H_{net\ rxn} = H_{rxn\ 1} + H_{rxn\ 2} + \ldots$$

A **standard** thermodynamic value occurs with all components at 25 °C and 100 kPa. This *thermodynamic standard state* is slightly different from the *standard temperature and pressure* (STP) often used for gas law problems (0 °C and 1 atm=101.325 kPa). Standard properties of common chemicals are listed in tables.

The **heat of formation** ΔH_f of a chemical is the heat required (positive) or emitted (negative) when elements react to form the chemical. It is also called the enthalpy of formation. The **standard heat of formation** $\Delta H_f°$ is the heat of formation with all reactants and products at 25 °C and 100 kPa.

Elements in their **most stable form** are assigned a value of $\Delta H_f° = 0$ kJ/mol. Different forms of an element in the same phase of matter are known as **allotropes**.

Example: The heat of formation for carbon as a gas is:

$\Delta H_f°$ for $C(g) = 718.4 \frac{kJ}{mol}$. C in the solid phase exists in three

allotropes. A C_{60} *buckyball* (one face is shown to the left), contains C atoms linked with aromatic bonds and arranged in the shape of a soccer ball. C_{60} was discovered in 1985. *Diamond* (below left) contains single C–C bonds in a three dimensional network. The most stable form at 25 °C is *graphite* (below right). Graphite is composed of C atoms with aromatic bonds in sheets.

$\Delta H_f°$ for C_{60}(*buckminsterfullerene* or *buckyball*) $= 38.0 \frac{kJ}{mol}$

$\Delta H_f°$ for C_∞ (*diamond*) $= 1.88 \frac{kJ}{mol}$

$\Delta H_f°$ for C_∞ (*graphite*) $= 0 \frac{kJ}{mol}$.

Heat of combustion ΔH_c (also called enthalpy of combustion) is the heat of reaction when a chemical **burns in O_2** to form completely oxidized products such as **CO_2 and H_2O**. It is also the heat of reaction for **nutritional molecules that are metabolized** in the body. The standard heat of combustion $\Delta H_c°$ takes place at 25 °C and 100 kPa. **Combustion is always exothermic**, so the negative sign for values of ΔH_c is often omitted. If a combustion reaction is used in Hess's Law, the value must be negative.

Example: Determine the standard heat of formation $\Delta H_f°$ for ethylene:
$$2C(graphite) + 2H_2(g) \to C_2H_4(g).$$
Use the heat of combustion for ethylene:

$\Delta H_c° = 1411.2 \frac{kJ}{mol\ C_2H_4}$ for $C_2H_4(g) + 3O_2(g) \to 2CO_2(g) + 2H_2O(l)$

and the following two heats of formation for CO_2 and H_2O:

$\Delta H_f° = -393.5 \frac{kJ}{mol\ C}$ for $C(graphite) + O_2(g) \to CO_2(g)$

$\Delta H_f° = -285.9 \frac{kJ}{mol\ H_2}$ for $H_2(g) + \frac{1}{2}O_2(g) \to H_2O(l)$.

Solution: Use Hess's Law after rearranging the given reactions so they cancel to yield the reaction of interest. Combustion is exothermic, so ΔH for this reaction is negative. We are interested in C_2H_4 as a product, so we take the opposite (endothermic) reaction. The given ΔH are multiplied by stoichiometric coefficients to give the reaction of interest as the sum of the three:

$$2CO_2(g) + 2H_2O(l) \rightarrow C_2H_4(g) + 3O_2(g) \quad \Delta H = 1411.2 \frac{kJ}{mol\ reaction}$$

$$2C(graphite) + 2O_2(g) \rightarrow 2CO_2(g) \quad \Delta H = -787.0 \frac{kJ}{mol\ reaction}$$

$$2H_2(g) + O_2(g) \rightarrow 2H_2O(l) \quad \Delta H = -571.8 \frac{kJ}{mol\ reaction}$$

$$2C(graphite) + 2H_2(g) \rightarrow C_2H_4(g) \quad \Delta H_f^\circ = 52.4 \frac{kJ}{mol}$$

Whether a substance exists as a gas, liquid, or solid depends on the nature of its intermolecular attractive forces and on its temperature and pressure. This information is often visualized as a **phase diagram** for the substance.

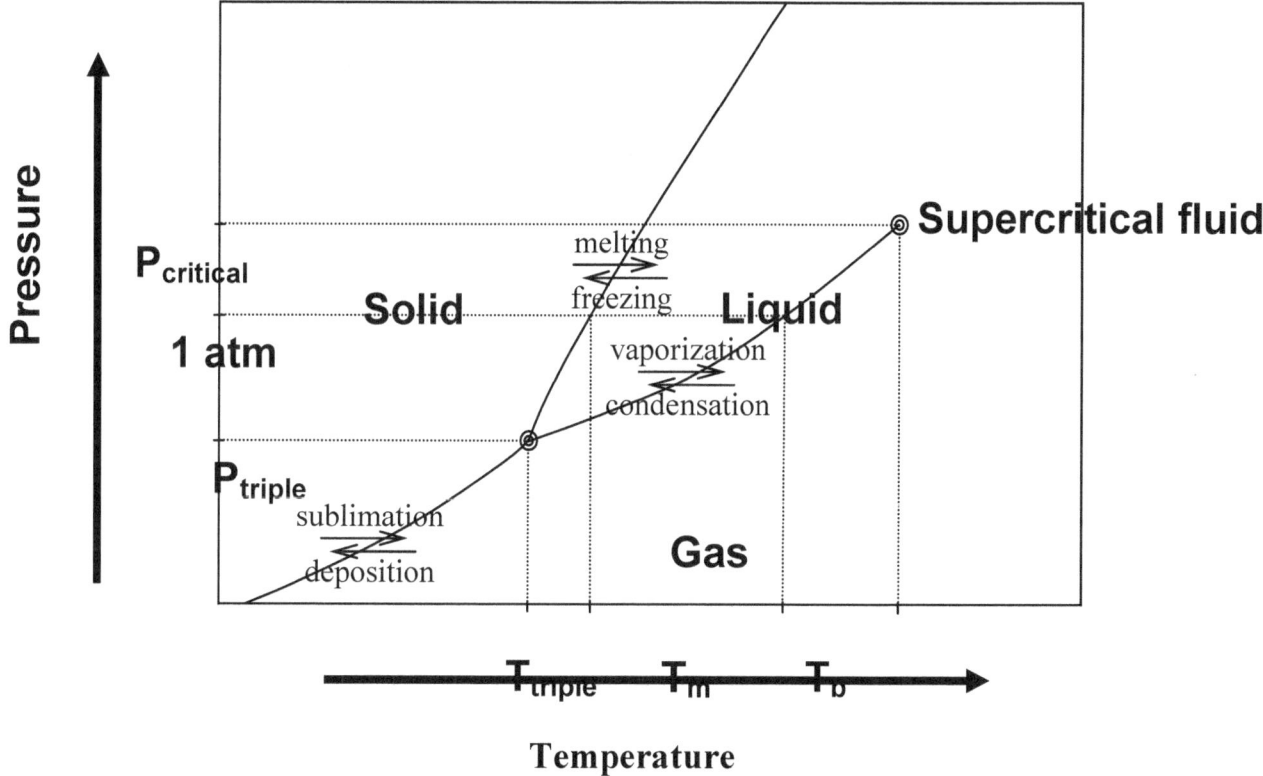

A region on the phase diagram represents each phase. Solid lines dividing these regions are located at conditions under which two phases may exist at equilibrium (see competency 6) and a phase change may occur. All three phases may coexist at the **triple point** of a substance. The triple point pressure of CO_2 is greater than 1 atm, so dry ice sublimates at atmospheric pressure with no liquid phase. **Vapor pressure** at a given temperature is the pressure of the phase transition line to a gas at that temperature. **Normal melting point** (T_m) and **normal boiling point** (T_b) are defined at 1 atm. Note that freezing point and melting point refer to an identical temperature approached from different directions, but they represent the same concept. At temperatures and pressures above the **critical point**, the substance becomes too dense with too much kinetic energy for a gas-liquid interface to form. Matter under these conditions forms a **supercritical fluid** with properties of gases and of liquids.

The phase diagram for water (shown below) is unusual. The solid/liquid phase boundary slopes to the left with increasing pressure because the melting point of water decreases with increasing pressure. Note that the normal melting point of water is lower than its triple point. The diagram is not drawn to a uniform scale. Many anomalous properties of water are discussed here: http://www.lsbu.ac.uk/water/anmlies.html.

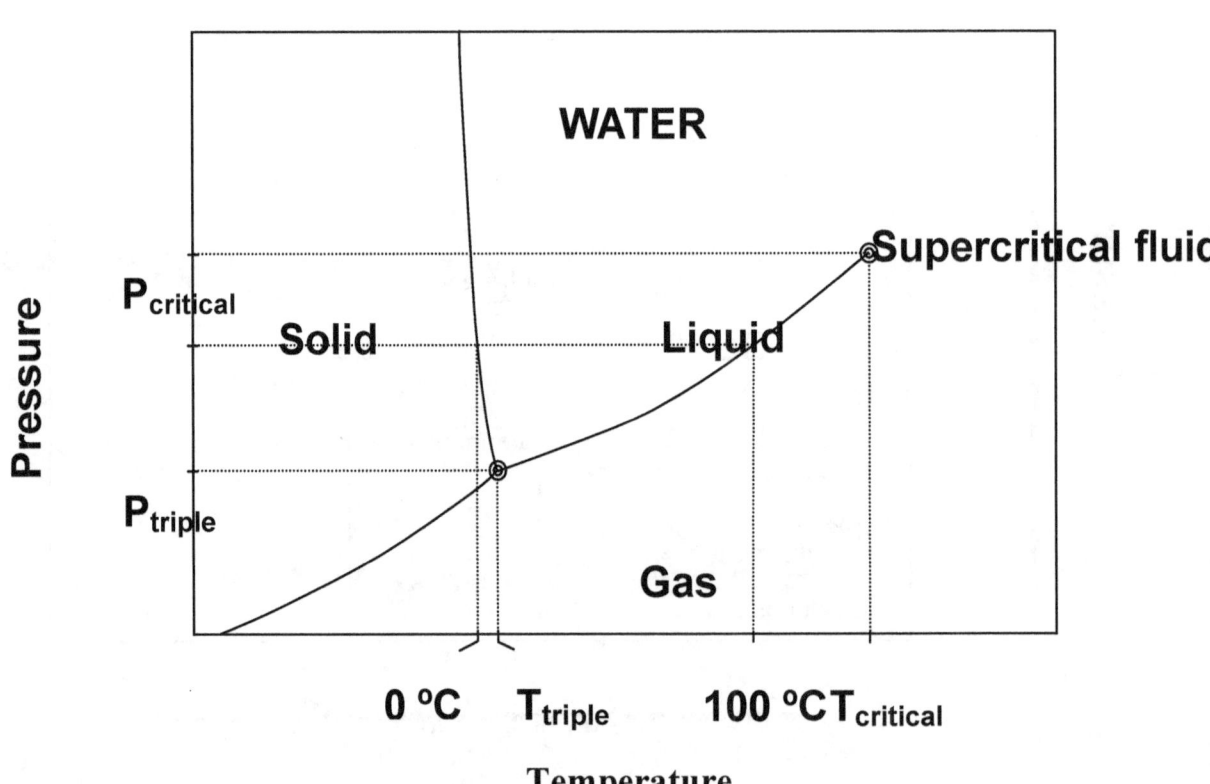

Competency 0012: Understand energy relationships in chemical bonding and chemical reactions.

Chemical energy is the **energy stored in substances due to the arrangement of atoms** within the substance. When atoms are rearranged during chemical reactions, energy is either released or consumed. It is the energy released from chemical reactions that fuels our economy and powers our bodies. Most of the electricity produced on the planet comes from chemical energy released by the burning of petroleum, coal and natural gas. ATP is the molecule used by our body to carry chemical energy form cell to cell.

The energy in molecules is located in the **bonds between the atoms** in the molecule. To break these bonds requires energy. Once broken apart, the atoms, ions or molecules rearrange themselves to form new substances, making new bonds. Making new bonds releases energy.

If during a chemical reaction, **more energy is needed to break the reactant bonds than released when product bonds form, the reaction is endothermic** and heat is absorbed. The environment becomes colder.

On the other hand, if **more energy is released due to product bonds forming than is needed to break reactant bonds the reaction is exothermic** and the excess energy is released to the environment as heat. The temperature of the environment goes up.

Bond energies
The total energy absorbed or released in the reaction can be determined by **using heats of formation** or by using **bond energies**. The total energy change of the reaction is equal to the total energy of all of the bonds of the products minus the total energy of all of the bonds of the reactants.

Burning gasoline as a fuel would be a complex example to consider because gasoline is a mixture of hydrocarbons ranging from 5 to 12 carbon atom chains.

Propane (C_3H_8) is a better example to consider of chemical energy stored in fuel. Propane is a common fuel used in heating homes and backyard grills. When burned, the combustion reaction shown below takes place, and excess energy is released and used to cook our food

$$C_3H_8\ (g) + 5\ O_2\ (g) \rightarrow 3\ CO_2\ (g) + 4\ H_2O(l)$$

The total energy of the products is from the bonds found in the carbon dioxide molecules and the water molecules.

$$3\ O=C=O\ +\ 4\ H\text{-}O\text{-}H$$

or 6 C=O bonds and 8 H-O bonds.

A table of bond energies gives the following information:
    C=O   743 kJ/mol   H-O   463 kJ/mol

For these molecules there would be: (6 x –743 kJ/mol) + (8 x –463 kJ/mol) =–8162 kJ of energy released when these molecules form. Negative values are used to indicate energy released for this exothermic process of bond formation.

The reactants are these:

```
    H   H   H
    |   |   |
H — C — C — C — H
    |   |   |
    H   H   H        + 5  O = O
```

or 2 C-C bonds, 8 C-H bonds, and 5 O=O bonds.

These bonds require the following energy to break:
C-C   348 kJ/ mol   C-H   412 kJ/mol   O=O 498 kJ/mol.

The total energy required for the reactants would be:
(2 x 348 kJ) + (8 x 412 kJ) +(5 x 498 kJ) = 6482 kJ of energy required. Positive values are used to indicate energy required for the endothermic process of bond destruction.

The total energy change that occurs during the combustion of propane is found from the sum of the energy released by the formation of the product bonds and the energy required to break the reactant bonds:

–8162 kJ + 6482 kJ = –1680 kJ of energy is released for every mole of propane that burns.

Chemical energy transformed into heat for propulsion
Hydrogen burns with oxygen in the propulsion engine of the space shuttle. Very hot water vapor is produced by the exothermic reaction, and this vapor expands with great force to generate the upward thrust needed for launch. This water vapor is at a much higher temperature than the hydrogen and oxygen reactants. This increase in the kinetic energy of atoms is due to the transformation of chemical energy to heat, and results in the kinetic energy of the shuttle itself.

Competency 0013: Understand the types of bonds between atoms (including ionic, covalent, and metallic bonds), the formation of these bonds, and the properties of substances containing the different bonds.

The relation of valence electrons to bonding is reviewed in **Competency 0007**.

An **ionic bond** occurs **between a metal and a nonmetal**. In an ionic bond, the metal "gives" an electron to the nonmetal. A **covalent bond is favored between nonmetals**. In a covalent bond both atoms attract electrons and share electrons between them. A **metallic bond is favored between metals**. In a metallic bond, atoms lose electrons to a matrix of free electrons surrounding them. Many bonds have some characteristics of more than one of the above basic bond types.

Ionic bonds
An **ionic bond** describes the electrostatic forces that exist between **particles of opposite charge**. Elements that form an ionic bond with each other have a large difference in their electronegativity. Anions and cations pack together into a crystal **lattice** as shown to the right for NaCl. Ionic compounds are also known as **salts**.

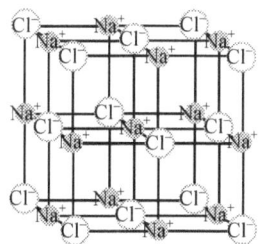

All common salts are solids at room temperature. **Salts are brittle, have a high melting point**, and do not conduct electricity because their ions are not free to move in the crystal lattice. Salts do conduct electricity in molten form. The formation of a salt from a metal and a nonmetal is a highly exothermic reaction.

Salts in solid form are generally stable compounds, but in molten form or in solution, their component ions often react to form a more stable salt.

Some salts decompose to form more stable salts, as in the decomposition of molten potassium chlorate to form potassium chloride and oxygen:
$$2KClO_3(l) \rightarrow 2KCl(s) + 3O_2(g).$$

Single and multiple covalent bonds
Nonmetals typically react with other nonmetals to form **covalent bonds**. A covalent bond is formed between two atoms by **sharing a pair of electrons**. The simplest covalent bond is between the two single electrons of hydrogen atoms. Covalent bonds may be represented by an electron pair (a pair of dots) or a line as shown below. The shared pair of electrons provides each H atom with two electrons in its valence shell (the 1s orbital), so both have the stable electron configuration of helium.

H· + ·H $\longrightarrow$ H:H
                          H—H

CHEMISTRY

Chlorine molecules have 7 electrons in their valence shell and share a pair of electrons so both have the stable electron configuration of argon.

$$:\!\ddot{\underset{..}{Cl}}\!\cdot \;+\; \cdot\!\ddot{\underset{..}{Cl}}\!: \;\longrightarrow\; :\!\ddot{\underset{..}{Cl}}\!:\!\ddot{\underset{..}{Cl}}\!:$$

$$Cl\!-\!Cl$$

In the previous two examples, a single pair of electrons was shared, and the resulting bond is referred to as a **single bond**. When two electron pairs are shared, two lines are drawn, representing a **double bond**, and three shared pairs of electrons represents a **triple bond** as shown below for CO_2 and N_2. The remaining electrons are in **unshared pairs**.

$$\ddot{O}::C::\ddot{O} \qquad :N:::N:$$

$$O=C=O \qquad N\equiv N$$

Covalent bonds in a network solid
A covalent network solid may be considered **one large molecule connected by covalent bonds**. These materials are **very hard, strong, and have a high melting point**. Diamond, C_n or C_∞, and quartz, $(SiO_2)_n$ or $(SiO_2)_\infty$, are two examples.

Electronegativity and polar/nonpolar covalent bonds
Electron pairs shared between **two atoms of the same element are shared equally**. At the other extreme, **for ionic bonding there is no electron sharing** because the electron is transferred completely from one atom to the other. Most bonds fall somewhere between these two extremes, and the electrons are **shared unequally**. This will increase the probability that the shared electrons will be located on one of the two atoms, giving that atom a **partial negative charge**, and the other atom a **partial positive charge** as shown below for gaseous HCl. Such bonds are referred to as **polar bonds**. A particle with a positive and a negative region is called a **dipole**. A lower-case delta (δ) is used to indicate partial charge or an arrow is draw from the partial positive to the partial negative atom.

$$\overset{\delta+}{H}\!-\!\overset{\delta-}{Cl} \qquad \overset{\longrightarrow}{H\!-\!Cl}$$

Electronegativity is a measure of **the ability of an atom to attract electrons** in a chemical bond. Metallic elements have low electronegativities and nonmetallic elements have high electronegativities.

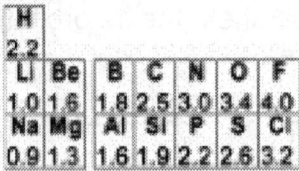

Linus Pauling developed the concept of electronegativity and its relationship to different types of bonds in the 1930s.

A **large electronegativity difference** (greater than 1.7) results in an **ionic bond**. Any bond composed of two different atoms will be slightly polar, but for a **small electronegativity difference** (less than 0.4), the distribution of charge in the bond is so nearly equal that the result is called a **nonpolar covalent bond**. An **intermediate electronegativity difference** (from 0.4 to 1.7) results in a **polar covalent bond**. HCl is polar covalent because Cl has a very high electronegativity (it is near F in the periodic table) and H is a nonmetal (and so it will form a covalent bond with Cl), but H is near the dividing line between metals and nonmetals, so there is still a significant electronegativity difference between H and Cl. Using the numbers in the table above, the electronegativity for Cl is 3.2 and it is 2.2 for H. The difference of 3.2 – 2.2 = 1.0 places this bond in the middle of the range for polar covalent bonds.

Bond type is actually a continuum as shown in the following chart for common bonds. Note that the **C-H bond** is considered **nonpolar**.

Type of bonding	Electronegativity difference	Bond
Very ionic		Fr^+—F^-
		Na^+—F^-
	3.0	
Ionic		Na^+—Cl^-
	2.0	Na^+—Br^-
Mostly ionic		Na^+—I^-
Mostly polar covalent	1.5	$C^{\delta+}$—$F^{\delta-}$
		$H^{\delta+}$—$O^{\delta-}$
Polar covalent	1.0	$H^{\delta+}$—$Cl^{\delta-}$
		$C^{\delta+}$=$O^{\delta-}$
		$H^{\delta+}$—$N^{\delta-}$
		$C^{\delta+}$—$Cl^{\delta-}$
	0.5	$C^{\delta+}$≡$N^{\delta-}$
Mostly nonpolar covalent		C—H
Fully nonpolar covalent	0	H_2, N_2, O_2, F_2, Cl_2, Br_2, I_2, C—C, S—S

⇑ Increasing ionic character

Metallic bonds

The physical properties of metals are attributed to the **electron sea model of metallic bonds** shown on the right. Metals **conduct heat and electricity** because electrons are not associated with the bonding between two specific atoms and they are able to flow through the material. They are called **delocalized** electrons. Metals are **lustrous** because electrons at their surface reflect light at many different wavelengths. Metals are **malleable** and **ductile** because the electrons are able to rearrange their positions to maintain the integrity of the solid when the metallic lattice is deformed, acting like glue between the cations. The strengths of different metallic bonds can be related to the relative amounts and positions of electrons in this glue.

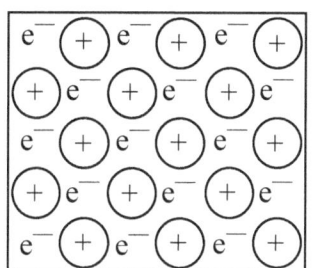

Alkali metals contain only one valence electron ("less glue"), and that electron is a considerable distance away from the nucleus ("weaker glue") because it is shielded from nuclear attraction by the noble gas configuration of the remaining electrons. The result is a weak metallic bond and a low melting point. Heavier alkali metals contain a valence electron even further from the nucleus, resulting in a very weak metallic bond and a lowering of the melting point. With two valence electrons and smaller atoms, alkaline earth metals have stronger metallic bonds than the alkali metals.

The metal with the weakest metallic bonds is mercury. Hg is a liquid at room temperature because Hg atoms hold on tightly to a stable valence configuration of full s, f, and d subshells. Fewer electrons are shared to create bonds than in other metals.

The reactivity of metals increases with lower electronegativity in reactions with nonmetals to form ionic bonds.

Hydrogen bonds

Except in larger molecules, hydrogen bonds are usually an intermolecular force, not a bonding mechanism within a single molecule. Intermolecular forces are also sometimes described as "secondary molecular bonds".

Noble gases have stable electron configurations because the subshells corresponding to their valence electrons are completely filled. Atoms often gain, lose, or share electrons in order to achieve the **same number of electrons as the noble gas nearest to them in the periodic table**. Helium has a $1s^2$ valence electron configuration, and every other noble gas has an ns^2np^6 valence electron configuration for a total of **eight valence electrons**. The observation that **many reaction products have eight valence electrons** is known as the **octet rule**.

TEACHER CERTIFICATION EXAM

Lewis dot structures are a method for keeping track of each atom's valence electrons in a molecule. Drawing Lewis structures is a three-step process:

1) Add the number of valence shell electrons for each atom. If the compound is an anion, add the charge of the ion to the total electron count because anions have "extra" electrons. If the compound is a cation, subtract the charge of the ion.
2) Write the symbols for each atom showing how the atoms connect to each other.
3) Draw a single bond (one pair of electron dots or a line) between each pair of connected atoms. Place the remaining electrons around the atoms as unshared pairs. If every atom has an octet of electrons except H atoms with two electrons, the Lewis structure is complete. Shared electrons count towards both atoms. If there are too few electron pairs to do this, draw multiple bonds (two or three pairs of electron dots between the atoms) until an octet is around each atom (except H atoms with two). If there are two many electron pairs to complete the octets with single bonds then the octet rule Is broken for this compound.

Example: Draw the Lewis structure of HCN.
Solution:
1) From their locations in the main group of the periodic table, we know that each atom contributes the following number of electrons: H—1, C—4, N—5. Because it is a neutral compound, the molecule will have a total of 10 valence electrons.
2) The atoms are connected with C at the center and will be drawn as: H C N.
Having H as the central atom is impossible because H has one valence electron and will always only have a single bond to one other atom. If N were the central atom then the formula would probably be written as HNC.
3) Connecting the atoms with 10 electrons in single bonds gives
the structure to the right. H has two electrons to fill its valence subshells, but C and N only have six each. A triple bond between these atoms fulfills the octet rule for C and N and is the correct Lewis structure.

$$H : C ::: N :$$

Resonance

O_2 contains a total of 12 valence electrons and the following Lewis structure:

Ozone, O_3, has a total of 18 valence electrons, and two Lewis structures are possible for this molecule

CHEMISTRY

Equivalent Lewis structures are called **resonance forms**. A double-headed arrow is used to indicate resonance. The actual molecule does not have a double bond on one bond and a single bond on the other. The **molecular structure is in an average state between the resonance forms**.

Hybridized atomic orbitals

Electron shell structures are built up by considering different energy levels for different subshells to explain spectroscopic data about individual atoms. However, when Lewis dot structures are drawn or molecular geometries are determined (later in this skill), all valence electrons are treated identically to explain the bonding between atoms regardless of whether the electrons once belonged to the s or the p subshell of their atom. Reconciling these views of the individual and the bonded atom requires a theory known as hybridization.

Hybridization describes the pre-bonding **promotion of one or more electrons** from a lower energy subshell to a higher energy subshell followed by a **combination** of the orbitals into degenerate **hybrid orbitals**.

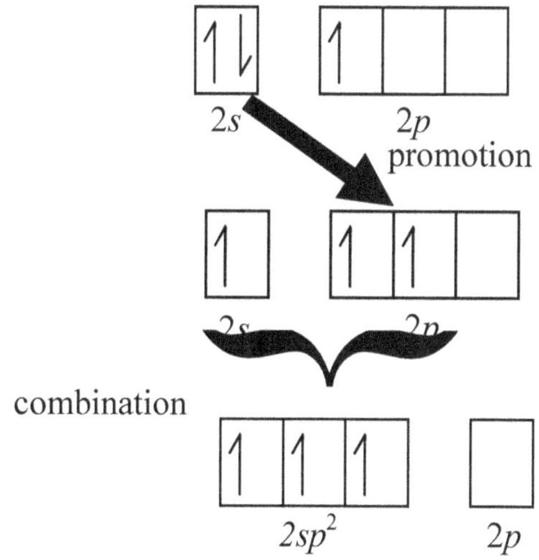

Example: A boron atom has the valence electron configuration $2s^2 2p^1$ as shown to the right. Before bonding to three other atoms, the capability to form three equivalent bonds is achieved by hybridization. First a $2s$ electron is promoted to an empty p orbital. Next the occupied orbitals combine into three hybrid $2sp^2$ orbitals. Now three electrons in degenerate orbitals are available to create covalent bonds with three atoms.

Hybridization occurs for atoms with a valence electron configuration of ns^2, ns^2np^1, or ns^2p^2. For period 2, this corresponds with Be, B, C, and N in the NH_3^+ ion.

An atom joined to its neighbor by **multiple covalent bonds** is prepared for bonding by hybridization with incomplete combination. Electrons that remain in p orbitals can contribute additional bonds between the same two atoms.

CHEMISTRY

Example: An isolated carbon atom has the valence electron configuration $2s^2 2p^2$. Hybridization to four $2sp^3$ orbitals occurs before bonding to four atoms. Three hybrid sp^2 orbitals form if there is a double bond so the C atom is bonded to three atoms and one electron remains in the p orbital. Two hybrid sp orbitals occur if there is a triple bond or two double bonds. In this case, C is bonded to two atoms with two electrons remaining in p orbitals.

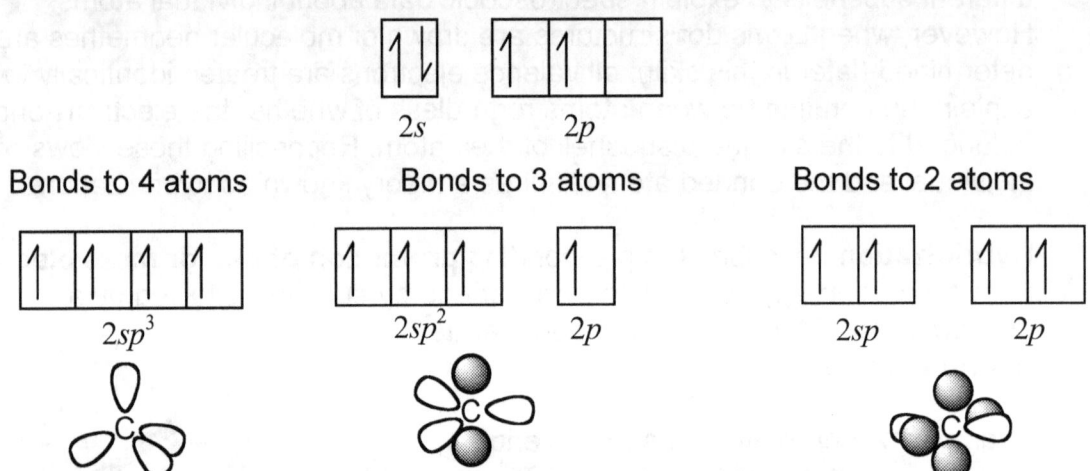

Note: p orbitals are shaded in the diagrams. These models are meant to illustrate the **locations** and **angles** of hybrid and p orbitals relative to the central atom. A mathematical solution would also show that each type of hybrid orbital (sp^3, sp^2, and sp) has a slightly different shape from the other two.

See http://www.mhhe.com/physsci/chemistry/essentialchemistry/flash/hybrv18.swf for a flash animation tutorial of hybridization.

Molecular Orbital Theory

The electron configurations of isolated atoms are found in atomic orbitals; the configurations of atoms about to bond are represented by atomic and hybridized atomic orbitals; and **the electron configurations of molecules are represented by molecular orbitals**. Molecular orbital theory is an advanced topic, but it may be simplified to representing the **bonds between atoms as overlapping electron density shapes from atomic orbitals**. There are two typical locations for molecular orbitals.

The **bonding sigma orbital** (σ) surrounds a **line drawn between the two atoms** in a bond. At least one electron pair in every bond is in a bonding σ orbital. Sigma bonds get their name from s orbitals because the spherical electron density shapes of two s orbitals overlap to form a σ orbital. A drawing of this overlap and the resulting molecular orbital is shown to the right for H_2. Hybrid or p atomic orbitals also form a σ orbital when they overlap such that the axis between the bonded atoms runs through the center of the combined electron density.

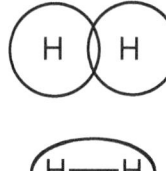

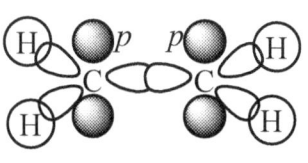

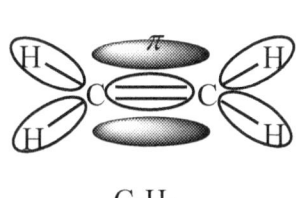

C_2H_4

The **bonding pi orbital** (π) follows regions **separate from a line drawn between the two atoms** in a bond. Two overlapping p orbitals will form π bonds to contain the additional shared electrons in molecules with double or triple bonds. π bonds prevent atoms from rotating about the central axis between them. The atomic orbitals that form the compound C_2H_4 are shown above to the left. Each H atom contains one electron in an s orbital and each C atom contains 4 valence electrons in three hybrid sp^2 orbitals and one p orbital. The compound itself contains the molecular orbitals shown below to the left. There are five σ bonds (white ovals) and one π bond (the shaded shapes).

Molecular orbital theory also predicts **antibonding orbitals** that **prevent bonding** because they are at a higher energy level than the electrons on individual atoms. Antibonding electrons play a role in explaining why molecules like H_2 form while molecules like He_2 do not, but they are not required to predict molecular structures. For more on this aspect of molecular orbital theory, see http://www.chem.ufl.edu/~chm2040/Notes/Chapter_12/theory.html.

TEACHER CERTIFICATION EXAM

Electron Pairs
Molecular geometry is predicted using the valence-shell electron-pair repulsion or **VSEPR** model. VSEPR uses the fact that **electron pairs around the central atom of a molecule repel each other**. Imagine you are one of two pairs of electrons in bonds around a central atom (like a bonds in BeH₂ in the table below). You want to be as far away from the other electron pair as possible, so you will be on one side of the atom and the other pair will be on the other side. There is a straight line (or a 180° angle) between you to the other electron pair on the other side of the nucleus. In general, electron pairs lie at the **largest possible angles** from each other.

Electron pairs	Geometrical arrangement		Predicted bond angles	Example
2	:—X—:	Linear	180°	H—Be—H
3		Trigonal planar	120°	BF₃
4		Tetrahedral	109.5°	CH₄
5		Trigonal bipyramidal	120° and 90°	PF₅
6		Octahedral	90°	SF₆

X represents a generic central atom. Lone pair electrons on F are not shown in the example molecules.

CHEMISTRY

Unshared Electron Pairs

The **shape of a molecule is given by the location of its atoms**. These are connected to central atoms by shared electrons, but unshared electrons also have an important impact on molecular shape. Unshared electrons may determine the angles between atoms. Molecular shapes in the following table take into account total and unshared electron pairs.

Electron pairs	Molecular shape				
	All shared pairs	1 unshared pair	2 unshared pairs	3 unshared pairs	4 unshared pairs
2	A—X—A Linear				
3	Trigonal planar	Bent			
4	Tetrahedral	Trigonal pyramidal	Bent		
5	Trigonal bipyramidal	Seesaw or sawhorse	T-shaped	Linear	
6	Octohedral	Square pyramidal	Square planar	T-shaped	Linear

X represents a generic central atom bonded to atoms labeled A.

Altered Bond Angles

Unpaired electrons also have a less dramatic impact on molecular shape. Imagine you are an unshared electron pair around a molecule's central atom. The shared electron pairs are each attracted partially to the central atom and partially to the other atom in the bond, but you are different. You are attracted to the central atom, but there's nothing on your other side, so you are free to expand in that direction. That expansion means that you take up more room than the other electron pairs, and they are all squeezed a little closer together because of you. Multiple bonds have a similar effect because more space is required for more electrons. In general, **unshared electron pairs and multiple bonds decrease the angles between the remaining bonds**. A few examples are shown in the following tables.

Compound	CH_4	NH_3	H_2O
Unshared electrons	0	1	2
Shape	109.5° Tetrahedral	107° Trigonal pyramidal	104.5° Bent

Compound	BF_3	C_2H_4 (ethylene)
Multiple bonds	0	1
Shape	120°, 120°, 120° Trigonal planar	121.5°, 117° Trigonal planar

Summary

In order to use VSEPR to predict molecular geometry, perform the following steps:

1) Write out Lewis dot structures.
2) Use the Lewis structure to determine the number of unshared electron pairs and bonds around each central atom counting multiple bonds as one (for now).
3) The second table of this skill gives the arrangement of total and unshared electron pairs to account for electron repulsions around each central atom.

4) For multiple bonds or unshared electron pairs, decrease the angles slightly between the remaining bonds around the central atom.
5) Combine results from the previous two steps to determine the molecular shape.

http://www.shef.ac.uk/chemistry/vsepr/ is a good site for explaining and visualizing molecular geometries using VSEPR.
http://cowtownproductions.com/cowtown/genchem/09_16T.htm provides more practice.

Polar and nonpolar molecules

A **polar molecule** has positive and negative regions as shown below for HCl.

$$\overset{\delta+}{H}\!-\!\overset{\delta-}{Cl} \qquad \overset{\longrightarrow}{H\!-\!Cl}$$

Bond polarity is **necessary but not sufficient for molecular polarity**. A molecule containing polar bonds will still be nonpolar if the most negative and most positive location occurs at the same point. In other words, **in a polar molecule, bond polarities must not cancel**.

To determine if a molecule is polar perform the following steps.

1) Draw the molecular structure.
2) Assign a polarity to each bond with an arrow (remember C-H is nonpolar). If none of the bonds are polar, the molecule is nonpolar.
3) Determine if the polarities cancel each other in space. If they do, the molecule is nonpolar. Otherwise the molecule is polar.

TEACHER CERTIFICATION EXAM

Examples: Which of the following are polar molecules: CO_2, CH_2Cl_2, CCl_4.

Solution:

1) [Structures of CO_2 (linear O=C=O), CH_2Cl_2 (tetrahedral with 2 Cl and 2 H on C), and CCl_4 (tetrahedral with 4 Cl on C)]

2) [Dipole arrows shown on each structure: CO_2 — opposing arrows cancel; CH_2Cl_2 — arrows give net dipole; CCl_4 — arrows cancel]

3) charges cancel   net dipole   charges cancel

       nonpolar   polar   nonpolar

The polarity of molecules is critical for determining a good solvent for a given solute. Additional practice on the topic of polar bonds and molecules is available at http://cowtownproductions.com/cowtown/genchem/09_17M.htm.

CHEMISTRY

Competency 0014: Understand types and characteristics of molecular interaction and properties of substances containing different types of interaction forces between molecules.

The following intermolecular forces between molecules are usually weaker than covalent, ionic, and metallic bonds. They are listed from the strongest force to the weakest.

Ion-dipole interactions
Salts tend to dissolve in several polar solvents. An ion with a full charge in a polar solvent will **orient nearby solvent molecules** so that their opposite partial charges are pointing towards the ion. In aqueous solution, certain salts react to form solid **precipitates** if a combination of their ions is insoluble.

Hydrogen bonds
Hydrogen bonds are particularly **strong dipole-dipole interactions** that form between the H-atom of one molecule and an **F, O, or N** atom of an adjacent molecule. The partial positive charge on the hydrogen atom is attracted to the partial negative charge on the electron pair of the other atom. The hydrogen bond between two water molecules is shown as the dashed line below:

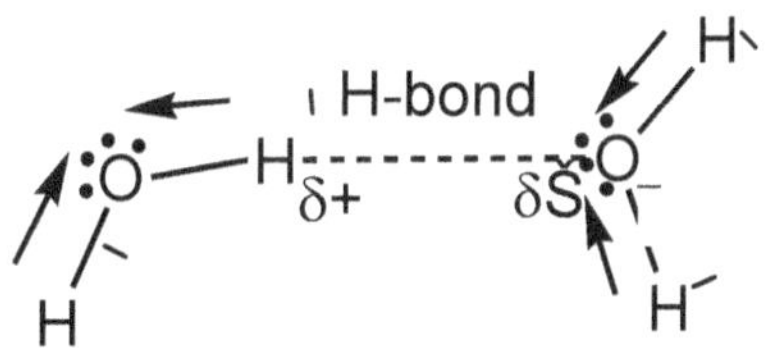

Dipole-dipole interactions
The intermolecular forces between polar molecules are known as dipole-dipole interactions. The partial positive charge of one molecule is attracted to the partial negative charge of its neighbor.

Ion-induced dipole
When a nonpolar molecule (or a noble gas atom) encounters an ion, its **electron density is temporarily distorted** resulting in an **induced dipole** that will be attracted to the ion. Intermolecular attractions due to induced dipoles in a nonpolar molecule are known as **London forces or Van der Waals interactions**. These are very weak intermolecular forces.

For example, carbon tetrachloride, CCl_4, has polar bonds but is a nonpolar molecule due to the symmetry of those bonds. An aluminum cation will draw the unbonded electrons of the chlorine atom towards it, distorting the molecule (this distortion has been exaggerated in the figure) and creating an attractive force as shown by the dashed line below.

[Diagram: CCl4 molecule with dipole interaction showing δ+C...Cl δ— ------ Al³⁺]

Dipole-induced dipole
The partial charge of **a permanent dipole may also induce a dipole in a nonpolar molecule** resulting in an attraction similar to—but weaker than—that created by an ion.

London dispersion force: induced dipole-induced dipole
The above two examples required a permanent charge to induce a dipole in a nonpolar molecule. A nonpolar molecule may also induce a temporary dipole on its identical neighbor in a pure substance. These forces occur because at any given moment, electrons are located within a certain region of the molecule, and **the instantaneous location of electrons will induce a temporary dipole** on neighboring molecules. For example, an isolated helium atom consists of a nucleus with a 2+ charge and two electrons in a spherical electron density cloud. An attraction of He atoms due to London dispersion forces (shown below by the dashed line) occurs because when the electrons happen to be distributed unevenly on one atom, a dipole is induced on its neighbor. This dipole is due to intermolecular repulsion of electrons and the attraction of electrons to neighboring nuclei.

The strength of London dispersion forces **increases for larger molecules** because a larger electron cloud is more easily polarized. The strength of London dispersion forces also **increases for molecules with a larger surface area** because there is greater opportunity for electrons to influence neighboring molecules if there is more potential contact between the molecules.
Paraffin in candles is an example of a solid held together by weak London forces between large molecules. These materials are soft.

Impact on physical properties

The impact of intermolecular forces on substances is best understood by imagining ourselves shrinking down to the size of molecules and picturing what happens when we stick more strongly to molecules nearby. It will take more energy (higher temperatures) to pull us away from our neighbors.

If two substances are being compared, the material with the **greater intermolecular attractive forces** (i.e. the stronger intermolecular bond) will have the following properties relative to the other substance:

For solids:
Higher melting point
Higher enthalpy of fusion
Greater hardness
Lower vapor pressure

For liquids:
Higher boiling point
Higher critical temperature
Higher critical pressure
Higher enthalpy of vaporization
Higher viscosity
Higher surface tension
Lower vapor pressure

For gases:
Intermolecular attractive forces are neglected for ideal gases.

For example, covalent networks, salts, and metals are nearly always solids at room temperature because the strength of these bonds results in a high melting point. H_2O and NH_3 are liquids at room temperature because they contain hydrogen bonds. These bonds are of intermediate strength, so the melting point of these compounds is lower than room temperature and their boiling point is higher than room temperature. H_2S contains weaker dipole-dipole interactions than H_2O because the sulfer atoms do not form hydrogen bonds. Therefore, H_2S is a gas at room temperature due to its low boiling point. Finally, small non-polar molecules such as CO_2 (44.01 u), N_2, or atoms such as He will be gases at room temperature due to very weak London forces, but larger non-polar molecules such as octane (114.22 u) or CCl_4 (153.82 u) may be liquids, and very large non-polar molecules such as paraffins will be soft solids.

Competency 0015: Understand the nomenclature and structure of organic compounds.

The IUPAC is the **International Union of Pure and Applied Chemistry**. **Organic compounds contain carbon,** and have their own branch of chemistry because of the huge number of carbon compounds in nature, including nearly all the molecules in living things. The 1979 IUPAC organic nomenclature is used and taught most often today, and it is the nomenclature described here.

The simplest organic compounds are called **hydrocarbons** because they **contain only carbon and hydrogen**. Hydrocarbon molecules may be divided into the classes of **cyclic** and **open-chain** depending on whether they contain a ring of carbon atoms. Open-chain molecules may be divided into **branched** or **straight-chain** categories.

Hydrocarbons are also divided into classes called **aliphatic** and **aromatic**. Aromatic hydrocarbons are related to benzene and are always cyclic. Aliphatic hydrocarbons may be open-chain or cyclic. Aliphatic cyclic hydrocarbons are called **alicyclic**. Aliphatic hydrocarbons are one of three types: alkanes, alkenes, and alkynes.

Alkanes
Alkanes contain only single bonds. Alkanes have the maximum number of hydrogen atoms possible for their carbon backbone, so they are called **saturated**. Alkenes, alkynes, and aromatics are **unsaturated** because they have fewer hydrogens.

Straight-chain alkanes are also called **normal alkanes**. These are the simplest hydrocarbons. They consist of a linear chain of carbon atoms. The names of these molecules contain the suffix –*ane* and a **root based on the number of carbons in the chain** according to the table on the following page. The first four roots, *meth–*, *eth–*, *prop–*, and *but–* have historical origins in chemistry, and the remaining alkanes contain common Greek number prefixes. Alkanes have the general formula C_nH_{2n+2}.

A single molecule may be represented in multiple ways. Methane and ethane in the table are shown as three-dimensional structures with dashed wedge shapes attaching atoms behind the page and thick wedge shapes attaching atoms in front of the page.

Number of carbons	Name	Formula	Structure
1	Methane	CH_4	
2	Ethane	C_2H_6	
3	Propane	C_3H_8	
4	Butane	C_4H_{10}	
5	Pentane	C_5H_{12}	
6	Hexane	C_6H_{14}	
7	Heptane	C_7H_{16}	
8	Octane	C_8H_{18}	

Additional ways that pentane might be represented are:

n-pentane (the n represents a normal alkane)

CH₃CH₂CH₂CH₂CH₃

CH₃(CH₂)₃CH₃

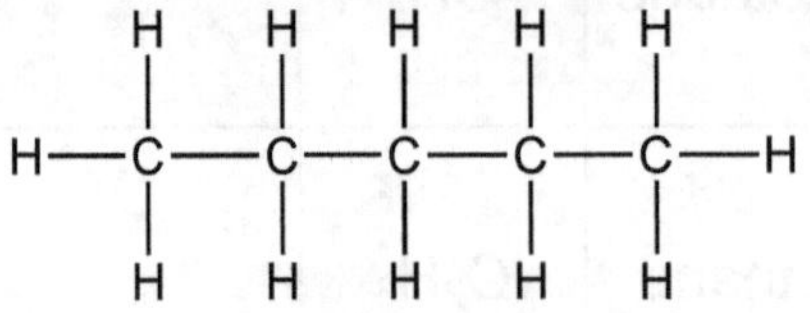

[Structural formula of pentane showing 5 carbons each bonded to hydrogens, and a zig-zag skeletal formula]

If one hydrogen is removed from an alkane, the residue is called an **alkyl** group. The –ane suffix is replaced by an –yl– infix when this residue is used as **functional group**. Functional groups are used to systematically build up the names of organic molecules.

Branched alkanes are named using a four-step process:

1) Find the longest continuous carbon chain. This is the parent hydrocarbon.
2) Number the atoms on this chain beginning at the end near the first branch point, so the lowest locant numbers are used. Number functional groups from the attachment point.
3) Determine the numbered locations and names of the substituted alkyl groups. Use di–, tri–, and similar prefixes for alkyl groups represented more than once. Separate numbers by commas and groups by dashes.
4) List the locations and names of alkyl groups in alphabetical order by their name (ignoring the di–, tri– prefixes) and end the name with the parent hydrocarbon.

Example—Name the following hydrocarbon:

$$\begin{array}{c} CH_2 \\ H_3C-CH \\ \diagdown \\ CH-CH_3 \\ H_2C-CH CH_3 \\ H_3C H_2C-CH_2 \end{array}$$

Solution—
1) The longest chain is seven carbons in length, as shown by the bold lines below. This molecule is a heptane.
2) The atoms are numbered from the end nearest the first branch as shown:

$$\begin{array}{c} \overset{1}{CH_3} \\ H_3C-\overset{2}{CH} \\ \overset{3}{CH}-CH_3 \\ H_2C-\overset{4}{CH} \overset{7}{CH_3} \\ H_3C \underset{5}{H_2C}-\underset{6}{CH_2} \end{array}$$

3) Methyl groups are located at carbons 2 and 3 (2,3-dimethyl), and an ethyl group is located at carbon 4.
4) "Ethyl" precedes "methyl" alphabetically. The hydrocarbon name is:
4-ethyl-2,3-dimethylheptane.

TEACHER CERTIFICATION EXAM

The following branched alkanes have IUPAC-accepted common names:

Structure	Systematic name	Common name
(CH₃)₂CH—CH₃	2-methylpropane	isobutane
CH₃CH₂—CH(CH₃)—CH₃	2-methylbutane	isopentane
C(CH₃)₄	2,2-dimethylpropane	neopentane

The following alkyl groups have IUPAC-accepted common names. The systematic names assign a locant number of 1 to the attachment point:

Structure	Systematic name	Common name
(H₃C)₂CH—	1-methylethyl	isopropyl
(H₃C)₂CH—CH₂—	2-methylpropyl	isobutyl
H₃C—CH₂—CH(CH₃)—	1-methylpropyl	*sec*-butyl
(H₃C)₃C—	1,1-dimethylethyl	*tert*-butyl

Alkenes

Alkenes contain one or more double bonds. Alkenes are also called olefins. The suffix used in the naming of alkenes is *–ene*, and the number roots are those used for alkanes of the same length.

A number preceding the name shows the location of the double bond for alkenes of length four and above. Alkenes with one double bond have the general formula C_nH_{2n}. Multiple double bonds are named using *–diene*, *–triene*, etc. The suffix *–enyl–* is used for functional groups after a hydrogen is removed from an alkene. Ethene and propene have the common names **ethylene** and **propylene**. The ethenyl group has the common name **vinyl** and the 2-propenyl group has the common name **allyl**.

$H_2C = CH_2$ is ethylene or ethene.

is a vinyl or ethenyl group.

is propylene or propene.

is an allyl or 2-propenyl group.

is 2-hexene.

is 2-methyl-1,3-butadiene (common name: isoprene).

Cis-trans isomerism is often part of the complete name for an alkene. Note that isoprene contains two adjacent double bonds, so it is a **conjugated** molecule.

Alkynes and alkenynes

Alkynes contain one or more triple bonds. They are named in a similar way to alkenes. The suffix used for alkynes is *–yne*. Ethyne is often called **acetylene**. Alkynes with one triple bond have the general formula C_nH_{2n-2}. Multiple triple bonds are named using *–diyne*, *–triyne*, etc. The infix *–ynyl–* is used for functional groups composed of alkynes after the removal of a hydrogen atom.

Hydrocarbons with **both double and triple bonds are known as alkenynes**. The locant number for the double bond precedes the name, and the locant for the triple bond follows the suffix –en– and precedes the suffix –yne.

Examples: HC≡CH is acetylene or ethyne.

HC≡C—CH₂—CH(CH₃) is 1-butyne.

HC≡C—C≡C—CH₃ is 1,3-pentadiyne.

H₃C—C≡C—CH₂—CH₂—CH₂— is a 4-hexynyl group.

H₂C=CH—C≡CH is 1-buten-3-yne. This compound has the common name of vinylacetylene

<u>Cycloalkanes, –enes, and –ynes</u>
Alicyclic hydrocarbons use the prefix *cyclo*– before the number root for the molecule. The structures for these molecules are often written as if the molecule lay entirely within the plane of the paper even though in reality, these rings dip above and below a single plane. When there is more than one substitution on the ring, numbering begins with the first substitution listed in alphabetical order.

Examples: (cyclopropane structure) is cyclopropane

(methylcyclohexane structures)

is methylcyclohexane.

CHEMISTRY

is 1,3-cyclohexadiene.

is 1-ethyl-3-propylcyclobutane.

Cis-trans isomerism is often part of the complete name for a cycloalkane.

Aromatic hydrocarbons
Aromatic hydrocarbons are structurally related to benzene or made up of benzene molecules fused together. These molecules are called **arenes** to distinguish them from alkanes, alkenes, and alkynes. All atoms in arenes lie in the same plane. In other words, aromatic hydrocarbons are flat. Aromatic molecules have electrons in delocalized π orbitals that are free to migrate throughout the molecule.

Substitutions onto the benzene ring are named in alphabetical order using the lowest possible locant numbers. The prefix *phenyl–* may be used for C_6H_5- (benzene less a hydrogen) attached as a functional group to a larger hydrocarbon residue. Arenes in general form aryl functional groups. A phenyl group may be represented in a structure by the symbol Ø. The prefix *benzyl–* may used for $C_6H_5CH_2-$ (methylbenzene with a hydrogen removed from the methyl group) attached as a functional group.

Examples: [benzene structure] or [benzene structure] is benzene.

[structure] is 2-isopropyl-1,4-dimethylbenzene.

[structure] is 3-phenyloctane or (1-ethylhexyl)benzene.

The most often used common names for aromatic hydrocarbons are listed in the following table. Naphthalene is the simplest molecule formed by fused benzene rings.

Structure	Systematic name	Common name
(methylbenzene structure)	methylbenzene	toluene
(1,2-dimethylbenzene structure)	1,2-dimethylbenzene	ortho-xylene or o-xylene
(1,3-dimethylbenzene structure)	1,3-dimethylbenzene	meta-xylene or m-xylene
(1,4-dimethylbenzene structure)	1,4-dimethylbenzene	para-xylene or p-xylene
(ethenylbenzene structure)	ethenylbenzene	styrene
(naphthalene structure)		naphthalene

Hydrocarbons consist entirely of nonpolar C-H bonds with no unpaired electrons. These compounds are relatively unreactive. The substitution of one or more atoms with unpaired electrons into the hydrocarbon backbone creates a **hydrocarbon derivative**. The unpaired electrons result in polar or charged portions of these molecules. These atoms fall into categories known as **functional groups**, and they create **local regions of reactivity**. Alkyl, alkenyl, alkynyl, and aryl groups may also be considered functional groups in some circumstances as described in the previous skill.

Two types of names are often used for the same hydrocarbon derivative. For **substitutive names**, the hydrocarbon name is written out and the correct prefix or suffix is added for the derivative group. For **functional class names**, the hydrocarbon is written as a functional group and the derivative is added as a second word.

Examples: CH_3Br may be called bromomethane (substitutive name) or methyl bromide (functional class name). CH_3CH_2OH is ethanol (substitutive name) or ethyl alcohol (functional class name).

In the tables on the following pages, the symbols R and R' represent hydrocarbons in covalent linkage to the functional group. Many derivatives are named in a similar manner to alkenes and alkynes, but the location and suffix of the functional group is used in place of –ene and –yne.

The **acyl group** is
$$R-\overset{\overset{\displaystyle O}{\|}}{C}-$$

There are non-systematic number roots for hydrocarbon derivatives containing acyl groups or derived from acyl groups. These are the ketones, carboxylic acids, esters, nitriles, and amides:

Number of carbons (including the acyl carbon)	Systematic prefix	Accepted prefix for acyl and nitrile functional groups
1	meth–	form–
2	eth–	acet–
3	prop–	propion–
4	but–	butyr–
5	pent–	pent–
6 and above	same for larger numbers	

Several functional groups utilize oxygen.

Class of molecule	Functional group	Structure	Affix	Example
Alcohol	Hydroxyl —OH	primary: R—CH$_2$—OH secondary: R$_1$R$_2$CH—OH tertiary: R$_1$R$_2$R$_3$C—OH	–ol	H$_3$C—CH$_2$—OH ethanol
Ether	Oxy \\O/	R$_1$—O—R$_2$	–oxy–	H$_3$C—O—CH$_2$—CH$_3$ methoxyethane or ethyl methyl ether
Aldehyde	Carbonyl C=O	R—C(=O)—H	–al	H—C(=O)—CH$_2$—CH$_3$ propionaldehyde or propanal
Ketone	Carbonyl C=O	R$_1$—C(=O)—R$_2$	–one	H$_3$C—C(=O)—CH$_3$ acetone
Carboxylic acid	Carboxyl —C(=O)OH	R—C(=O)—OH	–oic acid	HC(=O)—OH formic acid or methanoic acid

CHEMISTRY

Class of molecule	Functional group	Structure	Affix	Example
Ester	Oxycarbonyl $\overset{O}{\underset{}{\overset{\|}{C}}}{-}O{-}$	$R_2{-}\overset{:\ddot{O}:}{\underset{}{\overset{\|}{C}}}{-}\ddot{\underset{..}{O}}{-}R_1$	–yl –oate	$CH_3CH_2CH_2C(O)OCH_3$ methyl butyrate or methyl butanoate
Acid anhydride	Carbonyloxycarbonyl $\overset{O}{\underset{}{\overset{\|}{C}}}{-}O{-}\overset{O}{\underset{}{\overset{\|}{C}}}{-}$	$R_1{-}\overset{:\ddot{O}:}{\underset{}{\overset{\|}{C}}}{-}\ddot{\underset{..}{O}}{-}\overset{:\ddot{O}:}{\underset{}{\overset{\|}{C}}}{-}R_2$	–oic anhydride	$H_3C{-}C(O){-}O{-}C(O){-}CH_3$ acetic anhydride or ethanoic anhydride

Derivatives utilizing other atoms are also common.

Class of molecule	Functional group	Structure	Affix	Example
Nitrile	Cyanide —C≡N	R—C≡N:	–nitrile	$H_3C-C≡N$ acetonitrile or ethanonitrile
Amine	Amino —N—	primary R—NH₂; secondary R₁—NH—R₂; tertiary R₁—N(R₂)—R₃	–amine	$H_3C-CH_2-NH_2$ ethanamine
Amide	Aminocarbonyl (C(=O)—N)	primary R—C(=O)—NH₂; secondary R₂—C(=O)—NH—R₁; tertiary R₃—C(=O)—N(R₁)(R₂)	–amide	$H_3C-CH_2-C(=O)-NH_2$ propionamide or propanamide
Alkyl halide	Halide —X (where X is F, Cl, Br, or I)	R—X:	fluoro– chloro– bromo– iodo–	2-bromobutane ($CH_3-CHBr-CH_2-CH_3$)

Hydrocarbon derivatives and functional groups may be identified using the tables found in the previous skill. One way to memorize the derivatives utilizing oxygen is to divide them into pairs with a hydrogen atom in the first element of the pair replaced by a hydrocarbon in the second element. These pairs are:

1) alcohol/ether.
2) aldehyde/ketone.
3) carboxylic acid/ester.

SUBAREA IV- CHEMICAL REACTIONS

Competency 0016: Understand factors that affect reaction rates and methods of measuring reaction rates.

Introduction to reaction rates
The rate of any process is measured by its change per unit time. The speed of a car is measured by its change in position with time using units of miles per hour. The speed of a chemical reaction is usually measured by a change in the concentration of a reactant or product with time using units of **molarity per second** (M/s). The molarity of a chemical is represented in mathematical equations using brackets.

The **average reaction rate** is the change in concentration either reactant or product per unit time during a time interval:
$$\text{Average reaction rate} = \frac{\text{Change in concentration}}{\text{Change in time}}$$

Reaction rates are positive quantities. Product concentrations increase and reactant concentrations decrease with time, so a different formula is required depending on the identity of the component of interest:
$$\text{Average reaction rate} = \frac{[\text{product}]_{final} - [\text{product}]_{initial}}{\text{time}_{final} - \text{time}_{iniial}}$$
$$= \frac{[\text{reactant}]_{initial} - [\text{reactant}]_{final}}{\text{time}_{final} - \text{time}_{iniial}}$$

The **reaction rate** at a given time refers to the **instantaneous reaction rate**. This is found from the absolute value of the **slope of a curve of concentration vs. time**. An estimate of the reaction rate at time t may be found from the average reaction rate over a small time interval surrounding t. For those familiar with calculus notation, the following equations define reaction rate, but calculus is not needed for this skill:
$$\text{Reaction rate at time } t = \frac{d[\text{product}]}{dt} = -\frac{d[\text{reactant}]}{dt}.$$

Deriving rate laws from reaction rates
A **rate law** is an **equation relating a reaction rate to concentration**. The rate laws for most reactions discussed in high-school level chemistry are of the form:
$$\text{Rate} = k[\text{reactant 1}]^a [\text{reactant 2}]^b \ldots$$

In the above general equation, k is called the **rate constant**. a and b are called **reaction orders**. Most reactions considered in introductory chemistry have a reaction order of zero, one, or two. The sum of all reaction orders for a reaction is called the **overall reaction order**. Rate laws cannot be predicted from the stoichiometry of a reaction. They must be determined by experiment or derived from knowledge of reaction mechanism.

If a reaction is zero order for a reactant, the concentration of that reactant has no impact on rate as long as some reactant is present. If a reaction is first order for a reactant, the reaction rate is proportional to the reactant's concentration. For a reaction that is second order with respect to a reactant, doubling that reactant's concentration increases reaction rate by a factor of four. Rate laws are determined by finding the appropriate reaction order describing **the impact of reactant concentration on reaction rate**.

Reaction rates typically have units of M/s (moles/liter-sec) and concentrations have units of M (moles/liter). For units to cancel properly in the expression above, the units found on the rate constant k must vary with overall reaction order as shown in the following table. The value of k may be determined by finding the slope of a plot charting a function of concentration against time. These functions may be memorized or computed using calculus.

Overall reaction order	Units of rate constant k	Method to determine k for rate laws with one reactant
0	M/sec	–(slope) of a chart of [reactant] vs. t
1	sec^{-1}	–(slope) of a chart of ln[reactant] vs. t
2	$M^{-1}sec^{-1}$	slope of a chart of 1/[reactant] vs. t

As an alternative to using the rate constant k, the course of **first order reactions** may be expressed in terms of a **half-life**, $t_{halflife}$. The half-life of a reaction is the time required for reactant concentration to reach half of its initial value. First order rate constants and half-lives are inversely proportional:

$$t_{halflife} = \frac{\ln 2}{k_{first\ order}} = \frac{0.693}{k_{first\ order}}$$

Example: Derive a rate law for the reaction $2N_2O_5 \rightarrow 4NO_2 + O_2$ using data from the previous example.

Solution: Three methods will be used to solve this problem.

1) In the previous example, we found the following two **instantaneous reaction rates**:

Time (sec)	[N₂O₅] (M)	Reaction rate (M/sec)
0	0.0200	1.00×10^{-5}
4000	0.0029	1.5×10^{-6}

A decrease in reactant concentration to 0.0029/0.0200=14.5% of its initial value led to a nearly proportional decrease in reaction rate to 15% of its initial value. In other words, reaction rate remains proportional to reactant concentration. The reaction is first order:

$$\text{Rate} = k[N_2O_5].$$

We may estimate a value for the rate constant by dividing reaction rates by the concentration:

$$k_{\text{first order}} = \frac{\text{Rate}}{[N_2O_5]}.$$

Time (sec)	[N₂O₅] (M)	Reaction rate (M/sec)	k (sec⁻¹)
0	0.0200	1.00×10^{-5}	5.00×10^{-4}
4000	0.0029	1.5×10^{-6}	5.2×10^{-4}

2) We could estimate this rate constant by finding **average reaction rates** in each small time interval and assuming this rate occurs halfway between the two concentrations:

Time (sec)	[N₂O₅] (M)	Average rate (M/sec)	Halfway [N₂O₅] (M)	k (sec⁻¹)
0	0.0200	8.00×10^{-6}	0.0160	5.00×10^{-4}
1000	0.0120	4.6×10^{-6}	0.0097	4.7×10^{-4}
2000	0.0074	2.8×10^{-6}	0.0060	4.7×10^{-4}
3000	0.0046	1.7×10^{-6}	0.0038	4.5×10^{-4}
4000	0.0029	1.1×10^{-6}	0.0024	4.7×10^{-4}
5000	0.0018	4.8×10^{-7}	0.0012	4.0×10^{-4}
7500	0.0006	2×10^{-7}	0.0004	4×10^{-4}
10000	0.0002			

3) If **concentration data** are given then no rate data needs to be found to determine a rate constant. For a first order reaction, chart the natural logarithm of concentration against time and find the slope.

Time (sec)	[N$_2$O$_5$] (M)	ln[N$_2$O$_5$]
0	0.0200	-3.91
1000	0.0120	-4.41
2000	0.0074	-4.90
3000	0.0046	-5.37
4000	0.0029	-5.83
5000	0.0018	-6.30
7500	0.0006	-7.39
10000	0.0002	-8.46

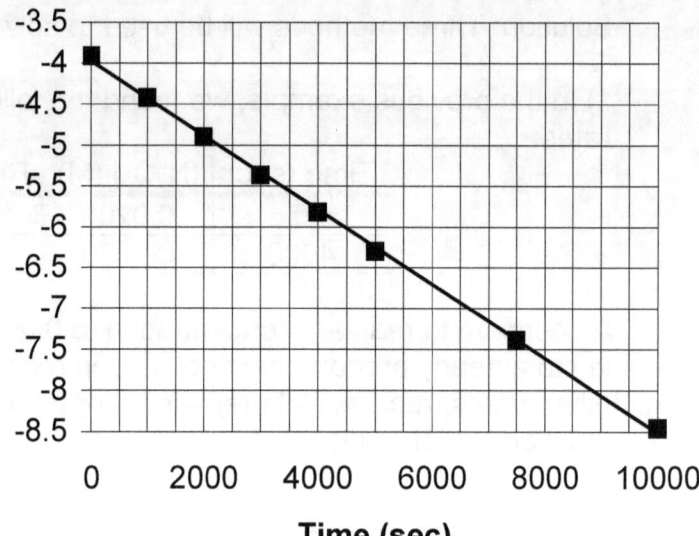

The slope may be determined from a best-fit method or it may be estimated from $\frac{-8.46-(-3.91)}{10000} = -5 \times 10^{-4}$. The rate law describing this reaction is:

$$\text{Rate} = \left(5 \times 10^{-4} \frac{M}{\text{sec}}\right)[N_2O_5]$$

Derive rate laws from simple reaction mechanisms
A **reaction mechanism** is a series of **elementary reactions** that explain how a reaction occurs. These elementary reactions are also called elementary processes or elementary steps. **A reaction mechanism cannot be determined from reaction stoichiometry**. Stoichiometry indicates the number of molecules of reactants and products in an **overall reaction**. Elementary steps represent a **single event**. This might be a collision between two molecules or a single rearrangement of electrons within a molecule.

The simplest reaction mechanisms consist of a single elementary reaction. The number of molecules required determines the rate laws for these processes. For a **unimolecular process**:

$$A \rightarrow products$$

the number of molecules of A that decompose in a given time will be proportional to the number of molecules of A present. Therefore unimolecular processes are first order:

$$Rate = k[A].$$

For **bimolecular processes**, the rate law will be second order.

For $A + A \rightarrow products$, $Rate = k[A]^2$

For $A + B \rightarrow products$, $Rate = k[A][B].$

Most reaction mechanisms are multi-step processes involving **reaction intermediates**. Intermediates are chemicals that are formed during one elementary step and consumed during another, but they are not overall reactants or products. In many cases one elementary reaction in particular is the slowest and determines the overall reaction rate. This slowest reaction in the series is called the **rate-limiting step** or rate determining step.

Example: The reaction $NO_2(g) + CO(g) \rightarrow NO(g) + CO_2(g)$ is composed of the following elementary reactions in the gas phase:

$$NO_2 + NO_2 \rightarrow NO + NO_3$$
$$NO_3 + CO \rightarrow NO_2 + CO_2.$$

The first elementary reaction is very slow compared to the second. Determine the rate law for the overall reaction if NO_2 and CO are both present in sufficient quantity for the reaction to occur. Also name all reaction intermediates.

Solution: The first step will be rate limiting because it is slower. In other words, almost as soon as NO_3 is available, it reacts with CO, so the rate-limiting step is the formation of NO_3. The first step is bimolecular.

Therefore, the rate law for the entire reaction is: $Rate = k[NO_2]^2$.

NO_3 is formed during the first step and consumed during the second. NO_3 is the only reaction intermediate because it is neither a reactant nor a product of the overall reaction.

Effect of reaction conditions on reaction rates
Kinetic molecular theory may be applied to reaction rates in addition to physical constants like pressure. **Reaction rates increase with reactant concentration** because more reactant molecules are present and more are likely to collide with one another in a certain volume at higher concentrations.

For ideal gases, the concentration of a reactant is its molar density, and this varies with pressure and temperature.

Kinetic molecular theory also predicts that **reaction rate increase with temperature** because of two reasons:
1) More reactant molecules will collide with each other per second.
2) These collisions will each occur at a higher energy that is more likely to overcome the activation energy of the reaction.

During a chemical reaction, only a fraction of the collisions between the appropriate reactant molecules convert them into product molecules. This occurs for two reasons:

1) Not all collisions occur with a **sufficiently high energy** for the reaction to occur.
2) Not all collisions **orient the molecules properly** for the reaction to occur.

The **activation energy**, E_a, of a reaction is the **minimum energy to overcome the barrier to the formation of products**. This is the minimum energy needed for the reaction to occur.

At the scale of individual molecules, a reaction typically involves a very small period of time when old bonds are broken and new bonds are formed. During this time, the molecules involved are in a **transition state** between reactants and products. A threshold of maximum energy is crossed when the arrangement of molecules is in an unfavorable intermediate between reactants and products known as the **activated complex**. Formulas and diagrams of activated complexes are often written within brackets to indicate they are transition states that are present for extremely small periods of time.

The activation energy, E_a, is the difference between the energy of reactants and the energy of the activated complex. The energy change during the reaction, ΔE, is the difference between the energy of the products and the energy of the reactants. The activation energy of the reverse reaction is $E_a - \Delta E$. These energy levels are represented in an **energy diagram** such as the one shown below for $NO_2 + CO \rightarrow NO + CO_2$.

This is an exothermic reaction because products are lower in energy than reactants.

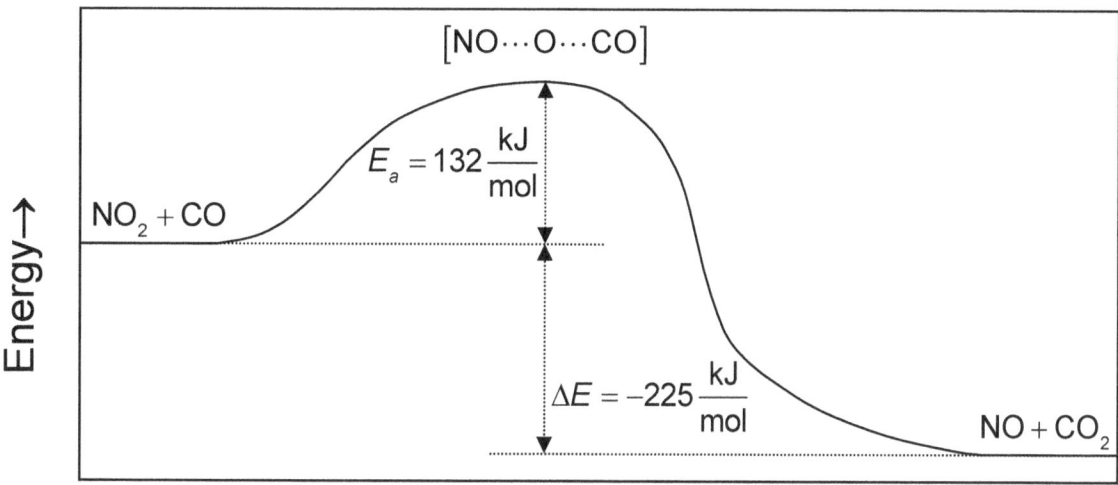

An energy diagram is a conceptual tool, so there is some variability in how its axes are labeled. The y-axis of the diagram is usually labeled energy (E), but it is sometimes labeled "enthalpy (H)" or (rarely) "free energy (G)." There is an even greater variability in how the x-axis is labeled. The terms "reaction pathway," "reaction coordinate," "course of reaction," or "reaction progress" may be used on the x-axis, or the x-axis may remain without a label.

The energy diagrams of an endothermic and exothermic reaction are compared below.

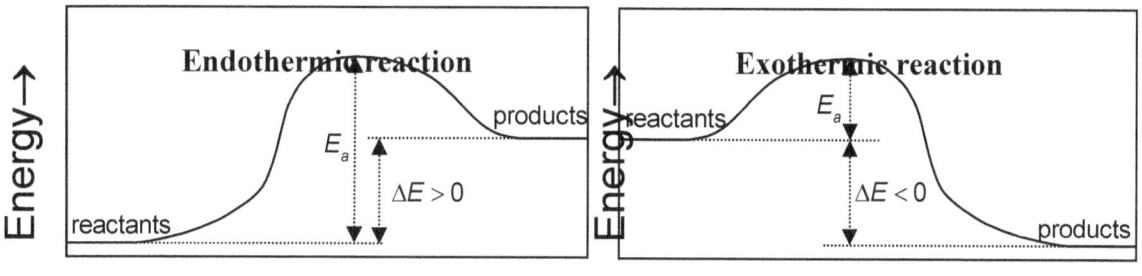

The rate of most simple reactions **increases with temperature** because a **greater fraction of molecules have the kinetic energy** required to overcome the reaction's activation energy. The chart below shows the effect of temperature on the distribution of kinetic energies in a sample of molecules. These curves are called **Maxwell-Boltzmann distributions**. The shaded areas represent the fraction of molecules containing sufficient kinetic energy for a reaction to occur. This area is larger at a higher temperature; so more molecules are above the activation energy and more molecules react per second.

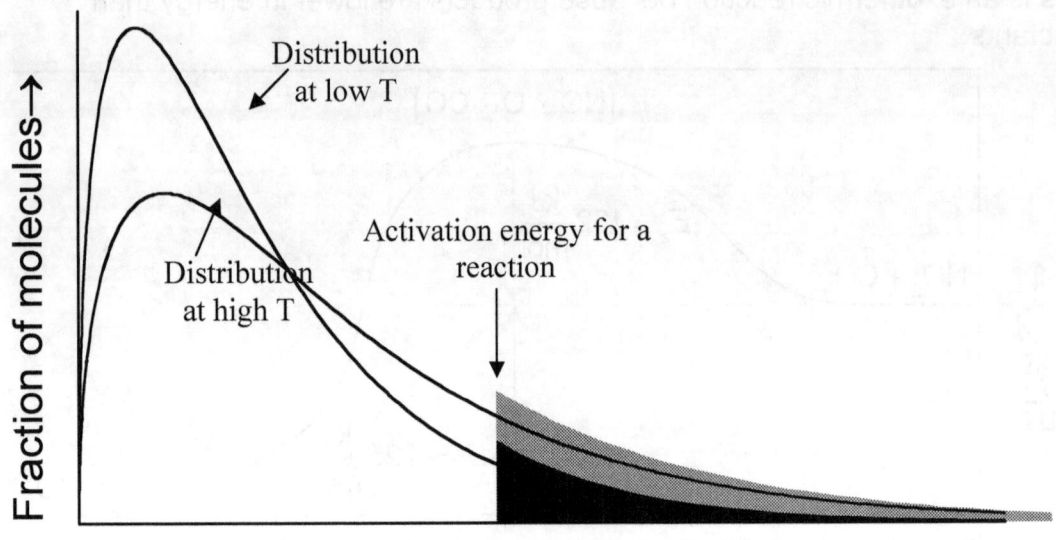

http://www.mhhe.com/physsci/chemistry/essentialchemistry/flash/activa2.swf provides an animated audio tutorial on energy diagrams.

A **catalyst** is a material that increases the rate of a chemical reaction without changing itself permanently in the process. Catalysts provide an alternate reaction mechanism for the reaction to proceed in the forward and in the reverse direction. Therefore, **catalysts have no impact on the chemical equilibrium** of a reaction. They will not make a less favorable reaction more favorable.

Catalysts reduce the activation energy of a reaction. This is the amount of energy needed for the reaction to begin. Molecules with such low energies that they would have taken a long time to react will react more rapidly if a catalyst is present. **A catalyst increases the rate of both the forward and reverse reactions by lowering the activation energy** for the reaction. Catalysts provide a different activated complex for the reaction at a lower energy state. The impact of a catalyst may be represented on an energy diagram as shown below.

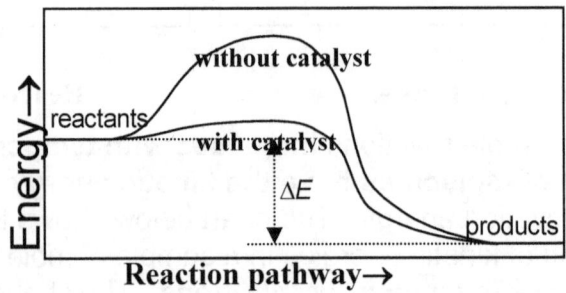

There are two types of catalysts: **Homogeneous catalysts** are in the same physical phase as the reactants. Biological catalysts are called **enzymes**, and most are homogeneous catalysts.

CHEMISTRY

A typical homogenous catalytic reaction mechanism involves an initial reaction with one reactant followed by a reaction with a second reactant and release of the catalyst:

$$A + C \rightarrow AC$$
$$B + AC \rightarrow AB + C$$

Net reaction: $A + B \xrightarrow{\text{catalyst C}} AB$

Heterogeneous catalysts are present in a different physical state from the reactants. A typical heterogeneous catalytic reaction involves a solid surface onto which molecules in a fluid phase temporarily attach themselves in such a way to favor a rapid reaction. Catalytic converters in cars utilize heterogeneous catalysis to break down harmful chemicals in exhaust.

Competency 0017: Understand the principles of chemical equilibrium.

Introduction to dynamic equilibrium
A dynamic equilibrium consists of two **opposing reversible processes** that both occur at the **same rate**. *Balance* is a synonym for equilibrium. A system at equilibrium is stable; it does not change with time. Equilibria are drawn with a double arrow.

When a process at equilibrium is observed, it often doesn't seem like anything is happening, but **at a microscopic scale, two events are taking place that balance each other**. An example is given to the right. Arrows in this diagram represent the movement of molecules. When water is placed in a closed container, the water evaporates until the air in the container is saturated. After this occurs, the water level no longer changes, so an observer at the macroscopic scale would say that evaporation has stopped, but the reality on a microscopic scale is that both evaporation and condensation are taking place at the same rate. All equilibria between different phases of matter have this dynamic character on a microscopic scale.

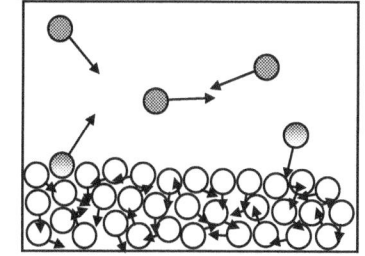

Liquid ⇌ Vapor (evaporation/condensation)

Chemical reactions often do not "go to completion." Instead, products are generated from reactants up to a certain point when the reaction no longer seems to occur, leaving some reactant unaltered. At this point, the system is in a state of **chemical equilibrium** because **the rate of the forward reaction is equal to the rate of the reverse reaction**. An example is shown to the right. Arrows in this diagram represent the chemical reactions of individual molecules. An observer at the macroscopic scale might say that no reaction is taking place at equilibrium, but at a microscopic scale, both the forward and reverse reactions are occurring at the same rate.

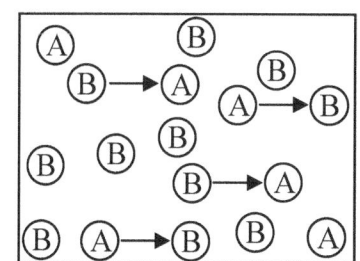

A ⇌ B

TEACHER CERTIFICATION EXAM

Homogeneous equilibrium refers to a chemical equilibrium among reactants and products that are all in the same phase of matter. **Heterogeneous equilibrium** takes place between two or more chemicals in different phases.

A reaction at equilibrium contains a constant ratio of chemical species. The nature of these ratios is determined by an **equilibrium constant**.

If equilibrium is disturbed by changing concentration, pressure, or temperature, the state of balance is upset for a period of time before the equilibrium shifts to achieve a new state of balance.
Le Chatelier's principle states that equilibrium will shift to partially offset the impact of an altered condition.

Le Chatelier: Change in reactant and product concentrations
If a chemical reaction is at equilibrium, Le Chatelier's principle predicts that **adding a substance**—either a reactant or a product—will shift the reaction so **a new equilibrium is established by consuming some of the added substance**. Removing a substance will cause the reaction to move in the direction that forms more of that substance.

Example: The reaction $CO + 2H_2 \rightleftharpoons CH_3OH$ is used to synthesize methanol. Equilibrium is established, and then additional CO is added to the reaction vessel. Predict the impact on each reaction component after CO is added.

Solution: Le Chatelier's principle states that the reaction will shift to partially offset the impact of the added CO. Therefore, CO concentration will decrease, and the reaction will "shift to the right." H_2 concentration will also decrease and CH_3OH concentration will increase.

Le Chatelier: Change in pressure for gases at equilibrium
If a chemical reaction is at equilibrium in the gas phase, Le Chatelier's principle predicts that **an increase in pressure** will shift the reaction so **a new equilibrium is established by decreasing the number of gas moles present**. A decrease in the number of moles partially offsets this rise in pressure. Decreasing pressure will cause the reaction to move in the direction that forms more moles of gas. These changes in pressure might result from altering the volume of the reaction vessel at constant temperature.

Example: The reaction $N_2 + 3H_2 \rightleftharpoons 2NH_3$ is used to synthesize ammonia. Equilibrium is established. Next the reaction vessel is expanded at constant temperature. Predict the impact on each reaction component after this expansion occurs.

Solution: The expansion will result in a decrease in pressure (Boyle's Law). Le Chatelier's principle states that the reaction will shift to partially offset this decrease by increasing the number of moles present. There are 4 moles on the left side of the equation and 2 moles on the right, so the reaction will shift to the left. N_2 and H_2 concentration will increase. NH_3 concentration will decrease.

Le Chatelier: Change in temperature
Le Chatelier's principle predicts that **when heat is added** at constant pressure to a system at equilibrium, **the reaction will shift in the direction that absorbs heat** until a new equilibrium is established. For an endothermic process, the reaction will shift to the right towards product formation.
For an exothermic process, the reaction will shift to the left towards reactant formation. If you understand the application of Le Chatelier's principle to concentration changes then writing "heat" on the appropriate side of the equation will help you understand its application to changes in temperature.

Example: $N_2 + 3H_2 \rightleftharpoons 2NH_3$ is an exothermic reaction. First equilibrium is established and then the temperature is decreased. Predict the impact of the lower temperature on each reaction component.

Solution: Since the reaction is exothermic, we may write it as:
$N_2 + 3H_2 \rightleftharpoons 2NH_3 + \text{Heat}$. For the purpose of finding the impact of temperature on equilibrium processes, we may consider heat as if it were a reaction component. Le Chatelier's principle states that after a temperature decrease, the reaction will shift to partially offset the impact of a loss of heat. Therefore more heat will be produced, and the reaction will shift to the right. N_2 and H_2 concentration will decrease. NH_3 concentration will increase.

A flash animation with audio that demonstrates Le Chatelier's principle is at http://www.mhhe.com/physsci/chemistry/essentialchemistry/flash/lechv17.swf.

The concentrations of reactants and products at equilibrium remain constant because the forward and reverse reactions take place at the same rate. This equilibrium responds to a perturbation in one concentration by altering every concentration in a well-defined way until equilibrium is reestablished. Now, we will present a mathematical expression that relates these concentrations and defines the law that governs equilibrium.

Consider the general balanced reaction:
$$mA + nB \rightleftharpoons pR + qS$$
where m, n, p, and q are stoichiometric coefficients and A, B, R, and S are chemical species. An **equilibrium expression** relating the concentrations of chemical species at equilibrium is determined by the equation:

$$K_{eq} = \frac{[R]^p [S]^q}{[A]^m [B]^n}$$

where K_{eq} is a constant value called the **equilibrium constant**. Product concentrations raised to the power of their stoichiometric coefficients are placed in the numerator and reactant concentrations raised to the power of their coefficients are placed in the denominator. Every reaction has a unique value of K_{eq} that varies only with temperature. Alternate subscripts are often given to the equilibrium constant. K_c or K with no subscript is often used instead of K_{eq} to represent the equilibrium constant. Other subscripts are used for specific situations.

Example: Write the equilibrium expression for the reaction
$2HI(g) \rightleftharpoons H_2(g) + I_2(g)$.

Solution: $K_{eq} = \dfrac{[H_2][I_2]}{[HI]^2}$.

The units associated with equilibrium constants in the expression above are molarity raised to the power of an integer that depends on the stoichiometric coefficients of the reaction, but it is common practice to write these constants as dimensionless values. Multiplying or dividing the equilibrium expression by 1 M as needed achieves these dimensionless values. **The equilibrium expression for a reaction written in one direction is the reciprocal of the expression for the reaction in the reverse direction**.

For a heterogeneous equilibrium (a chemical equilibrium with components in different phases), reactants or products may be pure liquids or solids. The concentration of a pure liquid or solid in moles/liter cannot change. It is a constant property of the material, and these constants are incorporated into the equilibrium constant. Therefore the concentrations of pure liquids and solids are absent from equilibrium expressions for heterogeneous equilibria.

Example: Write the equilibrium expression for the redox reaction between copper and silver: $Cu(s) + 2Ag^+(aq) \rightleftharpoons Cu^{2+}(aq) + 2Ag(s)$.

Solution: $K_{eq} = \dfrac{[Cu^{2+}]}{[Ag^+]^2}$. The solids do not appear in the equilibrium expression.

Equilibrium is established when the reaction rates of the forward and reverse reactions are equal. This is a fundamental concept of equilibrium. It's also important to know the converse statement. If the forward and reverse reactions are *unequal* then equilibrium is *not* established.

Competency 0018: Understand the theories, principles, and applications of acid-base chemistry.

It was recognized centuries ago that many substances could be divided into the two general categories. **Acids** have a sour taste (as in lemon juice), dissolve many metals, and turn litmus paper red. **Bases** have a bitter taste (as in soaps), feel slippery, and turn litmus paper blue. The chemical reaction between an acid and a base is called **neutralization**. The products of neutralization reactions are neither acids nor bases. Litmus paper is an example of an **acid-base indicator**, a substance that changes color when changing from an acid to a base.

Strong and weak acids and bases
Strong acids and bases are strong electrolytes, and weak acids and bases are weak electrolytes, so **strong acids and bases completely dissociate in water**, but weak acids and bases do not.

Examples: $HCl(aq) + H_2O(l) \rightarrow H_3O^+(aq) + Cl^-(aq)$ goes to completion. HCl is a strong acid. $HF(aq) + H_2O(l) \rightleftharpoons F^-(aq) + H_3O^+(aq)$ is an equilibrium reaction. Some HF and some F^- are present in solution. HF is a weak acid.

The aqueous dissociation constants K_a and K_b quantify acid and base strength. K_a and K_b are two examples of special equilibrium constants. Larger values for these constants indicate a stronger acid or base.

The **acid-dissociation constant**, K_a, is the equilibrium constant for the ionization of a weak acid to a hydrogen ion and its conjugate base:

$$HX(aq) \rightleftharpoons H^+(aq) + X^-(aq) \qquad K_a = \dfrac{[H^+][X^-]}{[HX]}.$$

Polyprotic acids have unique values for each dissociation: K_{a1}, K_{a2}, etc.

The **base-dissociation constant**, K_b, is the equilibrium constant for the addition of a proton to a weak base by water to form its conjugate acid and an OH^- ion. In these reactions, it is water that is dissociating as a result of reaction with the base:

$$\text{weak base}(aq) + H_2O(l) \rightleftharpoons \text{conjugate acid}(aq) + OH^-(aq)$$

$$K_b = \frac{[\text{conjugate acid}][OH^-]}{[\text{weak base}]}.$$

The concentration of water is nearly constant and is incorporated into the dissociation constant.

For ammonia (the most common weak base), the equilibrium reaction and base-dissociation constant are:

$$NH_3(aq) + H_2O(l) \rightleftharpoons NH_4^+(aq) + OH^-(aq)$$

$$K_b = \frac{[NH_4^+][OH^-]}{[NH_3]}$$

Another way of looking at acid dissociation is that strong acids transfer protons more readily than H_3O^+ transfers protons, so they protonate water, the conjugate base of H_3O^+. In general, **if two acid/base conjugate pairs are present, the stronger acid will transfer a proton to the conjugate base of the weaker acid**.

Acid and base **strength is not related to safety**. Weak acids like HF may be extremely corrosive and dangerous.

The most **common strong acids and bases** are listed in the following table:

Strong acid		Strong base	
HCl	Hydrochloric acid	LiOH	Lithium hydroxide
HBr	Hydrobromic acid	NaOH	Sodium hydroxide
HI	Hydroiodic acid	KOH	Potassium hydroxide
HNO_3	Nitric acid	$Ca(OH)_2$	Calcium hydroxide
H_2SO_4	Sulfuric acid	$Sr(OH)_2$	Strontium hydroxide
$HClO_4$	Perchloric acid	$Ba(OH)_2$	Barium hydroxide

A flash animation tutorial demonstrating the difference between strong and weak acids is located at
http://www.mhhe.com/physsci/chemistry/essentialchemistry/flash/acid13.swf.

Chemical trends in acid and base strength

The strongest acid in a polyprotic series is always **the acid with the most protons** (e.g. H_2SO_4 is a stronger acid than HSO_4^-). The strongest acid in a series with the same central atom is always **the acid with the central atom at the highest oxidation number** (e.g. $HClO_4 > HClO_3 > HClO_2 > HClO$ in terms of acid strength. The strongest acid in a series with different central atoms at the same oxidation number is usually **the acid with the central atom at the highest electronegativity** (e.g. the K_a of $HClO > HBrO > HIO$). This electronegativity trend stretches across the periodic table for oxides.

The $H^+(aq)$ ion

In acid-base systems, **"protonated water" or "$H^+(aq)$" are shorthand for a mixture of water ions**. For example, HCl reacting in water may be represented as a dissociation:

$$HCl(aq) \rightarrow H^+(aq) + Cl^-(aq).$$

The same reaction may be described as the transfer of a proton to water to form H_3O^+:

$$HCl(aq) + H_2O(l) \rightarrow Cl^-(aq) + H_3O^+(aq).$$

H_3O^+ is called a **hydronium ion**. Its Lewis structure is shown below to the left. In reality, the hydrogen bonds in water are so strong that H^+ ions exist in water as a mixture of species in a hydrogen bond network. Two of them are shown below at center and to the right. Hydrogen bonds are shown as dashed lines.

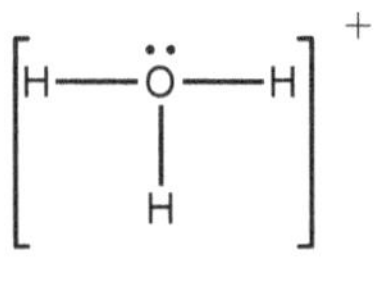

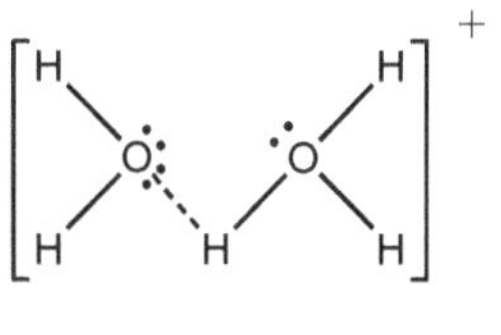

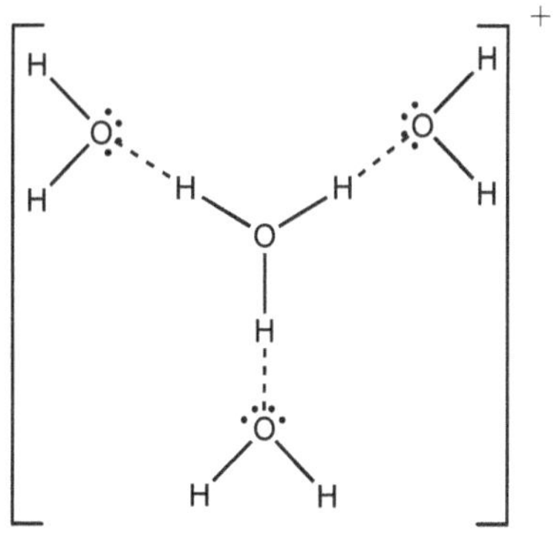

Ion-product constant, K_w

The **ion-product constant for water**, K_w is the equilibrium constant for the dissociation of H_2O. Water molecules may donate protons to other water molecules in a process known as autoionization:

$$2H_2O(l) \rightleftharpoons H_3O^+(aq) + OH^-(aq)$$

The above equation may be rewritten as the following reaction that defines K_w. As with K_b, the concentration of water is nearly constant.

$$H_2O(l) \rightleftharpoons H^+(aq) + OH^-(aq)$$
$$K_w = [H^+][OH^-] = 1.0 \times 10^{-14} \text{ at } 25°C.$$

Pure water at equilibrium has an equal concentration of the two ions: $[H^+] = [OH^-]$. Therefore $K_w = [H^+]^2 = 1.0 \times 10^{-14}$. Solving for $[H^+]$ yields $[H^+] = 1.0 \times 10^{-7}$ M **for pure water**.

The **product of K_a for an acid and K_b for its conjugate base will always be K_w**. This is demonstrated below for the weak acid, HF and its conjugate base, F^-:

$$HF(aq) \rightleftharpoons H^+(aq) + F^-(aq) \qquad K_a = \frac{[H^+][F^-]}{[HF]}.$$

$$F^-(aq) + H_2O(l) \rightleftharpoons HF(aq) + OH^-(aq) \qquad K_b = \frac{[HF][OH^-]}{[F^-]}$$

Multiplication of K_a and K_b yields:
$$K_a \times K_b = \left(\frac{[H^+][F^-]}{[HF]}\right)\left(\frac{[HF][OH^-]}{[F^-]}\right)$$
$$= [H^+][OH^-] = K_w$$

Definition of pH and pK_a

The concentration of $H^+(aq)$ ions is often expressed in terms of pH. **The pH of a solution is the negative base-10 logarithm of the hydrogen-ion molarity.**

$$pH = -\log[H^+] = \log\left(\frac{1}{[H^+]}\right).$$

A ten-fold increase in [H$^+$] decreases the pH by one unit. [H$^+$] may be found from pH using the expression:

$$[H^+] = 10^{-pH}.$$

Because $[H^+] = 10^{-7}$ M for pure water, **the pH of a neutral solution is 7**. In an **acidic solution**, $[H^+] > 10^{-7}$ M and **pH < 7**. In a basic solution, $[H^+] < 10^{-7}$ M and **pH > 7**.

CHEMISTRY

Example: An aqueous solution has an H^+ ion concentration of 4.0×10^{-9}. Is the solution acidic or basic? What is the pH of the solution?

Solution: The solution is basic because $[H^+] < 10^{-7}$ M.
$$pH = -\log[H^+] = -\log 4 \times 10^{-9}$$
$$= 8.4.$$

The negative base-10 log is a convenient way of representing other small numbers used in chemistry by placing the letter "p" before the symbol. Values of K_a are often represented as pK_a, with $pK_a = -\log K_a$.

Buffer solutions

A **buffer solution** is a solution that **resists a change in pH** after addition of small amounts of an acid or a base. Buffer solutions require the presence of an acid to neutralize an added base and also the presence of a base to neutralize an added acid. These two components present in the buffer also must not neutralize each other! A **conjugate acid-base pair is present in buffers** to fulfill these requirements.

Buffers are prepared by mixing together **a weak acid or base and a salt of the acid or base** that provides the conjugate.

Consider the buffer solution prepared by mixing together acetic acid—$HC_2H_3O_2$—and sodium acetate—$C_2H_3O_2^-$ containing Na^+ as a spectator ion. The equilibrium reaction for this acid/conjugate base pair is:
$$HC_2H_3O_2 \rightleftharpoons C_2H_3O_2^- + H^+.$$

If H^+ ions from a strong acid are added to this buffer solution, Le Chatelier's principle predicts that the reaction will shift to the left and much of this H^+ will be consumed to create more $HC_2H_3O_2$ from $C_2H_3O_2^-$. If a strong base that consumes H^+ is added to this buffer solution, Le Chatelier's principle predicts that the reaction will shift to the right and much of the consumed H^+ will be replaced by the dissociation of $HC_2H_3O_2$. The net effect is that **buffer solutions prevent large changes in pH that occur when an acid or base is added to pure water** or to an unbuffered solution.

The amount of acid or base that a buffer solution can neutralize before dramatic pH changes begins to occur is called its **buffering capacity**. Blood and seawater both contain several conjugate acid-base pairs to buffer the solution's pH and decrease the impact of acids and bases on living things.

An excellent flash animation with audio to explain the action of buffering solutions is found at
http://www.mhhe.com/physsci/chemistry/essentialchemistry/flash/buffer12.swf.

Calculating pH and H^+ concentration

The pH and $[H^+]$ of a **solution containing a strong acid or strong base** may be found using stoichiometry alone for a strong acid, and stoichiometry together with K_w for a base.

Example: What is the pH of a solution of 0.020 M $Ca(OH)_2$?

Solution: $Ca(OH)_2$ is a strong base, so it completely dissociates:

$$Ca(OH)_2(aq) \rightarrow Ca^{2+}(aq) + 2OH^-(aq).$$

The stoichiometry of the dissociation may be used to determine $[OH^-]$:

$$\frac{0.020 \text{ mol } Ca(OH)_2}{L} \times \frac{2 \text{ mol } OH^-}{1 \text{ mol } Ca(OH)_2} = \frac{0.040 \text{ mol } OH^-}{L} = 0.040 \text{ M } OH^-$$

Using the ion-product constant of water, we may find $[H^+]$:

$$K_w = 1.0 \times 10^{-14} = [H^+][OH^-] = [H^+](0.040).$$

Therefore, $[H^+] = \dfrac{1.0 \times 10^{-14}}{0.040} = 2.5 \times 10^{-13} \text{ M}.$

Finally, we determine the pH of the solution from its hydrogen ion concentration:

$$pH = -\log[H^+] = -\log(2.5 \times 10^{-13}) = 12.6.$$

The pH and $[H^+]$ of a **solution containing a weak acid or weak base** may be found using K_a or K_b (together with K_w for a base). If more than 5% of the electrolyte is ionized, the quadratic equation should be used. A review of the quadratic equation in the context of chemical equilibrium may be found at http://www.chem.tamu.edu/class/fyp/mathrev/mr-quadr.html.

Example: $K_a = 3.0 \times 10^{-8}$ for hypochlorous acid, HClO. What is the pH of a solution of 0.50 M HClO?

Solution: The dissociation HClO(aq) ⇌ H$^+$(aq) + ClO$^-$(aq) has the equilibrium constant:

$$K_a = \frac{[H^+][ClO^-]}{[HClO]} = 3.0 \times 10^{-8}.$$

There is only HClO at 0.50 M initially. Let $x = [H^+]$ at equilibrium. We may then arrange the initial and equilibrium concentrations into a table based on what is consumed and produced according to reaction stoichiometry:

	HClO(aq) ⇌	H$^+$(aq) +	ClO$^-$(aq)
Initial:	0.50 M	0 M	0 M
Equilibrium:	(0.50 − x) M	x M	x M

Substitution into the equilibrium constant gives us:

$$K_a = \frac{[H^+][ClO^-]}{[HClO]} = \frac{(x)(x)}{0.50 - x} = 3.0 \times 10^{-8}.$$

The expression $\frac{x^2}{0.50 - x} = 3.0 \times 10^{-8}$ may be rearranged to yield the quadratic: $x^2 + 3.0 \times 10^{-8} x - 1.5 \times 10^{-8} = 0$

and we could solve for x using the quadratic formula:

$x = \frac{-b \pm \sqrt{b^2 - 4ac}}{2a}$ where $a = 1$, $b = 3.0 \times 10^{-8}$, and $c = -1.5 \times 10^{-8}$

However, it will usually be safe to estimate that x (the H$^+$ concentration) is sufficiently small to avoid doing this. For this example, we require that x is less than 5% of 0.50 M (i.e., $x <$ 0.05×0.50 M or 2.5×10^{-2} M).

In that case 0.50 − x is roughly 0.50, and the expression $\frac{x^2}{0.50 - x} = 3.0 \times 10^{-8}$ simplifies to:

$$\frac{x^2}{0.50} = 3.0 \times 10^{-8}.$$

Solving for x gives us:

$$x = \sqrt{1.5 \times 10^{-8}} = 1.2 \times 10^{-4} \text{ M H}^+.$$

This value is less than 2.5×10^{-2} M, so the quadratic equation was not needed.

Finally, we determine the pH: $\text{pH} = -\log(1.2 \times 10^{-4}) = 3.9$.

TEACHER CERTIFICATION EXAM

The pH and [H⁺] of **a buffer solution may be estimated using the Henderson-Hasselbalch equation**:

$$pH = pK_a + \log\left(\frac{[\text{base}]}{[\text{acid}]}\right).$$

The logarithm is in numerical-base-10. This is also called the **buffer equation**.

Expressed in terms of H⁺ concentration and K_a, the Henderson-Hasselbalch equation is:

$$-\log[H^+] = -\log K_a + \log\left(\frac{[\text{base}]}{[\text{acid}]}\right).$$

Many assumptions are required to use these equations, but other methods of calculating the pH of buffers are too difficult to appear on an examination and are beyond the scope of high school chemistry. Therefore, if you are asked for the pH of a buffer solution on the teacher certification exam, you can use the buffer equation with confidence.

Example: A solution contains 0.050 M acetic acid, $HC_2H_3O_2$, and 0.020 M of acetate ion supplied by sodium acetate, $NaC_2H_3O_2$. The K_a of acetic acid is 1.8×10^{-5}. What is the pH of the solution?

Solution: $HC_2H_3O_2$ is a weak acid, and its dissociation reaction is:
$$HC_2H_3O_2 \rightleftharpoons C_2H_3O_2^- + H^+.$$

Sodium acetate provides the conjugate base, so we know we have a buffer problem with Na⁺ as a spectator ion. The pKa may be found from:

$$pK_a = -\log K_a = -\log(1.8 \times 10^{-5}) = 4.8.$$

From the Henderson-Hasselbalch equation:

$$pH = pK_a + \log\left(\frac{[\text{base}]}{[\text{acid}]}\right) = 4.8 + \log\left(\frac{0.02}{0.05}\right) = 4.8 + (-0.4)$$
$$= 4.4$$

A comprehensive set of lectures on pH calculation is presented at:
http://www.chembuddy.com/?left=pH-calculation&right=toc.

Arrhenius definition of acids and bases

Svante **Arrhenius** proposed in the 1880s that **acids form H⁺ ions and bases form OH⁻ ions in water**. The net ionic reaction for neutralization between an Arrhenius acid and base always produces water as shown below for nitric acid and sodium hydroxide:

$$HNO_3(aq) + NaOH(aq) \rightarrow NaNO_3(aq) + H_2O(l)$$

$$H^+(aq) + NO_3^-(aq) + Na^+(aq) + OH^-(aq) \rightarrow NO_3^-(aq) + Na^+(aq) + H_2O(l) \text{ (complete ionic)}$$

$$H^+(aq) + OH^-(aq) \rightarrow H_2O(l) \text{ (net ionic)}$$

Brønsted-Lowry definition of acids and bases

In the 1920s, Johannes **Brønsted** and Thomas **Lowry** recognized that **acids can transfer a proton to bases** regardless of whether an OH⁻ ion accepts the proton. In an equilibrium reaction, the direction of proton transfer depends on whether the reaction is read left to right or right to left, so **Brønsted acids and bases exist in conjugate pairs with and without a proton**. Acids that are able to transfer more than one proton are called **polyprotic acids**.

Examples:
1) In the reaction:

$$HF(aq) + H_2O(l) \rightleftharpoons F^-(aq) + H_3O^+(aq),$$

HF transfers a proton to water. Therefore HF is the Brønsted acid and H₂O is the Brønsted base. But in the reverse direction, hydronium ions transfer a proton to fluoride ions. H_3O^+ is the conjugate acid of H_2O because it has an additional proton, and F⁻ is the conjugate base of HF because it lacks a proton.

2) In the reaction:

$$NH_3(aq) + H_2O(l) \rightleftharpoons NH_4^+(aq) + OH^-(aq),$$

water transfers a proton to ammonia. H₂O is the Brønsted acid and OH⁻ is its conjugate base. NH₃ is the Brønsted base and NH₄⁺ is its conjugate acid.

3) In the reaction:

$$H_3PO_4 + HS^- \rightleftharpoons H_2PO_4^- + H_2S$$

H₃PO₄/H₂PO₄⁻ is one conjugate acid-base pair and H₂S/HS⁻ is the other.

4) H₃PO₄ is a polyprotic acid. It may further dissociate to transfer more than one proton:

$$H_3PO_4 \rightleftharpoons H_2PO_4^- + H^+$$
$$H_2PO_4^- \rightleftharpoons HPO_4^{2-} + H^+$$
$$HPO_4^{2-} \rightleftharpoons PO_4^{3-} + H^+$$

Lewis definition of acids and bases
The transfer of a proton from a Brønsted acid to a Brønsted base requires that the base accept the proton. When Lewis diagrams are used to draw the proton donation of Brønsted acid-base reactions, it is always clear that the base must contain an unshared electron pair to form a bond with the proton. For example, ammonia contains an unshared electron pair in the following reaction:

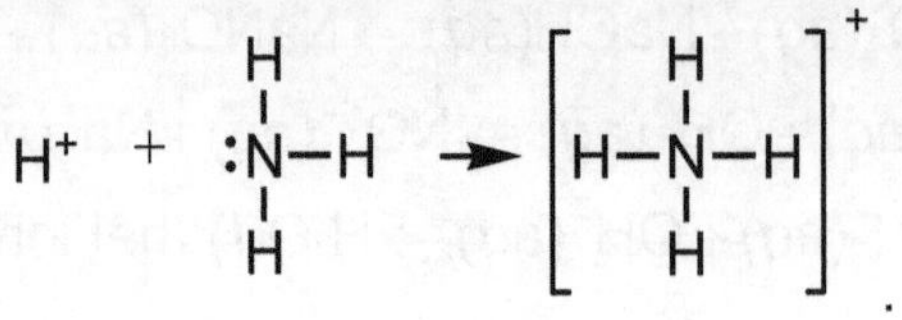

$$H^+ + :NH_3 \rightarrow [NH_4]^+$$

In the 1920s, Gilbert N. **Lewis** proposed that **bases donate unshared electron pairs to acids**, regardless of whether the donation is made to a proton or to another atom. Boron trifluoride is an example of a Lewis acid that is not a Brønsted acid because it is a chemical that accepts an electron pair without involving an H⁺ ion:.

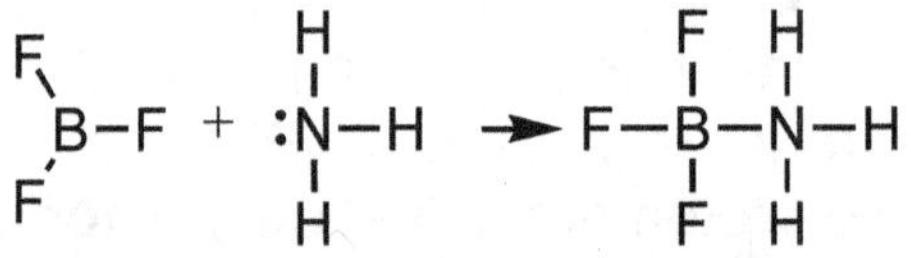

$$BF_3 + :NH_3 \rightarrow F_3B-NH_3$$

The Lewis theory of acids and bases is more general than Brønsted-Lowry theory, but Brønsted-Lowry's definition is used more frequently. The terms "acid" and "base" most often refer to Brønsted acids and bases, and the term "Lewis acid" is usually reserved for chemicals like BF_3 that are not also Brønsted acids.

Summary of definitions
A Lewis base transfers an electron pair to a Lewis acid. A Brønsted acid transfers a proton to a Brønsted base. These exist in conjugate pairs at equilibrium. In an Arrhenius base, the proton acceptor (electron pair donor) is OH^-. All Arrhenius acids/bases are Brønsted acids/bases and all Brønsted acids/bases are Lewis acids/bases. Each definition contains a subset of the one that comes after it.

Competency 0019: Understand redox reactions and electrochemistry.

Oxidation states

The **oxidation state of an ion is its charge**. The oxidation state of an atom sharing its electrons is **the charge it would have if the bonding were ionic**. Oxidation states are also called oxidation numbers. There are four rules for determining oxidation number:
1) The oxidation number of an element (i.e., a Cl atom in Cl_2) is zero because the electrons in the bond are shared equally.
2) In a compound, the more electronegative atoms are assigned negative oxidation numbers and the less electronegative atoms are assigned positive oxidation numbers equal to the number of shared electron-pair bonds. For example, hydrogen may only have an oxidation number of –1 when bonded to a less electronegative element or +1 when bonded to a more electronegative element. Oxygen almost always has an oxidation number of –2. Fluorine always has an oxidation number of –1 (except in F_2).
3) The oxidation numbers in a compound must add up to zero, and the sum of oxidation numbers in a polyatomic ion must equal the overall charge of the ion.

Example: What is the oxidation state of nitrogen in the nitrate ion, NO_3^-?
Oxygen has the oxidation number of –2 (rule 2), and the sum of the oxidation numbers must be –1 (rule 3). The oxidation number for N may be found by solving for x in the equation $x + 3 \times (-2) = -1$. The oxidation number of N in NO_3^- is +5.

Identifying oxidation-reduction reactions and their components

Reduction is the **gain of an electron** by a molecule, atom, or ion, thus decreasing its oxidation number. **Oxidation** is the **loss of an electron**, thus increasing the oxidation number of the molecule, atom, or ion. These two processes always occur together in **oxidation-reduction reactions, also called redox reactions**. Electrons lost by one substance are gained by the other.

The easiest redox processes to identify are those involving monatomic ions with altered charges. For example, the reaction
$$Zn(s) + Cu^{2+}(aq) \rightarrow Zn^{2+}(aq) + Cu(s)$$
is a redox process because electrons are transferred from Zn to Cu.

However, many redox reactions involve the transfer of electrons from one molecular compound to another. In these cases, **oxidation numbers must be determined**.

For example, the reaction
$$H_2 + F_2 \rightarrow 2HF$$
is a redox process because the oxidation numbers of atoms are altered. The oxidation numbers of elements are always zero, and oxidation numbers in a compound are never zero.

Fluorine is the more electronegative element, so in HF it has an oxidation number of –1 and hydrogen has an oxidation number of +1. This is a redox process where electrons are transferred from H_2 to F_2 to create HF.

In the reaction
$$HCl + NaOH \rightarrow NaCl + H_2O,$$
the H-atoms on both sides of the reaction have an oxidation number of +1, the atom of Cl has an oxidation number of –1, the Na-atom has an oxidation number of +1, and the atom of O has an oxidation number of –2. **This is not a redox process because oxidation numbers remain unchanged** by the reaction.

An **oxidizing agent** (also called an oxidant or oxidizer) has the ability to oxidize other substances by removing electrons from them. The **oxidizing agent is reduced** in the process. A **reducing agent** (also called a reductive agent, reductant or reducer) is a substance that has the ability to reduce other substances by transferring electrons to them. The **reducing agent is oxidized** in the process.

Redox reactions may always be written as **two half-reactions**, a **reduction half-reaction** with **electrons as a reactant** and an **oxidation half-reaction** with **electrons as a product**.

For example, the redox reactions considered previously:
$$Zn(s) + Cu^{2+}(aq) \rightarrow Zn^{2+}(aq) + Cu(s) \quad \text{and} \quad H_2 + F_2 \rightarrow 2HF$$
may be written in terms of the half-reactions:
$$2e^- + Cu^{2+}(aq) \rightarrow Cu(s) \qquad 2e^- + F_2 \rightarrow 2F^-$$
$$\text{and}$$
$$Zn(s) \rightarrow Zn^{2+}(aq) + 2e^-. \qquad H_2 \rightarrow 2H^+ + 2e^-.$$

An additional (non-redox) reaction, $2F^- + 2H^+ \rightarrow 2HF$, achieves the final products for the second reaction.

57 videos of redox experiments are presented here:
http://chemmovies.unl.edu/chemistry/redoxlp/redox000.html.

Charge balance
Balancing redox reactions requires an additional step because there must be a **charge balance.** For example, the equation:
$$Sn^{2+} + Fe^{3+} \rightarrow Sn^{4+} + Fe^{2+}$$
contains one Sn and one Fe atom on each side but it is not balanced because the sum of charges on the left side of the equation is +5 and the sum on the right side is +6. A charge balance is obtained by considering each half-reaction separately before multiplying by an appropriate factor so that the number of electrons gained by one half-reaction is the same as the number lost in the other. The two half-reactions may then be combined again into one reaction.

For the example presented above, one electron is gained in the reduction half-reaction ($Fe^{3+} + e^- \rightarrow Fe^{2+}$), but two are lost in the oxidation half-reaction ($Sn^{2+} \rightarrow Sn^{4+} + 2e^-$). A charge balance is obtained by multiplying the reduction half-reaction by two to obtain the half-reactions:
$$2Fe^{3+} + 2e^- \rightarrow 2Fe^{2+}$$
$$Sn^{2+} \rightarrow Sn^{4+} + 2e^-.$$

The equation:
$$Sn^{2+} + 2Fe^{3+} \rightarrow Sn^{4+} + 2Fe^{2+}$$
is properly balanced because both sides contain the same sum of charges (+8).

Oxidation states as a tool for balancing equations
Oxidation states are often useful to balance equations more rapidly than the method described above. For example, consider the unbalanced reaction between copper and nitric acid:
$$Cu(s) + HNO_3(aq) \rightarrow Cu(NO_3)_2(aq) + NO(g) + H_2O(g).$$

Let's first try balancing this equation using the method. There is one Cu on both sides, but none of the other atoms are balanced. If we assume that Cu(NO₃)₂ has a stoichiometric coefficient of one, then Cu(s) will also have a coefficient of one, but the other coefficients are difficult to balance right away. We could use algebra, and assign variable names to the other coefficients:
$$Cu(s) + xHNO_3(aq) \rightarrow Cu(NO_3)_2(aq) + yNO(g) + zH_2O(g)$$
Then we could solve these three equations:
    From the balance on H: $x = 2z$
    From the balance on N: $x = 2 + y$
    From the balance on O: $3x = 6 + y + z$

With a lot more work to solve three equations and three unknowns, we could determine that $x = 8/3$, $y = 2/3$, and $z = 4/3$, and we'd almost be finished.

Next let's try using oxidation states to help us balance the equation.

Cu is oxidized from an oxidation state of 0 to +2, an increase of 2. The N that will form NO is reduced from an oxidation state of +5 to +2, a decrease of 3. Therefore, three Cu atoms must be oxidized from Cu(s) (for a net change of +6) for every two N atoms that are reduced to NO(g) (for a net change of –6). We may write:

$$3Cu(s) + ?HNO_3(aq) \rightarrow ?Cu(NO_3)_2(aq) + 2NO(g) + ?H_2O(g).$$

A balance on Cu gives a stoichiometric coefficient of 3 for Cu(NO$_3$)$_2$. This means there are 8 N on the right. A balance on N gives a coefficient of 8 for HNO$_3$. This means there are 8 H on the left side. A balance on H gives a coefficient of 4 for H$_2$O. This yields the following equation:

$$3Cu(s) + 8HNO_3(aq) \rightarrow 3Cu(NO_3)_2(aq) + 2NO(g) + 4H_2O(g)$$

Before declaring that the equation is balanced, we also must confirm that the O atoms and the charges balance. There are 24 O on each side and there is a charge balance because all species are neutral.

Competency 0020: Understand the nature of organic reactions.

Carbon is almost unique among elements in its ability to form long molecular chains and rings that may also include nitrogen, oxygen, halogens, and many other atoms. These molecules may be large enough to bend and fold into distinct shapes with non-polar and polar regions. The polar regions may contain positive charges, negative charges, or hydrogen-bond-forming atoms that are all able to interact with neighboring molecules in specific ways. These interactions perform a wide variety of functions such as altering the shape and composition of molecules.

Carbon has a **great affinity for covalent bonding** with a wide variety of other atoms. Carbon also readily bonds to other carbon atoms to form polymers. **Carbon has four valence electrons**. It may share these electrons with four other atoms in single bonds to fulfill the octet rule. Bonding to four different atoms permits carbon to form compounds that are mirror images of of each other. Carbon also readily forms double and triple bonds. Carbon compounds containing oxygen and nitrogen are polar due to electronegativity differences, and these **polar regions of specific chemical activity are known as functional groups**. This leads to a wide variety of possible molecules. **Organic compounds contain carbon,** and they have their own branch of chemistry because of the huge number of carbon compounds in nature, including nearly all the molecules in living things.

Carbon is able to form sp, sp^2, and sp^3 hybridized atomic orbitals and σ and π molecular orbitals. For example, in CH$_4$, the electron density of the four sp^3 orbitals of C each overlap with an s orbital of H to form four σ bonds.

In C_2H_4 (an alkene), two sp^2 orbitals on each C overlap with H, the remaining sp^2 orbitals overlap with each other in a σ bond, and the p orbitals (drawn as shaded shapes) overlap with each other above and beneath the carbons in a π bond (also drawn as shaded shapes). In CO_2, the C atom has two sp hybrid orbitals and two p orbitals. These form one σ bond and one π bond with the two unfilled p orbitals on each O atom. In C_2H_2 (an alkyne), a triple bond forms with one σ and two π.

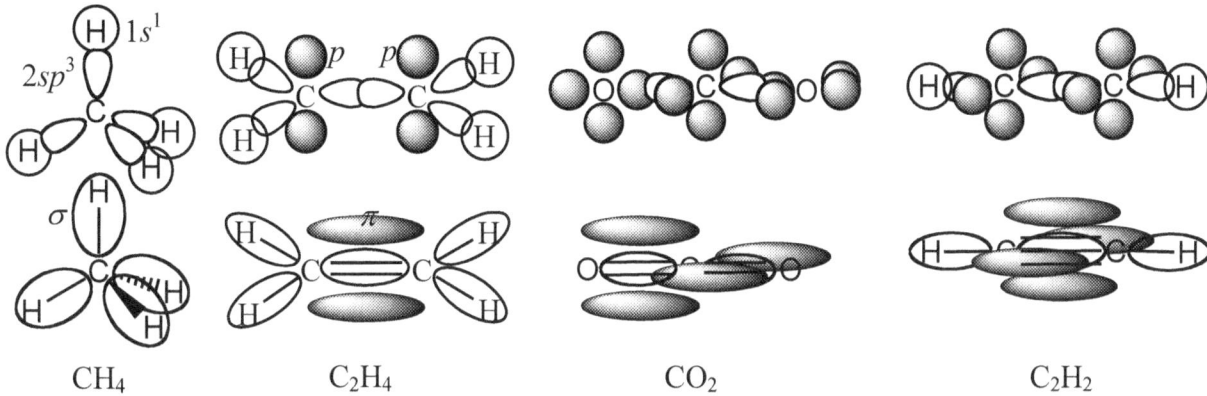

CH₄   C₂H₄   CO₂   C₂H₂

Molecules with double bonds next to each other and aromatic molecules based on benzene contain **more than two π orbitals on adjacent atoms**. The bonds and the entire molecules are described as being **conjugated**. Electrons in these molecules are free to move from one bond to the next **on the same molecule** and so are **delocalized**. Electron delocalization may extend throughout the entire substance in materials with metallic bonds.

Benzene (C_6H_6) has the following resonance forms:

$$\begin{array}{c} HC-CH \\ HC \diagup \diagdown CH \\ HC=CH \end{array} \longleftrightarrow \begin{array}{c} HC=CH \\ HC \diagdown \diagup CH \\ HC-CH \end{array}$$

Each carbon atom in benzene bonds to three atoms, so their electrons are in three sp^2 orbitals and one p orbital as we've seen for C_2H_4. The p orbitals are shown as the shaded shapes below on the left (only the C-C bonds are shown). The p atomic orbitals combine to form molecular orbitals with delocalized electrons as shown in the bonding π molecular orbital below to the right.

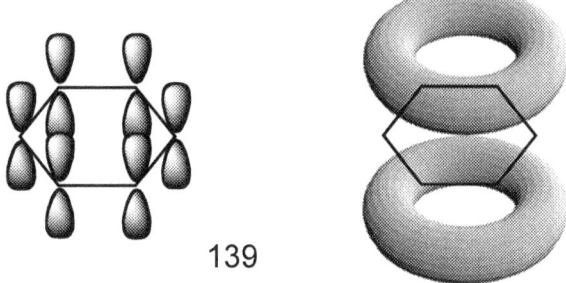

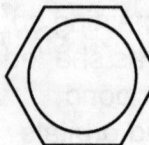 Aromatic molecules are often drawn with a circle in the center of their benzene rings (shown to the left) to show delocalized π electrons. The atoms of a benzene molecule are all located in the same plane. This is in contrast to molecules that contain only σ bonds as shown to the right for cyclohexane, C_6H_{12}.

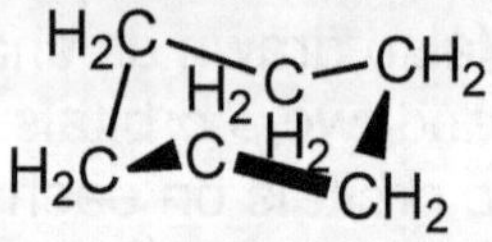

A few common reactions in organic chemistry are listed below:

Esterification occurs when a carboxylic acid and an alcohol react to **form an ester**:

$$H_3C\text{-}COOH + HO\text{-}CH_2\text{-}CH_3 \rightarrow H_3C\text{-}COO\text{-}CH_2\text{-}CH_3 + H_2O$$
$$\text{acetic acid} + \text{ethanol} \rightarrow \text{ethyl acetate} + \text{water}$$

Hydrolysis is a reaction in which **a molecule is split into two parts by reacting with water**. An example of a hydrolysis reaction is the reverse of the esterification reaction above.

Decarboxylation is any chemical reaction that **removes a carboxyl (-COOH) group from a compound, producing CO_2** in the process. Decarboxylation will convert a carboxylic acid into a hydrocarbon:

$$H_3C\text{-}COOH \rightarrow CH_4 + CO_2$$
$$\text{acetic acid} \rightarrow \text{methane} + \text{carbon dioxide}$$

TEACHER CERTIFICATION EXAM

SUBAREA V- QUANTITATIVE RELATIONSHIPS

Competency 0021: Understand the mole concept.

A single atom or molecule weighs very little in grams and cannot be measured using a balance the lab. It's useful to have a system that permits a large number of chemical particles to be described as one unit, analogous to a dozen as 12 of something or one gross as 144. A useful number of atoms, molecules, or formula units is **that number whose mass in grams is numerically equal to the atomic mass, molecular mass, or formula mass** of the substance. This quantity is called the **mole**, abbreviated mol. Because the ^{12}C isotope is assigned an exact value of 12 atomic mass units, there are exactly 12 g of ^{12}C in one mole of ^{12}C. The atomic mass unit is also called a Dalton, and either "u" (for "unified atomic mass unit") or "Da" may be used as an abbreviation. Older texts use "amu." To find the molar mass of a substance, use the periodic table before skill 1.1 to determine the molecular weight of each atom in the substance and multiply by the number of each atom present. For example:

$$Al_2(SO_4)_3 \text{ molecular weight} = 2(26.982 \text{ u for Al}) + 3(32.065 \text{ u for S}) + 12(15.999 \text{ u for O})$$
$$= 342.147 \text{ u.}$$

Therefore 1 mol $Al_2(SO_4)_3$ = 342.147 g $Al_2(SO_4)_3$.

It's been found experimentally that this number of atoms, ions, molecules, or anything else in one mole is 6.022045×10^{23}. For most purposes, three significant digits are sufficient, and $\mathbf{6.02 \times 10^{23}}$ will be used. This value was named in honor of Amedeo Avogadro after his death and it is referred to as **Avogadro's number**. The following table illustrates why the mole and Avogadro's number are useful. These concepts permit us to think about interactions among individual molecules and atoms while measuring many grams of a substance.

Name	Formula	Formula weight (u)	Mass of 1 mol of formula units (g)	Number and kind of particles in 1 mol
Atomic hydrogen	H	1.0079	1.0079	6.02×10^{23} H atoms
Molecular hydrogen	H_2	2.0158	2.0158	6.02×10^{23} H_2 molecules
				$2(6.02 \times 10^{23})$ H atoms
Silver	Ag	107.87	107.87	6.02×10^{23} Ag atoms
Silver ions	Ag^+	107.87	107.87	6.02×10^{23} Ag^+ ions
Barium chloride	$BaCl_2$	208.24	208.24	6.02×10^{23} $BaCl_2$ units
				6.02×10^{23} Ba^{2+} ions
				$2(6.02 \times 10^{23})$ Cl^- ions

CHEMISTRY

TEACHER CERTIFICATION EXAM

Many problems are given at "**standard temperature and pressure**" or "**STP**." Standard conditions are *exactly* **1 atm** (101.325 kPa) and **0 °C (273.15 K)**. At STP, one mole of an ideal gas has a volume of 22.4 L. This value is known as the **standard molar volume of any gas at STP.**

Competency 0022: Understand the relationship between the mole concept and chemical formulas.

The expression that shows the number and kind of each atom in a molecule is the chemical formula. Chemical formulas use the chemical symbol of the atom to express the type of atom and a subscript following the symbol to express the number of atoms in the molecule. If there is only one of a type of atom, no subscript is used. In addition to the number and type of atom, chemical formulas can (but don't have to) suggest the arrangement of the atoms.

The chemical formula tells the type and the ratio of atoms in a compound. Because the ratio is the same regardless of whether there is one molecule or millions, we use a "scale-up" factor to work with enough molecules to be easily manipulated. This factor, the SI unit for amount of substance, is a mole. The mole is just a specific number of things, in the case of chemistry either molecules or atoms. Because atoms and molecules are so small, this amount must be very large. The number of things in a mole is called Avogadro's number and has a value of 6.022×10^{23}. This number is used because whereas the mass of an atom is its atomic weight in atomic mass units, the mass of a mole of atoms is its atomic weight in grams. Since masses are additive, the mass of a molecule is the sum of the mass of each of its atoms in atomic mass units and the mass of a mole of the molecule is the sum of the mass of each of its atoms in grams. The mass of a mole of any substance is called molar mass. Also, since the ratios are the same in a mole as in a molecule, the molecular formula can be used to obtain mole ratios of elements in a compound.

NaCl represents the compound containing one atom of sodium and one atom of chlorine. The masses on these elements are too small to determine individually or as individual ionic units. However, using the mole we can determine the mass of the compound represented by the formula NaCl. One mole of sodium atoms has a mass of 23.0 grams and one mole of chlorine atoms has a mass of 35.5 grams. Therefore, one mole of sodium chloride molecules has a mass of 58.5 grams.

1. Molar masses of chemical compounds are equal to the sums of the molar masses of all the atoms in one molecule of that compound. If we have a chemical compound like NaCl, the molar mass will be equal to the molar mass of one atom of sodium plus the molar mass of one atom of chlorine. If we write this as a calculation, it looks like this:

(1 atom x 23 grams/mole Na) + (1 atom x 35.5 grams/mole Cl) = 58.5 grams/mole NaCl

2. If you have a subscript in a chemical formula, then you multiply the number of atoms of anything next to that subscript by the number of the subscript. For most compounds, this is easy. For example, in iron (II) chloride, or $FeCl_2$, you have one atom of iron and two atoms of chlorine. The molar mass will be equal to (1 atom x 56 grams/mole Fe) + (2 atoms x 35.5 grams/mole of chlorine) = 127 grams/mole of iron (II) chloride.

For other compounds, this might get a little bit more complicated. For example, take the example of zinc nitrate, or $Zn(NO_3)_2$. In this compound, we have one atom of zinc, two atoms of nitrogen (one atom inside the brackets multiplied by the subscript two) and six atoms of oxygen (three atoms in the brackets multiplied by the subscript two). The molar mass of zinc nitrate will be equal to:

 (1 atom x 65 grams/mole of zinc) + (two atoms x 14 grams/mole of nitrogen) + (six atoms x 16 grams/mole of oxygen) = 189 grams/mole of zinc nitrate.

Example: Determine the molar mass of potassium hydroxide.

Solution: The chemical formula for potassium hydroxide is KOH.
In potassium hydroxide, there is one atom of potassium, one atom of hydrogen, and one atom of oxygen. The molar mass will then be (1 mole K x 39 grams/ mol) + (1mol H x 1 gram/ mol) + (1mol O x 16 grams/ mol) = 56 grams/mole of potassium hydroxide

The **percent composition** of a substance is the **percentage by mass of each element**. Chemical composition is used to verify the purity of a compound in the lab. An impurity will make the actual composition vary from the expected one.

To determine percent composition from a formula, do the following:
1) Write down the **number of atoms each element contributes** to the formula.
2) Multiply these values by the molecular weight of the corresponding element to determine the **grams of each element in one mole** of the formula.
3) Add the values from step 2 to obtain the **formula mass**.
4) Divide each value from step 2 by the formula weight from step 3 and multiply by 100% to obtain the **percent composition**.

The first three steps are the same as those used to determine formula mass, but we use the intermediate results to obtain the composition.

TEACHER CERTIFICATION EXAM

Example: What is the chemical composition of ammonium carbonate $(NH_4)_2CO_3$?

Solution:

1) One $(NH_4)_2CO_3$ contains 2 N, 8 H, 1 C, and 3 O.

2) $\dfrac{2 \text{ mol N}}{\text{mol }(NH_4)CO_3} \times \dfrac{14.0 \text{ g N}}{\text{mol N}} = 28.0 \text{ g N/mol }(NH_4)CO_3$

$8(1.0) = 8.0 \text{ g H/mol }(NH_4)CO_3$

$1(12.0) = 12.0 \text{ g C/mol }(NH_4)CO_3$

$3(16.0) = 48.0 \text{ g O/mol }(NH_4)CO_3$

3) Sum is $\overline{96.0 \text{ g }(NH_4)CO_3/\text{mol }(NH_4)CO_3}$

4) $\%N = \dfrac{28.0 \text{ g N/mol }(NH_4)_2CO_3}{96.0 \text{ g }(NH_4)_2CO_3/\text{mol }(NH_4)_2CO_3} = 0.292 \text{ g N/g }(NH_4)_2CO_3 \times 100\% = 29.2\%$

$\%H = \dfrac{8.0}{96.0} \times 100\% = 8.3\% \quad \%C = \dfrac{12.0}{96.0} \times 100\% = 12.5\% \quad \%O = \dfrac{48.0}{96.0} \times 100\% = 50.0\%$

If we know the chemical composition of a compound, we can calculate an **empirical formula** for it. An empirical formula is the **simplest formula** using the smallest set of integers to express the **ratio of atoms** present in a molecule. To determine an empirical formula from a percent composition, do the following:

1) Change the "%" sign to grams for a basis of 100 g of the compound.
2) Determine the moles of each element in 100 g of the compound.
3) Divide the values from step 1 by the smallest value to obtain ratios.
4) Multiply by an integer if necessary to get a whole-number ratio.

Example: What is the empirical formula of a compound with a composition of 63.9% Cl, 32.5% C, and 3.6% H?

Solution:

1) We will use a basis of 100 g of the compound containing 63.9 g Cl, 32.5 g C, and 3.6 g H.

2) In 100 g, there are: $63.9 \text{ g Cl} \times \dfrac{\text{mol Cl}}{35.45 \text{ g Cl}} = 1.802 \text{ mol Cl}$

$32.5/12.01 = 2.706 \text{ mol C}$

$3.6/1.01 = 3.56 \text{ mol H}$

3) Dividing these values by the smallest yields:

$\dfrac{2.706 \text{ mol C}}{1.802 \text{ mol Cl}} = 1.502 \text{ mol C/mol Cl}$

$\dfrac{3.56 \text{ mol H}}{1.802 \text{ mol Cl}} = 1.97 \text{ mol H/mol Cl}$

Therefore, the elements are present in a ratio of C:H:Cl=1.50:2.0:1

CHEMISTRY

4) Multiply the entire ratio by 2 because you cannot have a fraction of an atom. This corresponds to a ratio of 3:4:2 for an empirical formula of $C_3H_4Cl_2$.

The **molecular formula** describing the **actual number of atoms in the molecule** might also be $C_3H_4Cl_2$ or it might be $C_6H_8Cl_4$ or some other multiple that maintains a 3:4:2 ratio.

Competency 0023: Understand the quantitative relationships expressed in chemical equations.

Balanced chemical equations

A properly written chemical equation must contain properly written formulas and must be **balanced**. Chemical equations are written to describe a certain number of moles of reactants becoming a certain number of moles of reaction products. The number of moles of each compound is indicated by its **stoichiometric coefficient**.

Example: In the reaction
$$2H_2(g) + O_2(g) \rightarrow 2H_2O(l),$$
hydrogen has a stoichiometric coefficient of two, oxygen has a coefficient of one, and water has a coefficient of two because 2 moles of hydrogen react with 1 mole of oxygen to form two moles of water.

In a balanced equation, the stoichiometric coefficients are chosen such that the equation contains an **equal number of each type of atom on each side**. In our example, there are four H atoms and two O atoms on both sides.

Antoine **Lavoisier** is called **the father of modern chemistry** because he carefully weighed material before and after chemical reactions to determine that **chemical reactions do not alter total mass**. This principle is called **conservation of matter**. It does not apply to nuclear reactions. The mass of individual atoms does not change, so placing an equal number of each type of atom on both sides of a chemical equation insures conservation of matter will be represented.

Reactions among ions in aqueous solution may often be represented in three ways. When solutions of hydrochloric acid and sodium hydroxide are mixed, a reaction occurs and heat is produced. The **molecular equation** for this reaction is:
$$HCl(aq) + NaOH(aq) \rightarrow H_2O(l) + NaCl(aq).$$

It is called a molecular equation because the **complete chemical formulas** of reactants and products are shown. But in reality, both HCl and NaOH are strong electrolytes and exist in solution as ions. This is represented by a **complete ionic equation** that shows all the dissolved ions:

$$H^+(aq) + Cl^-(aq) + Na^+(aq) + OH^-(aq) \rightarrow H_2O(l) + Na^+(aq) + Cl^-(aq).$$

Because $Na^+(aq)$ and $Cl^-(aq)$ appear as both reactants and products, they play no role in the reaction. Ions that appear in identical chemical forms on both sides of an ionic equation are called **spectator ions** because they aren't part of the action. When spectator ions are removed from a complete ionic equation, the result is a **net ionic equation** that shows the actual changes that occur to the chemicals when these two solutions are mixed together:

$$H^+(aq) + OH^-(aq) \rightarrow H_2O(l)$$

An additional requirement for **redox** reactions is that the equation contains an **equal charge on each side**. Redox reactions may be divided into half-reactions which either gain or lose electrons.

Balancing equations (other than redox reactions) is a four-step process.

1) Connect reactants to products, by an arrow creating an **unbalanced equation**.
2) Determine the **number of each type of atom on each side** of the equation to find if the equation is balanced.
3) Assume that **the molecule with the most atoms** has a stoichiometric coefficient of one, and determine the other stoichiometric coefficients required to create the **same number of atoms on each side** of the equation.
4) Multiply all the stoichiometric coefficients by a whole number if necessary to eliminate fractional coefficients.

Example: Balance the chemical equation describing the combustion of methanol (CH_4O) in oxygen to produce only CO_2 and water.
Solution:
    1) The unbalanced equation is: $CH_4O + O_2 \rightarrow CO_2 + H_2O$.

    2) On the left there are 1C, 4H, and 3O. On the right, there are 1C, 2H, and 3O. It seems close to being balanced, but there's work to do.

3) Assuming that CH_4O has a stoichiometric coefficient of one means that the left side has 1C and 4H that also must be present on the right. Therefore the stoichiometric coefficient of CO_2 will be 1 to balance C and the stoichiometric coefficient of H_2O will be 2 to balance H. Now we have:
$$CH_4O + ?O_2 \rightarrow CO_2 + 2H_2O.$$

and only oxygen remains unbalanced. There are 4O on the right and one of these is accounted for by methanol leaving 3O to be accounted for by O_2. This gives a stoichiometric coefficient of 3/2 and a balanced equation:
$$CH_4O + \frac{3}{2}O_2 \rightarrow CO_2 + 2H_2O.$$

4) Whole-number coefficients are achieved by multiplying by two:
$$2CH_4O + 3O_2 \rightarrow 2CO_2 + 4H_2O.$$

Mass-mass stoichiometry problems

In a mass-mass stoichiometry problem, the mass of one compound that participates in a reaction is given and the mass of a different compound is required. Solving these problems is a three-step process:

1) Grams of the given compound are converted to moles.
2) Moles of the given compound are related to moles of the second compound by relating their stoichiometric coefficients.
3) Moles of the second compound are converted to grams.

These steps are often combined in one series of multiplications, which may be described as **"grams to moles to moles to grams."**

Example: What mass of oxygen is required to consume 95.0 g of ethane in this reaction: $2C_2H_6 + 7O_2 \rightarrow 4CO_2 + 6H_2O$?

Solution:
$$95.0 \text{ g } C_2H_6 \times \underbrace{\frac{1 \text{ mol } C_2H_6}{30.1 \text{ g } C_2H_6}}_{\text{step 1}} \times \underbrace{\frac{7 \text{ mol } O_2}{2 \text{ mol } C_2H_6}}_{\text{step 2}} \times \underbrace{\frac{32.0 \text{ g } O_2}{1 \text{ mol } O_2}}_{\text{step 3}} = 359 \text{ g } O_2$$

Limiting reagent problems

The **limiting reagent** of a reaction is the **reactant that runs out first**. This reactant **determines the amount of product formed**, and any **other reactants remain unconverted** to product and are called **excess reagents**.

CHEMISTRY

Example: Consider the reaction $3H_2 + N_2 \rightarrow 2NH_3$ and suppose that 3 mol H_2 and 3 mol N_2 are available for this reaction. What is the limiting reagent?
Solution: The equation tells us that 3 mol H_2 will react with one mol N_2 to produce 2 mol NH_3. This means that 2 mol N_2 will remain and H_2 is the limiting reagent because it runs out first.

The limiting reagent may be determined by **dividing the number of moles of each reactant by its stoichiometric coefficient.** This determines the moles of reaction if each reactant were limiting. The **lowest result** will indicate the actual limiting reagent. Remember to use moles and not grams for these calculations.

Example: 50.0 g Al and 400. g Br_2 react according the the following equation:
$$2Al + 3Br_2 \rightarrow 2AlBr_3$$
until the limiting reagent is completely consumed. Find the limiting reagent, the mass of $AlBr_3$ expected to form, and the excess reagent expected to remain after the limiting reagent is consumed.

Solution: First convert both reactants to moles:
$$50.0 \text{ g Al} \times \frac{1 \text{ mol Al}}{26.982 \text{ g Al}} = 1.853 \text{ mol Al} \quad \text{and} \quad 400. \text{ g Br}_2 \times \frac{1 \text{ mol Br}_2}{159.808 \text{ g Br}_2} = 2.503 \text{ mol Br}_2.$$

The final digits in the intermediate results above are italicized because they are insignificant. Dividing by stoichiometric coefficients gives:

$$1.853 \text{ mol Al} \times \frac{\text{mol reaction}}{2 \text{ mol Al}} = 0.9265 \text{ mol reaction if Al is limiting}$$

$$2.503 \text{ mol Br}_2 \times \frac{\text{mol reaction}}{3 \text{ mol Br}_2} = 0.8343 \text{ mol reaction if Br}_2 \text{ is limiting.}$$

Br_2 is the lower value and is limiting reagent.
The reaction is expected to produce:

$$2.503 \text{ mol Br}_2 \times \frac{2 \text{ mol AlBr}_3}{3 \text{ mol Br}_2} \times \frac{266.694 \text{ g AlBr}_3}{\text{mol AlBr}_3} = 445 \text{ g AlBr}_3.$$

The reaction is expected to consume:

$$2.503 \text{ mol Br}_2 \times \frac{2 \text{ mol Al}}{3 \text{ mol Br}_2} \times \frac{26.982 \text{ g Al}}{\text{mol Al}} = 45.0 \text{ g Al.}$$

50.0 g Al – 45.0 g Al = 5.0 g Al are expected to remain.

Percent Yield

The **yield of a reaction is the amount of product** obtained. This value is nearly always less than what would be predicted from a stoichiometric balance because side-reactions may produce different products, the reverse reaction may occur, and some material may be lost during the procedure. The yield from a stoichiometric balance on the limiting reagent is called the theoretical yield.

Percent yield is the actual yield divided by the theoretical yield:

$$\text{Percent yield} = \frac{\text{Actual yield}}{\text{Theoretical yield}} \times 100\%.$$

Example: 387 g AlBr$_3$ are produced by the reaction described in the previous example. What is the percent yield?

Solution: $\dfrac{387 \text{ g AlBr}_3}{445 \text{ g AlBr}_3} \times 100\% = 87.0\%$ yield.

Competency 0024: Understand the properties of solutions and colloidal suspension, and analyze factors that affect solubility.

When two or more pure materials mix in a homogeneous way (with their molecules intermixing on a molecular level), the mixture is called a **solution**. Heterogeneous combinations of materials are called **mixtures**. Dispersions of small particles that are larger than molecules are called **colloids**. Liquid solutions are the most common, but any two phases may form a solution. When a pure liquid and a gas or solid form a liquid solution, the pure liquid is called the **solvent** and the non-liquids are called **solutes**. When all components in the solution were originally liquids, then the one present in the greatest amount is called the solvent and the others are called solutes. Solutions with water as the solvent are called **aqueous** solutions. The amount of solute in a solvent is called its **concentration**. A solution with a small concentration of solute is called **dilute**, and a solution with a large concentration of solute is called **concentrated**.

Particles in solution are free to move about and collide with each other, vastly increasing the likelihood that a reaction will occur compared with particles in a solid phase. Aqueous solutions may react to produce an insoluble substance that will fall out of solution as a solid or gas **precipitate** in a **precipitation reaction**. Aqueous solution may also react to form **additional water**, or a different chemical in aqueous solution.

Solubility rules for ionic compounds
Given a cation and anion in aqueous solution, we can determine if a precipitate will form according to some common **solubility rules**.

1) Salts with NH$_4^+$ or with a cation from group 1 of the periodic table are soluble in water.
2) Nitrates (NO$_3^-$), acetates (C$_2$H$_3$O$_2^-$), chlorates (ClO$_3^-$), and perchlorates are soluble.
3) Cl$^-$, Br$^-$, and I$^-$ salts are soluble except with Ag$^+$, Hg$_2^{2+}$, and Pb^{2+}.
4) Sulfates (SO$_4^{2-}$) are soluble except with Ca^{2+}, Ba^{2+}, Ag$^+$, Hg$_2^{2+}$, and Pb^{2+}.

5) Hydroxides (OH⁻) are <u>insoluble</u> except with cations from rule 1 and with Ca^{2+}, Sr^{2+}, and Ba^{2+}.
6) Sulfides (S^{2-}), sulfites (SO_3^{2-}), phosphates (PO_4^{3-}), and carbonates (CO_3^{2-}) are insoluble except with cations from rule 1.

The **molarity** (abbreviated M) of a solute in solution is defined as the number of moles of solute in a liter of solution.

$$\text{Molarity} = \frac{\text{moles solute}}{\text{volume of solution in liters}}$$

Molarity is the most frequently used concentration unit in chemical reactions because it reflects the number of solute moles available. By using Avogadro's number, the number of molecules in a flask--a difficult image to conceptualize in the lab--is expressed in terms of the volume of liquid in the flask—a straightforward image to visualize and actually manipulate. Molarity is useful for dilutions because the moles of solute remain unchanged if more solvent is added to the solution:

$$(\text{Initial molarity})(\text{Initial volume}) = (\text{molarity after dilution})(\text{final volume})$$

or

$$M_{initial}V_{initial} = M_{final}V_{final}$$

Mass percentage is frequently used to represent every component of a solution (possibly including the solvent) as a portion of the whole in terms of mass.

$$\text{Mass percentage of a component} = \frac{\text{mass of component in solution}}{\text{total mass of solution}} \times 100\%.$$

A concentration may be measured by a mass percentage, but, as described below, "percent composition" is usually a term applied to the elemental composition of a single compound, not to the solute composition of a solution.

Parts per million (or ppm) in solution usually refers to a dilute component of a solution as a portion of the whole in terms of mass. A solute present in one part per million would amount to one gram in one million grams of solution. This is also one mg of solute in one kg of solution.

$$\text{Parts per million of a component} = \frac{\text{mass of solute}}{\text{total mass of solution}} \times 10^6$$

$$= \frac{\text{number of mg of solute}}{\text{number of kg of solution}}$$

Strictly speaking, the expression above is a **"ppm by mass."** Parts per million is also sometimes used for ratios of moles or volumes.

A **mole fraction** is used to represent a component in a solution as a portion of the entire number of moles present. If you were able to pick out a molecule at random from a solution, the mole fraction of a component represents the probability that the molecule you picked would be that particular component. Mole fractions for all components must sum to one, and mole fractions are just numbers with no units.

$$\text{Mole fraction of a component} = \frac{\text{moles of component}}{\text{total moles of all components}}$$

The **percent composition** of a substance is the **percentage by mass of each element**. It is not a measure of concentration. Chemical composition is used to verify the purity of a compound in the lab. An impurity will make the actual composition vary from the expected one.

To determine percent composition from a formula, do the following:
  1) Write down the **number of atoms each element contributes** to the formula.
  2) Multiply these values by the molecular weight of the corresponding element to determine the **grams of each element in one mole** of the formula.
  3) Add the values from step 2 to obtain the **formula mass**.
  4) Divide each value from step 2 by the formula weight from step 3 and multiply by 100% to obtain the **percent composition**.

The first three steps are the same as those used to determine formula mass, but we use the intermediate results to obtain the composition.

Example: What is the chemical composition of ammonium carbonate $(NH_4)_2CO_3$?

Solution:
  1) One $(NH_4)_2CO_3$ contains 2 N, 8 H, 1 C, and 3 O.

  2) $\dfrac{2 \text{ mol N}}{\text{mol }(NH_4)CO_3} \times \dfrac{14.0 \text{ g N}}{\text{mol N}} = 28.0 \text{ g N/mol }(NH_4)CO_3$

  $\qquad\qquad\qquad\qquad 8(1.0) = 8.0 \text{ g H/mol }(NH_4)CO_3$
  $\qquad\qquad\qquad\qquad 1(12.0) = 12.0 \text{ g C/mol }(NH_4)CO_3$
  $\qquad\qquad\qquad\qquad 3(16.0) = 48.0 \text{ g O/mol }(NH_4)CO_3$

  3) $\qquad$ Sum is $\qquad 96.0 \text{ g }(NH_4)CO_3/\text{mol }(NH_4)CO_3$

  4) $\%N = \dfrac{28.0 \text{ g N/mol }(NH_4)_2CO_3}{96.0 \text{ g }(NH_4)_2CO_3/\text{mol }(NH_4)_2CO_3} = 0.292 \text{ g N/g }(NH_4)_2CO_3 \times 100\% = 29.2\%$

  $\%H = \dfrac{8.0}{96.0} \times 100\% = 8.3\% \quad \%C = \dfrac{12.0}{96.0} \times 100\% = 12.5\% \quad \%O = \dfrac{48.0}{96.0} \times 100\% = 50.0\%$

Gas solubility

Pressure does not dramatically alter the solubility of solids or liquids, but kinetic molecular theory predicts that **increasing the partial pressure of a gas will increase the solubility of the gas** in a liquid. If a substance is distributed between gas and solution phases and pressure is exerted, more gas molecules will impact the gas/liquid interface per second, so more will dissolve until a new equilibrium is reached at a higher solubility. **Henry's law** describes this relationship as a direct proportionality:

$$\text{Solubility of gas in liquid (in } \frac{\text{mol solute}}{\text{L solution}}) \propto P_{gas}$$

Carbonated drinks are bottled under high CO_2 pressure, permitting the gas to dissolve into aqueous solution. When the bottle is opened, the partial pressure of CO_2 in the gas phase rapidly decreases to the value in the atmosphere, and the gas bubbles out of solution. When the bottle is closed again, CO_2 gas pressure builds until a saturated solution at equilibrium is again obtained. The solubility of gases in a liquid also increases in the bloodstream of deep-sea divers when they experience high pressures. If they return to atmospheric pressure too rapidly, large bubbles of nitrogen gas will form in their blood and cause a potentially lethal condition known as **the bends** or **decompression sickness**. The diver must enter a hyperbaric (high pressure) chambers to redissolve the nitrogen back into the blood.

Increasing temperature will decrease the solubility of a gas in a liquid because kinetic energy opposes intermolecular attractions and permits more molecules to escape from the liquid phase. The vapor pressure of a pure liquid increases with temperature for the same reason. Greater kinetic energy will favor material in the gas phase.

Liquid and solid solubility

For solid and liquid solutes, the impact of temperature depends on whether the solution process requires or releases heat. The following brief analysis is applicable for the effect of temperature on solutions.

Three processes occur when a solution is formed:
1) Solute particles are separated from each other, and heat is required to break these bonds.
2) Solvent particles are separated from each other to create space for solute particles, and heat is required to break these bonds also.
3) Solute and solvent particles interact with each other forming new bonds, and releasing heat.

If the heat required for the first two processes is greater than the heat released by the third, then the entire reaction may be written as an endothermic process:

$$\text{Solute} + \text{Solvent} + \text{Heat} \rightleftharpoons \text{Solution}$$

and according to Le Chatelier's principle, **solubility will increase with increasing temperature for an endothermic solution process**. This occurs for most salts in water, including NaCl. There is a large increase for potassium nitrate—KNO_3.

However, heat is released when many solutes enter solution, and the entire reaction is exothermic:

$$\text{Solute} + \text{Solvent} \rightleftharpoons \text{Solution} + \text{Heat}.$$

Solubility will decrease with increasing temperature for an exothermic solution process. This is the case for cerium(III) sulfate—$Ce_2(SO_4)_3$—in water.

Summary
The following table summarizes the impact of temperature and pressure on solubility:

Effect on solution of an **increase** in one variable with the other constant	− = decrease, **0** = no/small change, **+** = increase, **++** = strong increase				
	Gas solute in liquid solvent			Solid and liquid solutes	
	Average kinetic energy of molecules	Collisions of gas with liquid interface	Solubility	Solubility for an endothermic heat of solution	Solubility for an exothermic heat of solution
Pressure	0	++	+	0	0
Temperature	+	+	−	+	−

Impact of surface area
Dissolution will only take place at the surface of a solute where the solvent molecules contact the solute. When this surface area is increased, the solute dissolves more rapidly. **The rate of solution is increased by surface area, but the solubility remains unchanged**. Solubility is the amount of solute that will saturate a solution, and this depends only on pressure, temperature, and the identity of the solute and solvent.

Granulated sugar, for example, will dissolve more rapidly in water than a sugar cube. This is because it takes very little time for water to dissolve through relatively thin layers of sugar in a small grain before reaching the center of each grain. This is in contrast to the sugar in the center of a sugar cube. The sugar in the center of a cube cannot dissolve for until the thicker layers of sugar around it has dissolved away into solution. However, the solubility of sugar in water does not depend on whether sugar cubes or granulated sugar is used.

TEACHER CERTIFICATION EXAM

SUBAREA VI - INTERACTIONS OF CHEMISTRY AND THE ENVIRONMENT

Competency 0025: Understand industrial and household chemistry.

An understanding of chemical reactions and processes is important outside of the laboratory. It is critical in a variety of "real world" applications.

Industrial Chemistry

The processing of crude oil is key to the manufacture of a vast variety of products from fuel oil to plastics. Crude oil contains a mixture of many compounds and is 50-95% hydrocarbon by weight. Distillation is first used to separate the different hydrocarbon fractions. The fractions themselves are also complex mixtures, since there are a number of factors that influence the boiling point of the hydrocarbons. These fractions are typically as follows, from lightest to heaviest: natural gas (C_1 to C_4), petroleum ether (C_5 to C_6), gasoline (C_5 to C_{12}, but mostly C_6 to C_8), kerosene (mostly C_{12} to C_{13}), fuel oils(C_{14} and higher), lubricants(C_{20} and above), asphalt or coke (polycyclic). Processes such as thermal or catalytic reforming are occasionally used to boost the octane number of the resultant gasoline. An even more important process is that of thermal cracking, which increases the amount of gasoline that can be obtained from a barrel of oil by "cracking" the hydrocarbons that usually end up in the kerosene or fuel oil fraction. In thermal cracking, high temperatures and pressures are used to break long-chain hydrocarbons into smaller pieces. More recently catalytic cracking has been used. In this case, the hydrocarbons are cracked with catalysts.

The vast majority of refined crude oil is used to produce fuels. The remainder is used for petroleum solvents, industrial greases and waxes, or as starting materials for the synthesis of **petro-chemicals**. Petroleum products are used to produce synthetic fibers such as nylon, orlon, and dacron, and other polymers such as polystyrene, polyethylene, and synthetic rubber. They also serve as raw materials in the production of refrigerants, aerosols, antifreeze, detergents, dyes, adhesives, alcohols, explosives, weed killers, insecticides, and insect repellents.

While refining crude oil and the processing of petro-chemicals is still the most economically important application of chemistry in industry, the increasing importance of **pharmaceuticals** means an understanding of organic and biochemistry is also necessary. **Organic synthesis**, the exploitation of the reactions between organic molecules, is necessary to research and develop new drugs. Large-scale manufacture of these drugs often relies on naturally occurring chemical processes such as **fermentation** or **cell-based expression of protein**. Careful controls are necessary to keep these processes producing efficiently and this, in turn, requires an understanding of chemical equilibrium, kinetics, rate laws, and the effects of temperature and pressure.

Household Chemistry

In the home, chemical reactions are all around us. An ancient example of the human exploitation of chemical reactions is the use of yeast. **Yeast is a fungus** (*Saccharomyces cerevisiae* is the species used by man) that feeds on sugars. It extracts energy from the sugar and the byproducts of this "digestion" are **carbon dioxide and alcohols**. Thus, when yeast is incorporated into bread dough, the trapped carbon dioxide makes the bread rise and alternately, when the yeast is combined with water and malted barley it makes beer.

Another commonly used leavener is **baking soda**, sodium bicarbonate. This basic compound combines with acidic molecules in the bread dough to make carbon dioxide. As with the yeast, this carbon dioxide gets trapped and causes the bread to rise. This production of carbon dioxide (and a **simple acid-base reaction**) is often demonstrated by combining baking soda with vinegar (dilute acetic acid). The reaction is as follows:

$$HC_2H_3O_2 + NaHCO_3 ===> NaC_2H_3O_2 + H_2CO_3$$

Note that, like all acid-base reaction, a salt (sodium acetate) is produced. In the reaction above, the carbonic acid further breaks down into carbon dioxide and water.

Other household chemistry can be rather more dangerous, particularly when it involves many common **fertilizers, pesticides, and cleaning chemicals**. Working with these chemicals requires the same care as working with chemicals in the laboratory. In fact, MSDS sheets for most household chemicals are available here: http://householdproducts.nlm.nih.gov/

It is critical to take appropriate safety measures (e.g., gloves, goggles, proper disposal, avoiding mixing with other chemicals). One particularly dangerous reaction between household chemicals is that of **bleach and ammonia**. Bleach is typically a 5% solution of NaOCl in water and ammonia (NH_3) is a component of many glass cleaners:

$$HOCl + NH_3 ====> NH_2Cl + H_2O$$

The products of this reaction are water and chloroamine, which is powerful respiratory irritant and can even be deadly.

CHEMISTRY

Competency 0026: Understand the uses and hazards of nuclear reactions.

Two important benefits of the use of radiation are in the fields of medicine and power generation.

Medicine
Medicine uses **X-rays** as a diagnostic tool and radioisotopes for **diagnostic radiology** and for **radiotherapy**. In diagnostic radiology, a radioisotope is introduced into the body and its location is monitored with a **gamma camera** or other imaging equipment. **Different isotopes are localized to different tissues at specific rates**. Abnormalities in internal organs and bone structure and function are found using these techniques. The isotopes typically emit only gamma rays because alpha and beta radiation are more likely to harm the patient. **Technetium-99m is a commonly used isotope for diagnostic radiology**. Many radioisotopes are used in diagnostic medicine outside the body for blood tests.

Radiotherapy uses radiation as part of **cancer treatment to destroy tumors**. Rapidly growing tumors are more vulnerable to radiation damage from β particles than non-malignant tissue. Radiotherapy works by damaging the DNA of these cells. The radioactive source may be outside the body (external radiotherapy) or introduced into the body. Isotopes used for internal radiotherapy may be injected into the body as a liquid or introduced temporarily through a catheter in a sealed container.

Cobalt-60 was a common isotope for external radiotherapy, but it has mostly been replaced by linear accelerators that provide high-energy electrons (β particles) without a dangerous isotope source. It is still used to irradiate some foods to destroy bacteria. **Iodine-131 is used to combat diseases of the thyroid** and of several types of cancer. A list of isotopes used in nuclear medicine may be found at http://www.cbvcp.com/nmrc/mia.html.

Power generation
Nuclear power currently provides 17% of the world's electricity. Heat is generated by **nuclear fission of uranium-235 or plutonium-239**. This heat is then converted to electricity by boiling water and forcing the steam through a turbine. Fission of ^{235}U and ^{239}Pu occurs when **a neutron strikes the nucleus and breaks it apart into smaller nuclei and additional neutrons**. One possible fission reaction is:

$$_0^1n + {}_{92}^{235}U \rightarrow {}_{56}^{141}Ba + {}_{36}^{92}Kr + 3\,_0^1n$$

Gamma radiation, kinetic energy from the neutrons themselves, and the decay of the fission products (^{141}Ba and ^{92}Kr in the example above) all produce heat. The neutrons produced by the reaction strike other uranium atoms and produce more neutrons and more energy in a **chain reaction**. If enough neutrons are lost, the chain reaction stops and the process is called **subcritical**. If the mass of uranium is large enough so that one neutron on average from each fission event triggers another fission, the reaction is said to be **critical**. If the mass is larger than this so that few neutrons escape, the reaction is called **supercritical**. The chain reaction then multiplies the number of fissions and the violent explosion of an atomic bomb will take place if the process is not stopped. The concentration of **fissile material** in nuclear power plants is sufficient for a critical reaction to occur but too low for a supercritical reaction to take place.

The alpha decay of **Plutonium-238 is used as a heat source for localized power generation** in space probes and in heart pacemakers from the 1970s.

The most promising nuclear reaction for producing power by **nuclear fusion** is:
$$^{2}_{1}H + ^{3}_{1}H \rightarrow ^{4}_{2}He + ^{1}_{0}n$$
Hydrogen-2 is called **deuterium** and is often represented by the symbol D. Hydrogen-3 is known as **tritium** and is often represented by the symbol T. Nuclear reactions between very light atoms similar to the reaction above are the energy source behind the sun and the hydrogen bomb.

Hazards

Radioactive contamination is the uncontrolled distribution of radioactive material in an environment. The hazards of ionizing radiation were first studied in detail after the **atomic bombs dropped on Hiroshima and Nagasaki in 1945**. The worst nuclear accident in history was the **Chernobyl nuclear power plant disaster in 1986**.

Acute exposure of large doses may cause **radiation poisoning** or **radiation burns**. Chronic exposure may result in **cancer or mutations in one's children** due damage to DNA. Organs with rapidly dividing cells such as bone marrow, intestines, and gonads are most vulnerable. Some effects do not appear until several years have passed. Other organisms in the environment are just as vulnerable as humans to this danger. Because of these risks, radioactive materials are shipped in shielded containers. The risks for medical and food-processing applications that utilize radioactivity are known to be very small compared to the potential benefits, but this is considered by many to be a controversial topic.

Current opinion is that **there is a small risk to human health from even low levels of exposure** to ionizing radiation, but there is also a known quantity of **natural background radiation** that the human species has always encountered.

TEACHER CERTIFICATION EXAM

In 1984, an employee at a nuclear power plant began to set off radiation alarms while walking *into* the plant. An investigation found that his home contained high levels of **radon gas** from natural minerals. Radon tests are now routinely performed in many homes.

Competency 0027: Understand factors and processes related to the release of chemicals into the environment.

A baby born today in the United States is expected to live 30 years longer on average than a baby born 100 years ago. A significant cause of this improvement is due to chemical technology. The manufacture and distribution of vaccines and antibiotics, an increase in understanding human nutritional needs, and the use of fertilizers in agriculture have all played a significant role in improving the length and the quality of human life. But the benefits of these technologies are almost always accompanied by problems and significant risks.

Pesticides are used to control or kill organisms that compete with humans for food, spread disease, or are considered a nuisance. Herbicides are pesticides that attack weeds; insecticides attack insects; fungicides attack molds and other fungus. Sulfur was used as a fungicide in ancient times. The development and use of new pesticides has exploded over the last 60 years, but these pesticides are often poisonous to humans.

The **insecticide DDT** was widely used in the 1940s and 1950s and is responsible for **eradicating malaria from Europe and North America**. It quickly became the most widely used pesticide in the world. In the 1960s, some claimed that DDT was preventing fish-eating birds from reproducing and that it was causing birth defects in humans. DDT is now banned in many countries, but it is still used in developing nations to prevent diseases carried by insects. Unfortunately, its use in agriculture has often led to resistant mosquito strains that have hindered its effectiveness to prevent diseases.

The **herbicide *Roundup*** kills all natural plants it encounters. It began to be used in the 1990s in combination with **genetically engineered crops** that include a gene intended to make the crop (and only the crop) resistant to the herbicide. This combination of chemical and genetic technology has been an economic success but it has raised many concerns about potential problems in the future.

CHEMISTRY

Most scientists believe the emission of greenhouse gases has already led to global warming due to an increase in the greenhouse effect. The greenhouse effect occurs when these gases in the atmosphere warm the planet by absorbing heat to prevent it from escaping into space. This is similar—but not identical—to what occurs in greenhouse buildings. Greenhouse buildings warm an interior space by preventing mixing with colder gases outside. Many greenhouse gases such as water vapor occur naturally and are important for life to exist on Earth. Human production of carbon dioxide from combustion of fossil fuels has increased the concentration of this important greenhouse gas to its highest value since millions of years ago. The precise impact of these changes in the atmosphere is difficult to predict and is a topic of international concern and political debate.

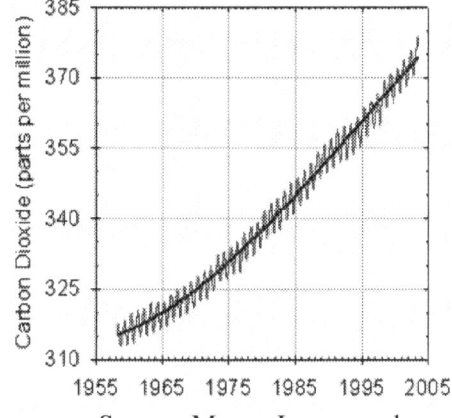

Source: Mauna Loa record, National Oceanic and Atmospheric Administration

Rain with a pH less than 5.6 is known as **acid rain**. Acid rain is caused by burning fossil fuels (especially coal) and by fertilizers used in intensive agriculture. These activities emit sulfur and nitrogen in gas compounds that are converted to sulfur oxides and nitrogen oxides. These in turn create sulfuric acid and nitric acid in rain. Acid rain may also be created from gases emitted by volcanoes and other natural sources. Acid rain harms fish and trees and triggers the release metal ions from minerals into water that can harm people. The problem of acid rain in the United States has been addressed in recent decades by the use of **scrubbers** in coal burning power plants and **catalytic converters** in vehicles.

Ozone is O_3. The ozone layer is a region of the stratosphere that contains higher concentrations of ozone than other parts of the atmosphere. The ozone layer is important for human health because it blocks ultraviolet radiation from the sun, and this helps to protect us from skin cancer. Research in the 1970s revealed that several gases used for refrigeration and other purposes were depleting the ozone layer.

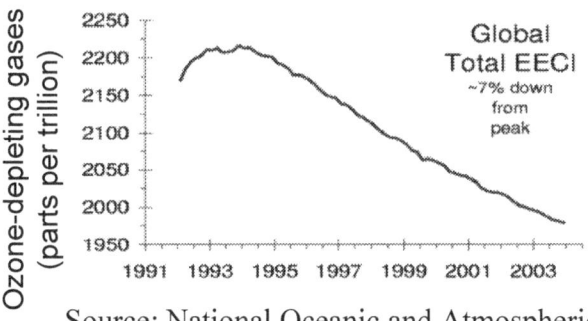

Source: National Oceanic and Atmospheric Administration

Many of these ozone-destroying molecules are short alkyl halides known as chlorofluorocarbons or CFCs. CCl_3F is one example. The widespread use of ozone-destroying gases was banned by an international agreement in the early 1990s. Other substances are used in their place such as CF_3CH_2F, a hydrofluorocarbon. Since that time the concentration of ozone-depleting gases in the atmosphere has been declining and the rate of ozone destruction has been decreasing. Many see this improvement as the most important positive example of international cooperation in helping the environment. The story of these new refrigerants is found at http://www.chemcases.com/fluoro/index.htm.

TEACHER CERTIFICATION EXAM

Sample Selected-Response Questions

Directions: Read each item and select the best response.

1. A piston compresses a gas at constant temperature. Which gas properties increase?

   I. Average speed of molecules
   II. Pressure
   III. Molecular collisions with container walls per second

   A. I and II
   B. I and III
   C. II and III
   D. I, II, and III

2. The temperature of a liquid is raised at atmospheric pressure. Which liquid property increases?

   A. critical pressure
   B. vapor pressure
   C. surface tension
   D. viscosity

3. Potassium crystallizes with two atoms contained in each unit cell. What is the mass of potassium found in a lattice 1.00×10^6 unit cells wide, 2.00×10^6 unit cells high, and 5.00×10^5 unit cells deep?

   A. 85.0 ng
   B. 32.5 µg
   C. 64.9 µg
   D. 130. µg

4. A gas is heated in a sealed container. Which of the following occur?

   A. gas pressure rises
   B. gas density decreases
   C. the average distance between molecules increases
   D. all of the above

5. How many molecules are in 2.20 pg of a protein with a molecular weight of 150. kDa?

   A. 8.83×10^9
   B. 1.82×10^9
   C. 8.83×10^6
   D. 1.82×10^6

6. At STP, 20. µL of O_2 contain 5.4×10^{16} molecules. According to Avogadro's hypothesis, how many molecules are in 20. µL of Ne?

   A. 5.4×10^{15}
   B. 1.0×10^{16}
   C. 2.7×10^{16}
   D. 5.4×10^{16}

CHEMISTRY

TEACHER CERTIFICATION EXAM

7. An ideal gas at 50.0 °C and 3.00 atm is in a 300. cm³ cylinder. The cylinder volume changes by moving a piston until the gas is at 50.0 °C and 1.00 atm. What is the final volume?

   A. 100. cm³
   B. 450. cm³
   C. 900. cm³
   D. 1.20 dm³

8. Which gas law may be used to solve the previous question?

   A. Charles's law
   B. Boyle's law
   C. Graham's law
   D. Avogadro's law

9. A blimp is filled with 5000. m³ of helium at 28.0 °C and 99.7 kPa. What is the mass of helium used?

   $R = 8.3144 \dfrac{J}{mol\text{-}K}$

   A. 797 kg
   B. 810. kg
   C. 879 kg
   D. 8.57×10^3 kg

10. Which of the following are able to flow from one place to another?

    I. Gases
    II. Liquids
    III. Solids
    IV. Supercritical fluids

    A. I and II
    B. II only
    C. I, II, and IV
    D. I, II, III, and IV

11. One mole of an ideal gas at STP occupies 22.4 L. At what temperature will one mole of an ideal gas at one atm occupy 31.0 L?

    A. 34.6 °C
    B. 105 °C
    C. 378 °C
    D. 442 °C

12. Why does $CaCl_2$ have a higher normal melting point than NH_3?

    A. Covalent bonds are stronger than London dispersion forces.
    B. Covalent bonds are stronger than hydrogen bonds.
    C. Ionic bonds are stronger than London dispersion forces.
    D. Ionic bonds are stronger than hydrogen bonds.

CHEMISTRY

13. Which intermolecular attraction explains the following trend in straight-chain alkanes?

Condensed structural formula	Boiling point (°C)
CH_4	-161.5
CH_3CH_3	-88.6
$CH_3CH_2CH_3$	-42.1
$CH_3CH_2CH_2CH_3$	-0.5
$CH_3CH_2CH_2CH_2CH_3$	36.0
$CH_3CH_2CH_2CH_2CH_2CH_3$	68.7

A. London dispersion forces
B. Dipole-dipole interactions
C. Hydrogen bonding
D. Ion-induced dipole interactions

14. List the substances NH_3, PH_3, $MgCl_2$, Ne, and N_2 in order of increasing melting point.

A. N_2 < Ne < PH_3 < NH_3 < $MgCl_2$
B. N_2 < NH_3 < Ne < $MgCl_2$ < PH_3
C. Ne < N_2 < NH_3 < PH_3 < $MgCl_2$
D. Ne < N_2 < PH_3 < NH_3 < $MgCl_2$

15. 1-butanol, ethanol, methanol, and 1-propanol are all liquids at room temperature. Rank them in order of increasing viscosity.

A. 1-butanol < 1-propanol < ethanol < methanol
B. methanol < ethanol < 1-propanol < 1-butanol
C. methanol < ethanol < 1-butanol < 1-propanol
D. 1-propanol < 1-butanol < ethanol < methanol

16. Which gas has a diffusion rate of 25% the rate for hydrogen?

A. helium
B. methane
C. nitrogen
D. oxygen

17. 2.00 L of an unknown gas at 1500. mm Hg and a temperature of 25.0 °C weighs 7.52 g. Assuming the ideal gas equation, what is the molecular mass of the gas?

760 mm Hg=1 atm
R=0.08206 L-atm/(mol-K)

A. 21.6 u
B. 23.3 u
C. 46.6 u
D. 93.2 u

18. Which substance is most likely to be a gas at room temperature?

A. SeO_2
B. F_2
C. $CaCl_2$
D. I_2

19. What pressure is exerted by a mixture of 2.7 g of H_2 and 59 g of Xe at STP on a 50. L container?

A. 0.69 atm
B. 0.76 atm
C. 0.80 atm
D. 0.97 atm

CHEMISTRY

20. A few minutes after opening a bottle of perfume, the scent is detected on the other side of the room. What law relates to this phenomenon?

   A. Graham's law
   B. Dalton's law
   C. Boyle's law
   D. Avogadro's law

21. Which of the following are true?

   A. Solids have no vapor pressure.
   B. Dissolving a solute in a liquid increases its vapor pressure.
   C. The vapor pressure of a pure substance is characteristic of that substance and its temperature.
   D. All of the above

22. Find the partial pressure of N_2 in a container at 150. kPa holding H_2O and N_2 at 50 °C. The vapor pressure of H_2O at 50 °C is 12 kPa.

   A. 12 kPa
   B. 138 kPa
   C. 162 kPa
   D. The value cannot be determined.

23. The normal boiling point of water on the Kelvin scale is closest to:

   A. 112 K
   B. 212 K
   C. 273 K
   D. 373 K
   E.

24. Which phase may be present at the triple point of a substance?

   I. Gas
   II. Liquid
   III. Solid
   IV. Supercritical fluid

   A. I, II, and III
   B. I, II, and IV
   C. II, III, and IV
   D. I, II, III, and IV

25. In the following phase diagram, _____ occurs as P is decreased from A to B at constant T and _____ occurs as T is increased from C to D at constant P.

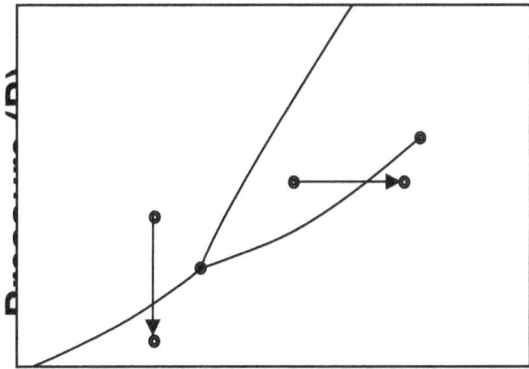

Temperature (T)

   A. deposition, melting
   B. sublimation, melting
   C. deposition, vaporization
   D. sublimation, vaporization

26. Heat is added to a pure solid at its melting point until it all becomes liquid at its freezing point. Which of the following occur?

   A. Intermolecular attractions are weakened.
   B. The kinetic energy of the molecules does not change.
   C. The freedom of the molecules to move about increases.
   D. All of the above.

27. Which of the following occur when NaCl dissolves in water?

   A. Heat is required to break bonds in the NaCl crystal lattice.
   B. Heat is released when hydrogen bonds in water are broken.
   C. Heat is required to form bonds of hydration.
   D. The oxygen end of the water molecule is attracted to the Cl^- ion.

28. The solubility of $CoCl_2$ is 54 g per 100 g of ethanol. Three flasks each contain 100 g of ethanol. Flask #1 also contains 40 g $CoCl_2$ in solution. Flask #2 contains 56 g $CoCl_2$ in solution. Flask #3 contains 5 g of solid $CoCl_2$ in equilibrium with 54 g $CoCl_2$ in solution. Which of the following describe the solutions present in the liquid phase of the flasks?

   A. #1-saturated, #2-supersaturated, #3-unsaturated.
   B. #1-unsaturated, #2-miscible, #3-saturated.
   C. #1-unsaturated, #2-supersaturated, #3-saturated.
   D. #1-unsaturated, #2-not at equilibrium, #3-miscible.

29. The solubility at 1.0 atm of pure CO_2 in water at 25 °C is 0.034 M. According to Henry's law, what is the solubility at 4.0 atm of pure CO_2 in water at 25 °C? Assume no chemical reaction occurs between CO_2 and H_2O.

   A. 0.0085 M
   B. 0.034 M
   C. 0.14 M
   D. 0.25 M

30. Carbonated water is bottled at 25 °C under pure CO_2 at 4.0 atm. Later the bottle is opened at 4 °C under air at 1.0 atm that has a partial pressure of 3×10^{-4} atm CO_2. Why do CO_2 bubbles form when the bottle is opened?

   A. CO_2 falls out of solution due to a drop in solubility at the lower total pressure.
   B. CO_2 falls out of solution due to a drop in solubility at the lower CO_2 pressure.
   C. CO_2 falls out of solution due to a drop in solubility at the lower temperature.
   D. CO_2 is formed by the decomposition of carbonic acid.

31. When KNO_3 dissolves in water, the water grows slightly colder. An increase in temperature will _____ the solubility of KNO_3.

   A. increase
   B. decrease
   C. have no effect on
   D. have an unknown effect with the information given on

32. An experiment requires 100. mL of a 0.500 M solution of $MgBr_2$. How many grams of $MgBr_2$ will be present in this solution?

   A. 9.21 g
   B. 11.7 g
   C. 12.4 g
   D. 15.6 g

33. 500. mg of RbOH are added to 500. g of ethanol (C_2H_6O) resulting in 395 mL of solution. Determine the molarity and molality of RbOH.

   A. 0.0124 M, 0.00488 m
   B. 0.0124 M, 0.00976 m
   C. 0.0223 M, 0.00488 m
   D. 0.0223 M, 0.00976 m

34. 20.0 g H_3PO_4 in 1.5 L of solution are intended to react with KOH according to the following reaction:
   $$H_3PO_4 + 3 KOH \rightarrow K_3PO_4 + 3 H_2O$$
   What is the molarity and normality of the H_3PO_4 solution?

   A. 0.41 M, 1.22 N
   B. 0.41 M, 0.20 N
   C. 0.14 M, 0.045 N
   D. 0.14 M, 0.41 N

35. Aluminum sulfate is a strong electrolyte. What is the concentration of all species in a 0.2 M solution of aluminum sulfate?

   A. 0.2 M Al^{3+}, 0.2 M SO_4^{2-}
   B. 0.4 M Al^{3+}, 0.6 M SO_4^{2-}
   C. 0.6 M Al^{3+}, 0.4 M SO_4^{2-}
   D. 0.2 M $Al_2(SO_4)_3$

36. 15 g of formaldehyde (CH_2O) are dissolved in 100. g of water. Calculate the weight percentage and mole fraction of formaldehyde in the solution.

   A. 13%, 0.090
   B. 15%, 0.090
   C. 13%, 0.083
   D. 15%, 0.083

37. Which of the following would make the best solvent for Br_2?

   A. H_2O
   B. CS_2
   C. NH_3
   D. molten NaCl

38. Which of the following is most likely to dissolve in water?

   A. H_2
   B. CCl_4
   C. SF_6
   D. CH_3OH

39. Which of the following is not a colligative property?

   A. Viscosity lowering
   B. Freezing point lowering
   C. Boiling point elevation
   D. Vapor pressure lowering

40. $BaCl_2(aq) + Na_2SO_4(aq) \rightarrow BaSO_4(s) + 2NaCl(aq)$
   is an example of a _____ reaction.

   A. acid-base
   B. precipitation
   C. redox
   D. nuclear

41. List the following aqueous solutions in order of increasing boiling point.

   I. 0.050 m $AlCl_3$
   II. 0.080 m $Ba(NO_3)_2$
   III. 0.090 m NaCl
   IV. 0.12 m ethylene glycol ($C_2H_6O_2$)

   A. I < II < III < IV
   B. I < III < IV < II
   C. IV < III < I < II
   D. IV < III < II < I

42. Osmotic pressure is the pressure required to prevent _____ flowing from low to high _____ concentration across a semipermeable membrane.

   A. solute, solute
   B. solute, solvent
   C. solvent, solute
   D. solvent, solvent

43. A solution of NaCl in water is heated on a mountain in an open container until it boils at 100. °C. The air pressure on the mountain is 0.92 atm. According to Raoult's law, what mole fraction of Na^+ and Cl^- are present in the solution?

   A. 0.04 Na^+, 0.04 Cl^-
   B. 0.08 Na^+, 0.08 Cl^-
   C. 0.46 Na^+, 0.46 Cl^-
   D. 0.92 Na^+, 0.92 Cl^-

44. Write a balanced nuclear equation for the emission of an alpha particle by polonium-209.

   A. $^{209}_{84}Po \rightarrow {}^{205}_{81}Pb + {}^{4}_{2}He$
   B. $^{209}_{84}Po \rightarrow {}^{205}_{82}Bi + {}^{4}_{2}He$
   C. $^{209}_{84}Po \rightarrow {}^{209}_{85}At + {}^{0}_{-1}e$
   D. $^{209}_{84}Po \rightarrow {}^{205}_{82}Pb + {}^{4}_{2}He$

45. Write a balanced nuclear equation for the decay of calcium-45 to scandium-45.

   A. $^{45}_{20}Ca \rightarrow {}^{41}_{18}Sc + {}^{4}_{2}He$
   B. $^{45}_{20}Ca + {}^{0}_{1}e \rightarrow {}^{45}_{21}Sc$
   C. $^{45}_{20}Ca \rightarrow {}^{45}_{21}Sc + {}^{0}_{-1}e$
   D. $^{45}_{20}Ca + {}^{0}_{1}p \rightarrow {}^{45}_{21}Sc$

46. $^{3}_{1}H$ decays with a half-life of 12 years. 3.0 g of pure $^{3}_{1}H$ were placed in a sealed container 24 years ago. How many grams of $^{3}_{1}H$ remain?

   A. 0.38 g
   B. 0.75 g
   C. 1.5 g
   D. 3.0 g

47. Oxygen-15 has a half-life of 122 seconds. What percentage of a sample of oxygen-15 has decayed after 300. seconds?

   A. 18.2%
   B. 21.3%
   C. 78.7%
   D. 81.8%

48. Which of the following isotopes is commonly used for medical imaging in the diagnose of diseases?

   A. cobalt-60
   B. technetium-99m
   C. tin-117m
   D. plutonium-238

49. Carbon-14 dating would be useful in obtaining the age of which object?

   A. a 20th century Picasso painting
   B. a mummy from ancient Egypt
   C. a dinosaur fossil
   D. all of the above

CHEMISTRY

50. Which of the following isotopes can create a chain reaction of nuclear fission?

   A. uranium-235
   B. uranium-238
   C. plutonium-238
   D. all of the above

51. List the following scientists in chronological order from earliest to most recent with respect to their most significant contribution to atomic theory:

   I. John Dalton
   II. Niels Bohr
   III. J. J. Thomson
   IV. Ernest Rutherford

   A. I, III, II, IV
   B. I, III, IV, II
   C. I, IV, III, II
   D. III, I, II, IV

52. Match the theory with the scientist who first proposed it:

   I. Electrons, atoms, and all objects with momentum also exist as waves.
   II. Electron density may be accurately described by a single mathematical equation.
   III. There is an inherent indeterminacy in the position and momentum of particles.
   IV. Radiant energy is transferred between particles in exact multiples of a discrete unit.

   A. I-de Broglie, II-Planck, III-Schrödinger, IV-Thomson
   B. I-Dalton, II-Bohr, III-Planck, IV-de Broglie
   C. I-Henry, II-Bohr, III-Heisenberg, IV-Schrödinger
   D. I-de Broglie, II-Schrödinger, III-Heisenberg, IV-Planck

53. How many neutrons are in $^{60}_{27}Co$?

   A. 27
   B. 33
   C. 60
   D. 87

54. The terrestrial composition of an element is: 50.7% as an isotope with an atomic mass of 78.9 u and 49.3% as an isotope with an atomic mass of 80.9 u. Both isotopes are stable. Calculate the atomic mass of the element.
   A. 79.0 u
   B. 79.8 u
   C. 79.9 u
   D. 80.8 u

55. Which of the following is a correct electron arrangement for oxygen?

   A.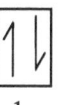

   B. $1s^2 1p^2 2s^2 2p^2$
   C. 2, 2, 4
   D. none of the above

56. Which of the following statements about radiant energy is not true?

   A. The energy change of an electron transition is directly proportional to the wavelength of the emitted or absorbed photon.
   B. The energy of an electron in a hydrogen atom depends only on the principle quantum number.
   C. The frequency of photons striking a metal determines whether the photoelectric effect will occur.
   D. The frequency of a wave of electromagnetic radiation is inversely proportional to its wavelength

57. Match the orbital diagram for the ground state of carbon with the rule/principle it violates:

   I.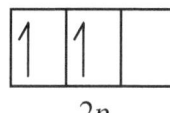

   II.

   III.

   IV.

   A. I-Pauli exclusion, II-Aufbau, III-no violation, IV-Hund's
   B. I-Aufbau, II-Pauli exclusion, III-no violation, IV-Hund's
   C. I-Hund's, II-no violation, III-Pauli exclusion, IV-Aufbau
   D. I-Hund's, II-no violation, III-Aufbau, IV-Pauli exclusion

58. Select the list of atoms that are arranged in order of increasing size.

   A. Mg, Na, Si, Cl
   B. Si, Cl, Mg, Na
   C. Cl, Si, Mg, Na
   D. Na, Mg, Si, Cl

59. Based on trends in the periodic table, which of the following properties would you expect to be greater for Rb than for K?

   I. Density
   II. Melting point
   III. Ionization energy
   IV. Oxidation number in a compound with chlorine

   A. I only
   B. I, II, and III
   C. II and III
   D. I, II, III, and IV

60. Which oxide forms the strongest acid in water?

   A. Al_2O_3
   B. Cl_2O_7
   C. As_2O_5
   D. CO_2

61. Rank the following bonds from least to most polar:

   C-H, C-Cl, H-H, C-F

   A. C-H < H-H < C-F < C-Cl
   B. H-H < C-H < C-F < C-Cl
   C. C-F < C-Cl < C-H < H-H
   D. H-H < C-H < C-Cl < C-F

62. At room temperature, $CaBr_2$ is expected to be:

   A. a ductile solid
   B. a brittle solid
   C. a soft solid
   D. a gas

63. Which of the following is a proper Lewis dot structure of CHClO?

   A. [structure]
   B. [structure]
   C. [structure]
   D. [structure]

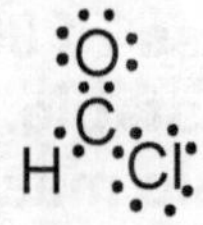

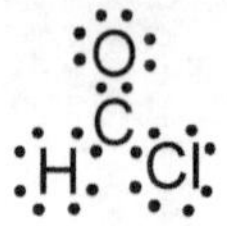

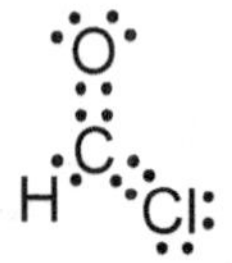

64. In C_2H_2, each carbon atom contains the following valence orbitals:

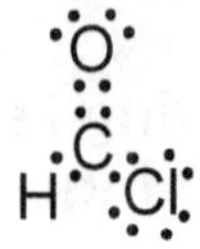

   A. *p* only
   B. *p* and *sp* hybrids
   C. *p* and sp^2 hybrids
   D. sp^3 hybrids only

CHEMISTRY

65. Which statement about molecular structures is false?

A. 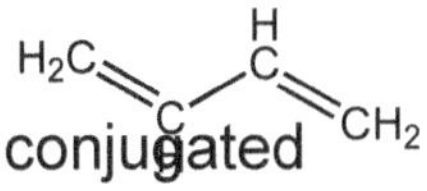 H₂C=CH-CH=CH₂ is a conjugated molecule
B. A bonding σ orbital connects two atoms by the straight line between them.
C. A bonding π orbital connects two atoms in a separate region from the straight line between them.
D. The anion with resonance forms

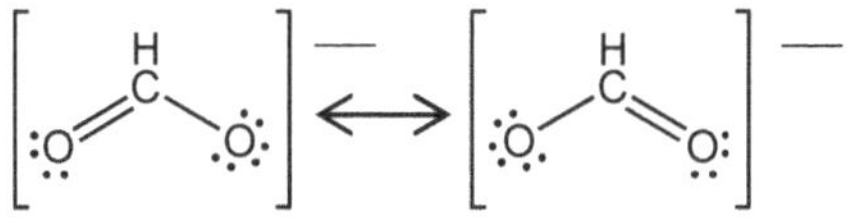

[resonance structures of formate anion shown]

will always exist in one form or the other.

66. What is the shape of the PH₃ molecule? Use the VSEPR model.

A. Trigonal pyramidal
B. Trigonal bipyramidal
C. Trigonal planar
D. Tetrahedral

67. What is the chemical composition of magnesium nitrate?

A. 11.1% Mg, 22.2% N, 66.7% O
B. 16.4% Mg, 18.9% N, 64.7% O
C. 20.9% Mg, 24.1% N, 55.0% O
D. 28.2% Mg, 16.2% N, 55.7% O

68. The IUPAC name for Cu₂SO₃ is:

A. Dicopper sulfur trioxide
B. Copper (II) sulfate
C. Copper (I) sulfite
D. Copper (II) sulfite

69. Which name or formula is **not** represented properly?

A. Cl₄S
B. KClO₃
C. Calcium dihydrogen phosphate
D. Sulfurous acid

70. Household "chlorine bleach" is sodium hypochlorite. Which of the following best represent the production of sodium hypochlorite, sodium chloride, and water by bubbling chlorine gas through aqueous sodium hydroxide?

A. 4Cl(g) + 4NaOH(aq) → NaClO₂(aq) + 3NaCl(aq) + 2H₂O(l)

B. 2Cl₂(g) + 4NaOH(aq) → NaClO₂(aq) + 3NaCl(aq) + 2H₂O(l)

C. 2Cl(g) + 2NaOH(aq) → NaClO(aq) + NaCl(aq) + H₂O(l)

D. Cl₂(g) + 2NaOH(aq) → NaClO(aq) + NaCl(aq) + H₂O(l)

71. Balance the equation for the neutralization reaction between phosphoric acid and calcium hydroxide by filling in the blank stoichiometric coefficients.

___H_3PO_4 + ___$Ca(OH)_2$ →
 ___$Ca_3(PO_4)_2$ + ___H_2O

A. 4, 3, 1, 4
B. 2, 3, 1, 8
C. 2, 3, 1, 6
D. 2, 1, 1, 2

72. Write an equation showing the reaction between calcium nitrate and lithium sulfate in aqueous solution. Include all products.

A. $CaNO_3(aq) + Li_2SO_4(aq) \rightarrow CaSO_4(s) + Li_2NO_3(aq)$

B. $Ca(NO_3)_2(aq) + Li_2SO_4(aq) \rightarrow CaSO_4(s) + 2LiNO_3(aq)$

C. $Ca(NO_3)_2(aq) + Li_2SO_4(aq) \rightarrow 2LiNO_3(s) + CaSO_4(aq)$

D. $Ca(NO_3)_2(aq) + Li_2SO_4(aq) + 2H_2O(l) \rightarrow 2LiNO_3(aq) + Ca(OH)_2(aq) + H_2SO_4(aq)$

73. Find the mass of CO_2 produced by the combustion of 15 kg of isopropyl alcohol in the reaction:

$2C_3H_7OH + 9O_2 \rightarrow 6CO_2 + 8H_2O$

A. 33 kg
B. 44 kg
C. 50 kg
D. 60 kg

74. What is the density of nitrogen gas at STP? Assume an ideal gas and a value of 0.08206 L·atm/(mol·K) for the gas constant.

A. 0.62 g/L
B. 1.14 g/L
C. 1.25 g/L
D. 2.03 g/L

75. Find the volume of methane that will produce 12 m³ of hydrogen in the reaction:

$CH_4(g) + H_2O(g) \rightarrow CO(g) + 3H_2(g)$

Assume temperature and pressure remain constant.

A. 4.0 m³
B. 32 m³
C. 36 m³
D. 64 m³

CHEMISTRY

76. A 100. L vessel of pure O_2 at 500. kPa and 20. °C is used for the combustion of butane:

$2C_4H_{10} + 13O_2 \rightarrow 8CO_2 + 10H_2O$

Find the mass of butane to consume all the O_2 in the vessel. Assume O_2 is an ideal gas and use a value of R = 8.314 J/(mol•K).

A. 183 g
B. 467 g
C. 1.83 kg
D. 7.75 kg

77. Consider the reaction between iron and hydrogen chloride gas:

$Fe(s) + 2HCl(g) \rightarrow FeCl_2(s) + H_2(g)$

7 moles of iron and 10 moles of HCl react until the limiting reagent is consumed. Which statements are true?

I. HCl is the excess reagent
II. HCl is the limiting reagent
III. 7 moles of H_2 are produced
IV. 2 moles of the excess reagent remain

A. I and III
B. I and IV
C. II and III
D. II and IV

78. 32.0 g of hydrogen and 32.0 grams of oxygen react to form water until the limiting reagent is consumed. What is present in the vessel after the reaction is complete?

A. 16.0 g O_2 and 48.0 g H_2O
B. 24.0 g H_2 and 40.0 g H_2O
C. 28.0 g H_2 and 36.0 g H_2O
D. 28.0 g H_2 and 34.0 g H_2O

79. Three experiments were performed at the same initial temperature and pressure to determine the rate of the reaction

$2ClO_2(g) + F_2(g) \rightarrow 2ClO_2F(g)$

Results are shown in the table below. Concentrations are given in millimoles per liter (mM).

Exp.	Initial $[ClO_2]$ (mM)	Initial $[F_2]$ (mM)	Initial rate of $[ClO_2F]$ increase (mM/sec)
1	5.0	5.0	0.63
2	5.0	20	2.5
3	10	10	2.5

What is the rate law for this reaction?

A. Rate = $k[F_2]$
B. Rate = $k[ClO_2][F_2]$
C. Rate = $k[ClO_2]^2[F_2]$
D. Rate = $k[ClO_2][F_2]^2$

CHEMISTRY

80. The reaction

(CH$_3$)$_3$CBr(aq) + OH$^-$(aq) →
　　(CH$_3$)$_3$COH(aq) + Br$^-$(aq)

occurs in three elementary steps:

(CH$_3$)$_3$CBr → (CH$_3$)$_3$C$^+$ + Br$^-$ is slow

(CH$_3$)$_3$C$^+$ + H$_2$O → (CH$_3$)$_3$COH$_2$$^+$ is fast

(CH$_3$)$_3$COH$_2$$^+$ + OH$^-$ → (CH$_3$)$_3$COH + H$_2$O is fast

What is the rate law for this reaction?

A. Rate = $k\left[(CH_3)_3CBr\right]$
B. Rate = $k\left[OH^-\right]$
C. Rate = $k\left[(CH_3)_3CBr\right]\left[OH^-\right]$
D. Rate = $k\left[(CH_3)_3CBr\right]^2$

81. Which statement about equilibrium is not true?

A. Equilibrium shifts to minimize the impact of changes.
B. Forward and reverse reactions have equal rates at equilibrium.
C. A closed container of air and water is at a vapor-liquid equilibrium if the humidity is constant.
D. The equilibrium between solid and dissolved forms is maintained when salt is added to an unsaturated solution.

82. Which statements about reaction rates are true?

I. Catalysts shift an equilibrium to favor product formation.
II. Catalysts increase the rate of forward and reverse reactions.
III. A greater temperature increases the chance that a molecular collision will overcome a reaction's activation energy.
IV. A catalytic converter contains a homogeneous catalyst.

A. I and II
B. II and III
C. II, III, and IV
D. I, III, and IV

83. Write the equilibrium expression K_{eq} for the reaction

CO$_2$(g) + H$_2$(g) ⇌ CO(g) + H$_2$O(l)

A. $\dfrac{[CO][H_2O]}{[CO_2][H_2]^2}$

B. $\dfrac{[CO_2][H_2]}{[CO][H_2O]}$

C. $\dfrac{[CO][H_2O]}{[CO_2][H_2]}$

D. $\dfrac{[CO]}{[CO_2][H_2]}$

CHEMISTRY

84. What could cause this change in the energy diagram of a reaction?

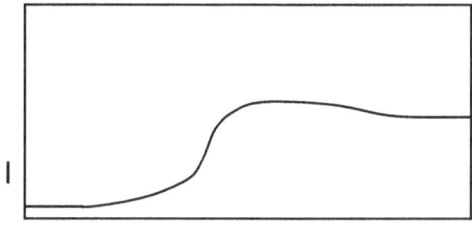

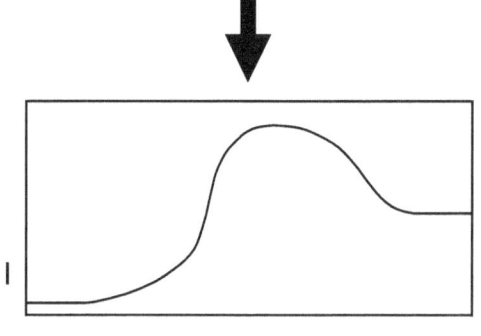

A. Adding catalyst to an endothermic reaction
B. Removing catalyst from an endothermic reaction
C. Adding catalyst to an exothermic reaction
D. Removing catalyst from an exothermic reaction

85. BaSO$_4$ (K_{sp} = 1X10^{-10}) is added to pure H$_2$O. How much is dissolved in 1 L of saturated solution?

A. 2 mg
B. 10 µg
C. 2 µg
D. 100 pg

86. The exothermic reaction
$2NO(g) + Br_2(g) \rightleftharpoons 2NOBr(g)$ is at equilibrium. According to LeChatelier's principle:

A. Adding Br$_2$ will increase [NO].
B. An increase in container volume (with T constant) will increase [NOBr].
C. An increase in pressure (with T constant) will increase [NOBr].
D. An increase in temperature (with P constant) will increase [NOBr].

87. At a certain temperature, T, the equilibrium constant for the reaction
$2NO(g) \rightleftharpoons N_2(g) + O_2(g)$ is K_{eq} = 2X10^3. If a 1.0 L container at this temperature contains 90 mM N$_2$, 20 mM O$_2$, and 5 mM NO, what will occur?

A. The reaction will make more N$_2$ and O$_2$.
B. The reaction is at equilibrium.
C. The reaction will make more NO.
D. The temperature, T, is required to solve this problem.

88. Which statement about acids and bases is not true?

A. All strong acids ionize in water.
B. All Lewis acids accept an electron pair.
C. All Brønsted bases use OH$^-$ as a proton acceptor
D. All Arrhenius acids form H$^+$ ions in water.

89. Which of the following are listed from weakest to strongest acid?

   A. H_2SO_3, H_2SeO_3, H_2TeO_3
   B. HBrO, $HBrO_2$, $HBrO_3$, $HBrO_4$
   C. HI, HBr, HCl, HF
   D. H_3PO_4, $H_2PO_4^-$, HPO_4^{2-}

90. NH_4F is dissolved in water. Which of the following are conjugate acid/base pairs present in the solution?

   I. NH_4^+/NH_4OH
   II. HF/F^-
   III. H_3O^+/H_2O
   IV. H_2O/OH^-

   A. I, II, and III
   B. I, III, and IV
   C. II and IV
   D. II, III, and IV

91. What are the pH and the pOH of 0.010 M $HNO_3(aq)$?

   A. pH = 1.0, pOH = 9.0
   B. pH = 2.0, pOH = 12.0
   C. pH = 2.0, pOH = 8.0
   D. pH = 8.0, pOH = 6.0

92. What is the pH of a buffer made of 0.128 M sodium formate (HCOONa) and 0.072 M formic acid (HCOOH)? The pK_a of formic acid is 3.75.

   A. 2.0
   B. 3.0
   C. 4.0
   D. 5.0

93. A sample of 50.0 ml KOH is titrated with 0.100 M $HClO_4$. The initial buret reading is 1.6 ml and the reading at the endpoint is 22.4 ml. What is [KOH]?

   A. 0.0416 M
   B. 0.0481 M
   C. 0.0832 M
   D. 0.0962 mM

94. Rank the following from lowest to highest pH. Assume a small volume for the component given in moles:

   I. 0.01 mol HCl added to 1 L H_2O
   II. 0.01 mol HI added to 1 L of an acetic acid/sodium acetate solution at pH 4.0
   III. 0.01 mol NH_3 added to 1 L H_2O
   IV. 0.1 mol HNO_3 added to 1 L of a 0.1 M $Ca(OH)_2$ solution

   A. I < II < III < IV
   B. I < II < IV < III
   C. II < I < III < IV
   D. II < I < IV < III

95. The curve below resulted from the titration of a _____ _____ with a _____ _____ titrant.

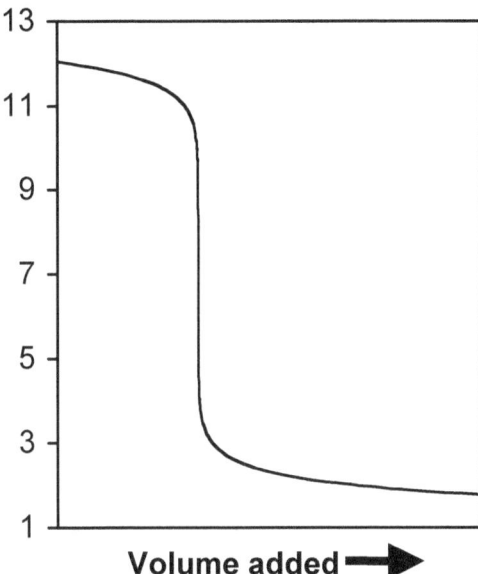

Volume added →

A. weak acid, strong base
B. weak base, strong acid
C. strong acid, strong base
D. strong base, strong acid

96. Which statement about thermochemistry is true?

A. Particles in a system move about less freely at high entropy
B. Water at 100 °C has the same internal energy as water vapor at 100°C
C. A decrease in the order of a system corresponds to an increase in entropy.
D. At its sublimation temperature, dry ice has a higher entropy than gaseous CO_2

97. What is the heat change of 36.0 g H_2O at atmospheric pressure when its temperature is reduced from 125 °C to 40. °C? Use the following data:

Values for water

Heat capacity of solid	37.6 J/mol•°C
Heat capacity of liquid	75.3 J/mol•°C
Heat capacity of gas	33.1 J/mol•°C
Heat of fusion	6.02 kJ/mol
Heat of vaporization	40.67 kJ/mol

A. −92.0 kJ
B. −10.8 kJ
C. 10.8 kJ
D. 92.0 kJ

98. What is the standard heat of combustion of $CH_4(g)$? Use the following data:

Standard heats of formation

$CH_4(g)$	−74.8 kJ/mol
$CO_2(g)$	−393.5 kJ/mol
$H_2O(l)$	−285.8 kJ/mol

A. −890.3 kJ/mol
B. −604.6 kJ/mol
C. −252.9 kJ/mol
D. −182.5 kJ/mol

99. Which reaction creates products at a lower total entropy than the reactants?

A. Dissolution of table salt:
$NaCl(s) \rightarrow Na^+(aq) + Cl^-(aq)$
B. Oxidation of iron:
$4Fe(s) + 3O_2(g) \rightarrow 2Fe_2O_3(s)$
C. Dissociation of ozone:
$O_3(g) \rightarrow O_2(g) + O(g)$
D. Vaporization of butane:
$C_4H_{10}(l) \rightarrow C_4H_{10}(g)$

100. Which statement about reactions is true?

A. All spontaneous reactions are both exothermic and cause an increase in entropy.
B. An endothermic reaction that increases the order of the system cannot be spontaneous.
C. A reaction can be non-spontaneous in one direction and also non-spontaneous in the opposite direction.
D. Melting snow is an exothermic process.

101. 10. kJ of heat are added to one kilogram of Iron at 10. °C. What is its final temperature? The specific heat of iron is 0.45 J/g•°C.

A. 22 °C
B. 27 °C
C. 32 °C
D. 37 °C

102. Which reaction is not a redox process?

A. Combustion of octane:
$2C_8H_{18} + 25O_2 \rightarrow 16CO_2 + 18H_2O$
B. Depletion of a lithium battery:
$Li + MnO_2 \rightarrow LiMnO_2$
C. Corrosion of aluminum by acid:
$2Al + 6HCl \rightarrow 2AlCl_3 + 3H_2$
D. Taking an antacid for heartburn:
$CaCO_3 + 2HCl \rightarrow CaCl_2 + H_2CO_3$
$\rightarrow CaCl_2 + CO_2 + H_2O$

103. Given the following heats of reaction:
$\Delta H = -0.3$ kJ / mol for
$Fe(s) + CO_2(g) \rightarrow FeO(s) + CO(g)$
$\Delta H = 5.7$ kJ / mol for
$2Fe(s) + 3CO_2(g) \rightarrow Fe_2O_3(s) + 3CO(g)$
and $\Delta H = 4.5$ kJ / mol for
$3FeO(s) + CO_2(g) \rightarrow Fe_3O_4(s) + CO(g)$

use Hess's Law to determine the heat of reaction for:
$3Fe_2O_3(s) + CO(g) \rightarrow 2Fe_3O_4(s) + CO_2(g)$

A. −10.8 kJ/mol
B. −9.9 kJ/mol
C. −9.0 kJ/mol
D. −8.1 kJ/mol

104. What is the oxidant in the reaction:

$2H_2S + SO_2 \rightarrow 3S + 2H_2O$?

A. H_2S
B. SO_2
C. S
D. H_2O

105. Molten NaCl is subjected to electrolysis. What reaction takes place at the cathode?

A. $2Cl^-(l) \rightarrow Cl_2(g) + 2e^-$
B. $Cl_2(g) + 2e^- \rightarrow 2Cl^-(l)$
C. $Na^+(l) + e^- \rightarrow Na(l)$
D. $Na^+(l) \rightarrow Na(l) + e^-$

106. What is the purpose of the salt bridge in an electrochemical cell?

A. To receive electrons from the oxidation half-reaction
B. To relieve the buildup of positive charge in the anode half-cell
C. To conduct electron flow
D. To permit positive ions to flow from the cathode half-cell to the anode half-cell

107. Given:
$E°=-2.37V$ for $Mg^{2+}(aq)+2e^- \rightarrow Mg(s)$
and
$E°=0.80$ V for $Ag^+(aq)+e^- \rightarrow Ag(s)$,
what is the standard potential of a voltaic cell composed of a piece of magnesium dipped in a 1 M Ag^+ solution and a piece of silver dipped in 1 M Mg^{2+}?

A. 0.77 V
B. 1.57 V
C. 3.17 V
D. 3.97 V

108.

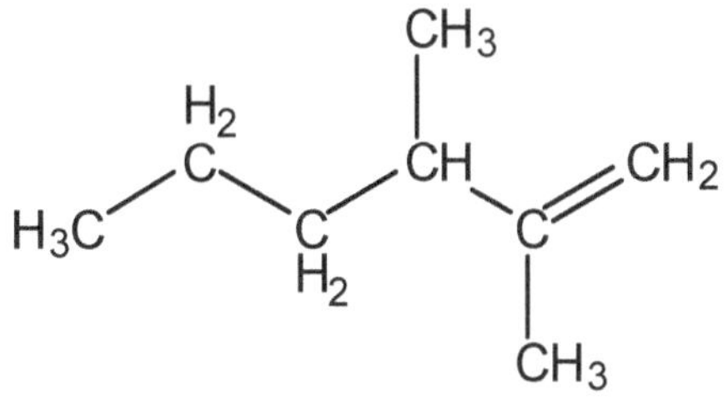

A proper name for this hydrocarbon is:

A. 4,5-dimethyl-6-hexene
B. 2,3-dimethyl-1-hexene
C. 4,5-dimethyl-6-hexyne
D. 2-methyl-3-propyl-1-butene

CHEMISTRY

109. An IUPAC approved name for this molecule is:

   A. butanal
   B. propanal
   C. butanoic acid
   D. propanoic acid

110. Which molecule has a systematic name of methyl ethanoate?

   A. 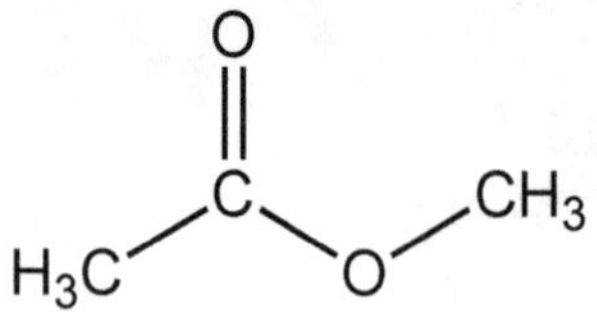
   B. 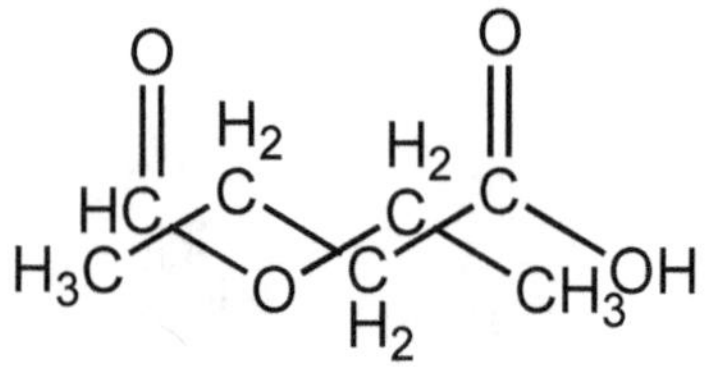
   C. 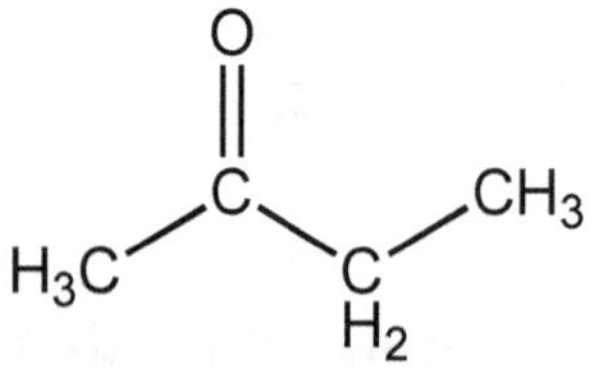
   D.

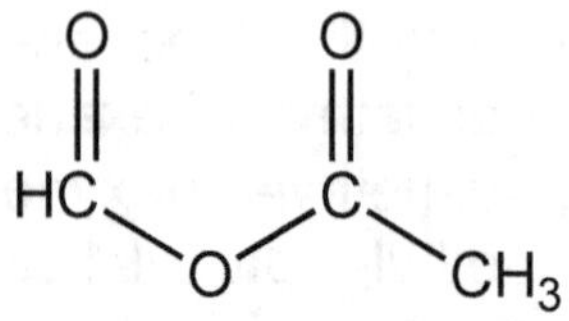

111. This compound

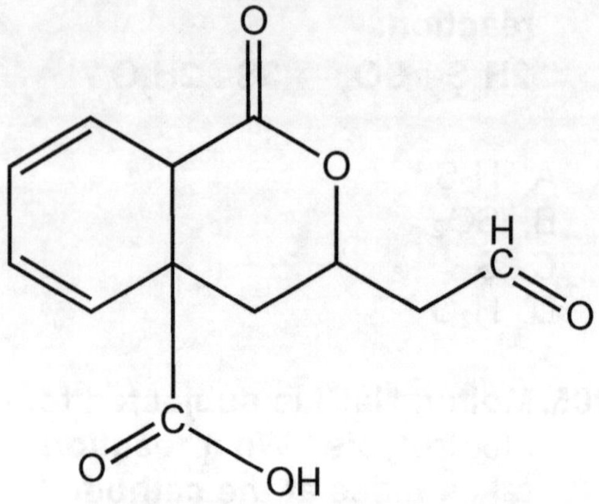

   contains an:

   A. alkene, carboxylic acid, ester, and ketone
   B. aldehyde, alkyne, ester, and ketone
   C. aldehyde, alkene, carboxylic acid, and ester
   D. acid anhydride, aldehyde, alkene, and amine

112. Which group of scientists made contributions in the same area of chemistry?

   A. Volta, Kekulé, Faraday, London
   B. Hess, Joule, Kelvin, Gibbs
   C. Boyle, Charles, Arrhenius, Pauli
   D. Davy, Mendeleev, Ramsay, Galvani

113. Which of the following pairs are isomers?

I. [structures of two N-N compounds with methyl groups]

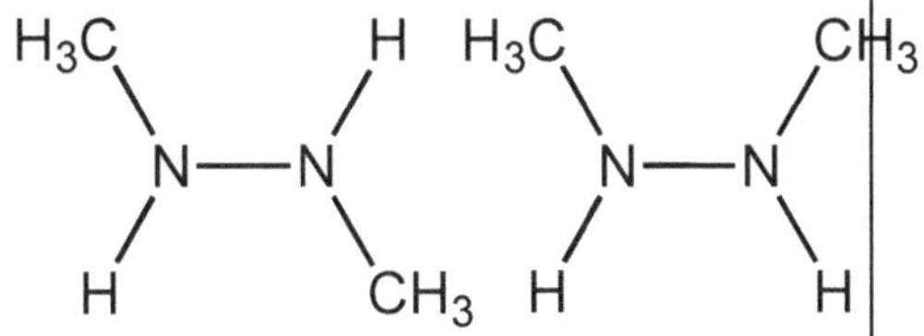

II. pentanal   2-pentanone

III. [two cyclopentane structures with Br substituents]

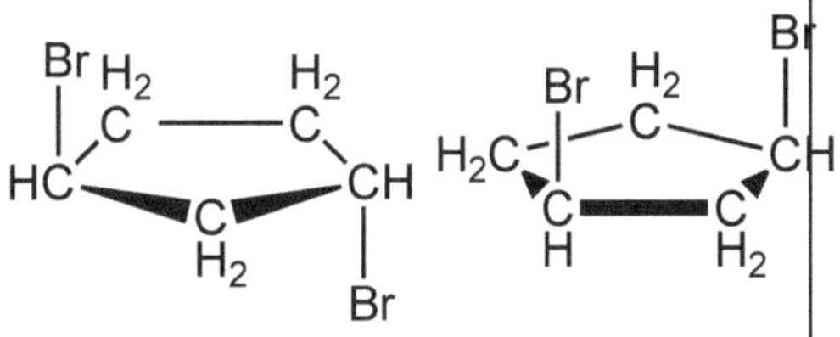

IV. [two chiral carbon structures with OH, F, CH3, H]

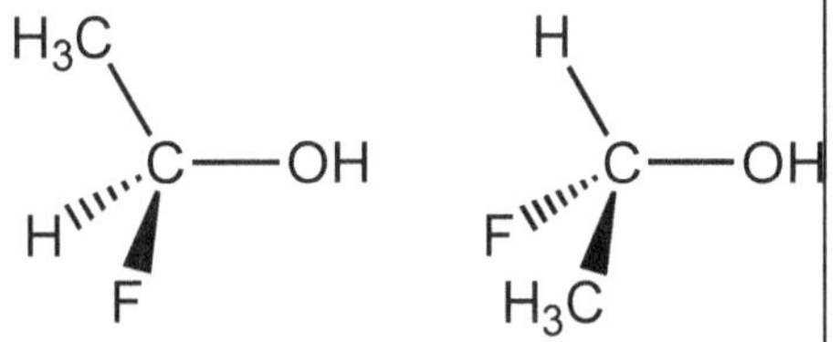

A. I and IV
B. II and III
C. I, II, and III
D. I, II, III, and IV

114. Which instrument would be most useful for separating two different proteins from a mixture?

A. UV/Vis spectrophotometer
B. Mass spectrometer
C. Gas chromatograph
D. Liquid chromatograph

115. Classify these biochemicals.

I. [cytidine monophosphate structure]

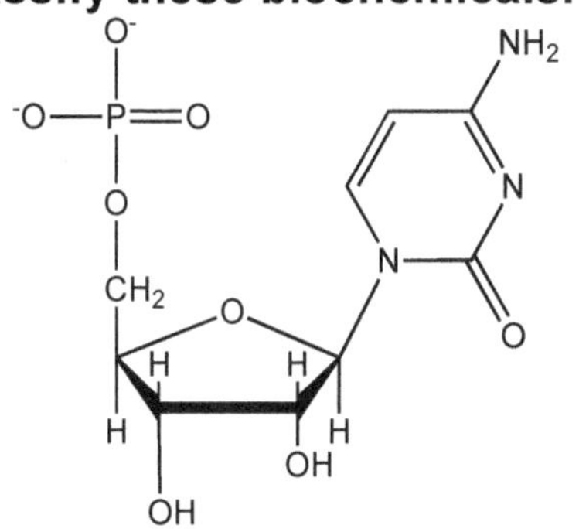

II. [sugar ring structure]

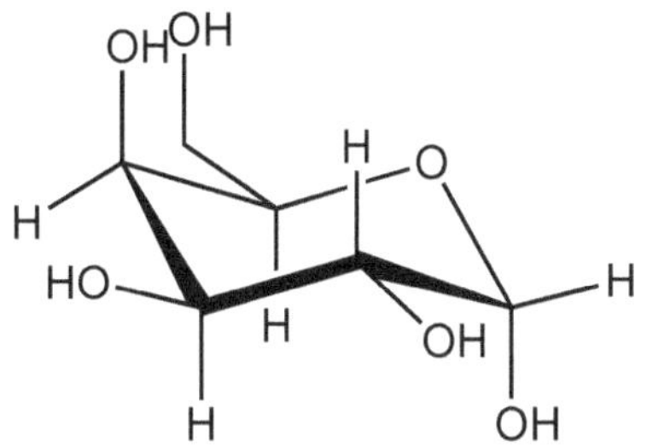

III. [tripeptide structure]

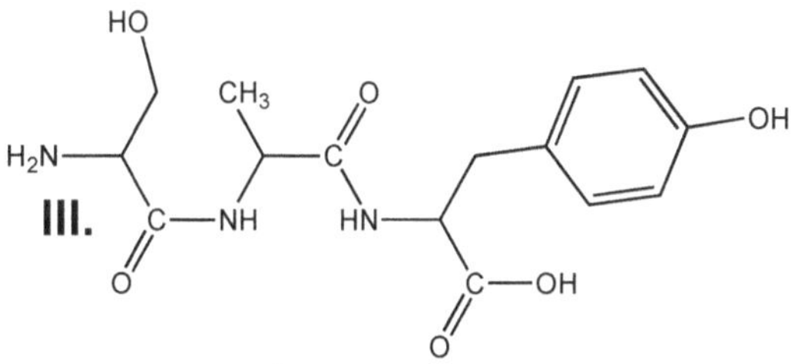

IV. [triglyceride structure]

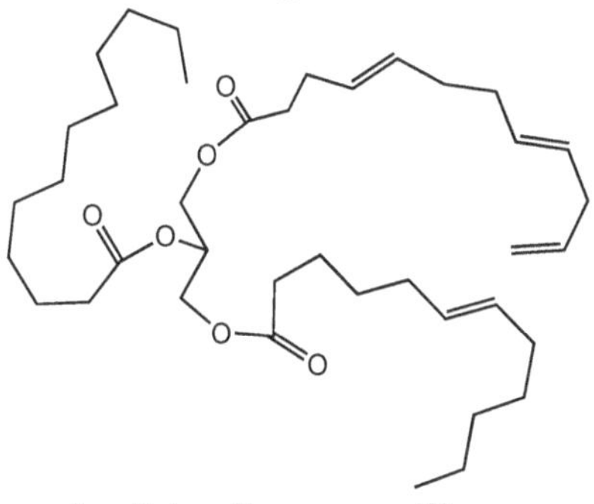

A. I-nucleotide, II-sugar, III-peptide, IV-fat
B. I-disaccharide, II-sugar, III-fatty acid, IV-polypeptide
C. I-disaccharide, II-amino acid, III-fatty acid, IV-polysaccharide
D. I I-nucleotide, II-sugar, III-triacylglyceride, and IV-DNA

116. You create a solution of 2.00 µg/ml of a pigment and divide the solution into 12 samples. You give four samples each to three teams of students. They use a spectrophotometer to determine the pigment concentration. Here is their data:

Team	Concentration (µg/ml)			
	sample 1	sample 2	sample 3	sample 4
1	1.98	1.93	1.92	1.88
2	1.70	1.72	1.69	1.70
3	1.78	1.99	2.87	2.20

Which of the following are true?

A. Team 1 has the most precise data
B. Team 3 has the most accurate data in spite of it having low precision
C. The data from team 2 is characteristic of a systematic error
D. The data from team 1 is more characteristic of random error than the data from team 3.

117. Which pair of measurements have an identical meaning?

A. 32 micrograms and 0.032 g
B. 26 nm and 2.60×10^{-8} m
C. 3.01×10^{-5} m^3 and 30.1 ml
D. 0.0020 L and 20 cm^3

118. Match the instrument with the quantity it measures

II. eudiometer
III. calorimeter
IV. manometer
V. hygrometer

A. I-volume, II-mass, III-radioactivity, IV-humidity
B. I-volume, II-heat, III-pressure, IV-humidity
C. I-viscosity, II-mass, III-pressure, IV-surface tension
D. I-viscosity, II-heat, III-radioactivity, IV-surface tension

119. Four nearly identical gems from the same mineral are weighed using different balances. Their masses are:

3.4533 g, 3.459 g, 3.4656 g, 3.464 g

The four gems are then collected and added to a volumetric cylinder containing 10.00 ml of liquid, and a new volume of 14.97 ml is read. What is the average mass of the four stones and what is the density of the mineral?

A. 3.460 g, and 2.78 g/ml
B. 3.460 g and 2.79 g/ml
C. 3.4605 g and 2.78 g/ml
D. 3.461 g and 2.79 g/ml

CHEMISTRY

120. Which list includes equipment that would not be used in vacuum filtration.

   A. Rubber tubing, Florence flask, Büchner funnel
   B. Vacuum pump, Hirsch funnel, rubber stopper with a single hole
   C. Aspirator, filter paper, filter flask
   D. Lab stand, clamp, filter trap

121. Which of the following statements about lab safety is not true?

   A. Corrosive chemicals should be stored below eye level.
   B. A chemical splash on the eye or skin should be rinsed for 15 minutes in cold water.
   C. MSDS means "Material Safety Data Sheet."
   D. A student should "stop, drop, and roll" if their clothing catches fire in the lab.

122. Which of the following lists consists entirely of chemicals that are considered safe enough to be in a high school lab?

   A. hydrochloric acid, lauric acid, potassium permanganate, calcium hydroxide
   B. ethyl ether, nitric acid, sodium benzoate, methanol
   C. cobalt (II) sulfide, ethylene glycol, benzoyl peroxide, ammonium chloride
   D. picric acid, hydrofluoric acid, cadmium chloride, carbon disulfide.

123. The following procedure was developed to find the specific heat capacity of metals:

   1. Place pieces of the metals in an ice-water bath so their initial temperature is 0 °C.
   2. Weigh a styrofoam cup.
   3. Add water at room temperature to the cup and weigh it again
   4. Add a cold metal from the bath to the cup and weigh the cup a third time.
   5. Monitor the temperature drop of the water until a final temperature at thermal equilibrium is found.

   _____ is also required as additional information in order to obtain heat capacities for the metals. The best control would be to follow the same protocol except to use _____ in step 4 instead of a cold metal.

   A. The heat capacity of water / a metal at 100 °C
   B. The heat of formation of water / ice from the 0 °C bath
   C. The heat of capacity of ice / glass at 0 °C
   D. The heat capacity of water / water from the 0 °C bath

CHEMISTRY

TEACHER CERTIFICATION EXAM

124. Which statement about the impact of chemistry on society is <u>not</u> true?

A. Partial hydrogenation creates *trans* fat.
B. The Haber Process incorporates nitrogen from the air into molecules for agricultural use.
C. The CO_2 concentration in the atmosphere has decreased in the last ten years.
D. The concentration of ozone-destroying chemicals in the stratosphere has decreased in the last ten years.

125. Which statement about everyday applications of chemistry is <u>true</u>?

A. Rainwater found near sources of air pollution will most likely be basic.
B. Batteries run down more quickly at low temperatures because chemical reactions are proceeding more slowly.
C. Benzyl alcohol is a detergent used in shampoo.
D. Adding salt decreases the time required for water to boil.

CHEMISTRY

TEACHER CERTIFICATION EXAM

Answer Key

1. C	26. D	51. B	76. A	101. C
2. B	27. A	52. D	77. D	102. D
3. D	28. C	53. B	78. C	103. B
4. A	29. C	54. C	79. B	104. B
5. C	30. B	55. D	80. A	105. C
6. D	31. A	56. A	81. D	106. D
7. C	32. A	57. C	82. B	107. C
8. B	33. B	58. C	83. D	108. B
9. A	34. D	59. A	84. B	109. C
10. C	35. B	60. B	85. A	110. A
11. B	36. C	61. D	86. C	111. C
12. D	37. B	62. B	87. A	112. B
13. A	38. D	63. C	88. C	113. B
14. D	39. A	64. B	89. B	114. D
15. B	40. B	65. D	90. D	115. A
16. D	41. C	66. A	91. B	116. C
17. C	42. C	67. B	92. C	117. C
18. B	43. A	68. C	93. A	118. B
19. C	44. D	69. A	94. A	119. B
20. A	45. C	70. D	95. D	120. A
21. C	46. B	71. C	96. C	121. D
22. B	47. D	72. B	97. A	122. A
23. D	48. B	73. A	98. A	123. D
24. A	49. B	74. C	99. B	124. C
25. D	50. A	75. A	100. B	125. B

CHEMISTRY

Answers with Solutions

Note: The first insignificant digit should be carried through intermediate calculations. This digit is shown using *italics* in the solutions below.

1. **A piston compresses a gas at constant temperature. Which gas properties increase?**

   II. Average speed of molecules
   III. Pressure
   IV. Molecular collisions with container walls per second

   A. I and II
   B. I and III
   C. II and III
   D. I, II, and III

C. A decrease in volume (V) occurs at constant temperature (T). Average molecular speed is determined only by temperature and will be constant. V and P are inversely related, so pressure will increase. With less wall area and at higher pressure, more collisions occur per second.

2. **The temperature of a liquid is raised at atmospheric pressure. Which liquid property increases?**

   A. critical pressure
   B. vapor pressure
   C. surface tension
   D. viscosity

B. The critical pressure of a liquid is its vapor pressure at the critical temperature and is always a constant value. A rising temperature increases the kinetic energy of molecules and decreases the importance of intermolecular attraction. More molecules will be free to escape to the vapor phase (vapor pressure increases), but the effect of attractions at the liquid-gas interface will fall (surface tension decreases) and molecules will flow against each other more easily (viscosity decreases).

TEACHER CERTIFICATION EXAM

3. Potassium crystallizes with two atoms contained in each unit cell. What is the mass of potassium found in a lattice 1.00×10^6 unit cells wide, 2.00×10^6 unit cells high, and 5.00×10^5 unit cells deep?

   A. 85.0 ng
   B. 32.5 µg
   C. 64.9 µg
   D. 130. µg

D. First we find the number of unit cells in the lattice by multiplying the number in each row, stack, and column:

1.00×10^6 unit cell lengths $\times$ 2.00×10^6 unit cell lengths $\times$ 5.00×10^5 unit cell lengths
$= 1.00 \times 10^{18}$ unit cells

Avogadro's number and the molecular weight of potassium (K) are used in the solution:

$$1.00 \times 10^{18} \text{ unit cells} \times \frac{2 \text{ atoms of K}}{\text{unit cell}} \times \frac{1 \text{ mole of K}}{6.02 \times 10^{23} \text{ atoms of K}} \times \frac{39.098 \text{ g K}}{1 \text{ mole of K}}$$
$$= 1.30 \times 10^{-4} \text{ g}$$
$$= 130. \text{ µg}$$

4. A gas is heated in a sealed container. Which of the following occur?

   A. gas pressure rises
   B. gas density decreases
   C. the average distance between molecules increases
   D. all of the above

A. The same material is kept in a constant volume, so neither density nor the distance between molecules will change. Pressure will rise because of increasing molecular kinetic energy impacting container walls.

TEACHER CERTIFICATION EXAM

5. How many molecules are in 2.20 pg of a protein with a molecular weight of 150. kDa?

   A. 8.83×10^9
   B. 1.82×10^9
   C. 8.83×10^6
   D. 1.82×10^6

C. The prefix "p" for "pico-" indicates 10^{-12}. A kilodalton is 1000 atomic mass units.

$$2.20 \text{ pg protein} \times \frac{10^{-12} \text{ g}}{1 \text{ pg}} \times \frac{1 \text{ mole protein}}{150 \times 10^3 \text{ g protein}} \times \frac{6.02 \times 10^{23} \text{ molecules protein}}{1 \text{ mole protein}} =$$
$$= 8.83 \times 10^6 \text{ molecules}$$

6. At STP, 20. μL of O_2 contain 5.4×10^{16} molecules. According to Avogadro's hypothesis, how many molecules are in 20. μL of Ne at STP?

   A. 5.4×10^{15}
   B. 1.0×10^{16}
   C. 2.7×10^{16}
   D. 5.4×10^{16}

D. Avogadro's hypothesis states that equal volumes of different gases at the same temperature and pressure contain equal numbers of molecules.

7. An ideal gas at 50.0 °C and 3.00 atm is in a 300. cm³ cylinder. The cylinder volume changes by moving a piston until the gas is at 50.0 °C and 1.00 atm. What is the final volume?

   A. 100. cm³
   B. 450. cm³
   C. 900. cm³
   D. 1.20 dm³

C. A three-fold decrease in pressure of a constant quantity of gas at constant temperature will cause a three-fold increase in gas volume.

CHEMISTRY

8. **Which gas law may be used to solve the previous question?**

   A. Charles's law
   B. Boyle's law
   C. Graham's law
   D. Avogadro's law

B. The inverse relationship between volume and pressure is Boyle's law.

9. **A blimp is filled with 5000. m³ of helium at 28.0 °C and 99.7 kPa. What is the mass of helium used?**

   $R = 8.3144 \dfrac{J}{mol\text{-}K}$

   A. 797 kg
   B. 810. kg
   C. 1.99×10^3 kg
   D. 8.57×10^3 kg

A. First the ideal gas law is manipulated to solve for moles.

$$PV = nRT \quad \Rightarrow \quad n = \dfrac{PV}{RT}$$

Temperature must be expressed in Kelvin: $T = (28.0 + 273.15)\,K = 301.15\,K$.

The ideal gas law is then used with the knowledge that joules are equivalent to Pa-m³:

$$n = \dfrac{PV}{RT} = \dfrac{(99.7 \times 10^3\,Pa)(5000.\,m^3)}{\left(8.3144 \dfrac{m^3\text{-}Pa}{mol\text{-}K}\right)(301.15\,K)} = 1.991 \times 10^3\,mol\,He.$$

Moles are then converted to grams using the molecular weight of helium:

$$1.991 \times 10^3\,mol\,He \times \dfrac{4.0026\,g\,He}{1\,mol\,He} = 797 \times 10^3\,g\,He = 797\,kg\,He.$$

TEACHER CERTIFICATION EXAM

10. Which of the following are able to flow from one place to another?

    I. Gases
    II. Liquids
    III. Solids
    IV. Supercritical fluids

    A. I and II
    B. II only
    C. I, II, and IV
    D. I, II, III, and IV

C. Gases and liquids both flow. Supercritical fluids have some traits in common with gases and some in common with liquids, and so they flow also. Solids have a fixed volume and shape.

11. One mole of an ideal gas at STP occupies 22.4 L. At what temperature will one mole of an ideal gas at one atm occupy 31.0 L?

    A. 34.6 °C
    B. 105 °C
    C. 378 °C
    D. 442 °C

B. Either Charles's law, the combined gas law, or the ideal gas law may be used with temperature in Kelvin.

Charles's law or the combined gas law with $P_1 = P_2$ may be manipulated to equate a ratio between temperature and volume when P and n are constant.

$$V \propto T \text{ or } \frac{P_1 V_1}{T_1} = \frac{P_2 V_2}{T_2} \Rightarrow \frac{T_1}{V_1} = \frac{T_2}{V_2} \Rightarrow T_2 = V_2 \frac{T_1}{V_1}$$

$$T_2 = 31.0 \text{ L} \frac{273.15 \text{ K}}{22.4 \text{ L}} = 378 \text{ K} = 105 \text{ °C}.$$

The ideal gas law may also be used with the appropriate gas constant:

$$PV = nRT \Rightarrow T = \frac{PV}{nR}$$

$$T = \frac{(1 \text{ atm})(31.0 \text{ L})}{(1 \text{ mol})\left(0.08206 \frac{\text{L-atm}}{\text{mol-K}}\right)} = 378 \text{ K} = 105 \text{ °C}.$$

12. Why does $CaCl_2$ have a higher normal melting point than NH_3?

   A. London dispersion forces in $CaCl_2$ are stronger than covalent bonds in NH_3.
   B. Covalent bonds in NH_3 are stronger than dipole-dipole bonds in $CaCl_2$.
   C. Ionic bonds in $CaCl_2$ are stronger than London dispersion forces in NH_3.
   D. Ionic bonds in $CaCl_2$ are stronger than hydrogen bonds in NH_3.

D. London dispersion forces are weaker than covalent bonds, eliminating choice A. A higher melting point will result from stronger intermolecular bonds, eliminating choice B. $CaCl_2$ is an ionic solid resulting from a cation on the left and an anion on the right of the periodic table. The dominant attractive forces between NH_3 molecules are hydrogen bonds.

13. Which intermolecular attraction explains the following trend in straight-chain alkanes?

Condensed structural formula	Boiling point (°C)
CH_4	-161.5
CH_3CH_3	-88.6
$CH_3CH_2CH_3$	-42.1
$CH_3CH_2CH_2CH_3$	-0.5
$CH_3CH_2CH_2CH_2CH_3$	36.0
$CH_3CH_2CH_2CH_2CH_2CH_3$	68.7

   A. London dispersion forces
   B. Dipole-dipole interactions
   C. Hydrogen bonding
   D. Ion-induced dipole interactions

A. Alkanes are composed entirely of non-polar C-C and C-H bonds, resulting in no dipole interactions or hydrogen bonding. London dispersion forces increase with the size of the molecule, resulting in a higher temperature requirement to break these bonds and a higher boiling point.

TEACHER CERTIFICATION EXAM

14. List NH_3, PH_3, $MgCl_2$, Ne, and N_2 in order of increasing melting point.

   A. N_2 < Ne < PH_3 < NH_3 < $MgCl_2$
   B. N_2 < NH_3 < Ne < $MgCl_2$ < PH_3
   C. Ne < N_2 < NH_3 < PH_3 < $MgCl_2$
   D. Ne < N_2 < PH_3 < NH_3 < $MgCl_2$

D. Higher melting points result from stronger intermolecular forces. $MgCl_2$ is the only material listed with ionic bonds and will have the highest melting point. Dipole-dipole interactions are present in NH_3 and PH_3 but not in Ne and N_2. Ne and N_2 are also small molecules expected to have very weak London dispersion forces and so will have lower melting points than NH_3 and PH_3. NH_3 will have stronger intermolecular attractions and a higher melting point than PH_3 because hydrogen bonding occurs in NH_3. Ne has a molecular weight of 20 and a spherical shape and N_2 has a molecular weight of 28 and is not spherical. Both of these factors predict stronger London dispersion forces and a higher melting point for N_2. Actual melting points are: Ne (25 K) < N_2 (63 K) < PH_3 (140 K) < NH_3 (195 K) < $MgCl_2$ (987 K).

15. 1-butanol, ethanol, methanol, and 1-propanol are all liquids at room temperature. Rank them in order of increasing viscosity.

   A. 1-butanol < 1-propanol < ethanol < methanol
   B. methanol < ethanol < 1-propanol < 1-butanol
   C. methanol < ethanol < 1-butanol < 1-propanol
   D. 1-propanol < 1-butanol < ethanol < methanol

B. Higher viscosities result from stronger intermolecular attractive forces. The molecules listed are all alcohols with the -OH functional group attached to the end of a straight-chain alkane. In other words, they all have the formula $CH_3(CH_2)_{n-1}OH$. The only difference between the molecules is the length of the alkane corresponding to the value of *n*. With all else identical, larger molecules have greater intermolecular attractive forces due to a greater molecular surface for the attractions. Therefore the viscosities are ranked: methanol (CH_3OH) < ethanol (CH_3CH_2OH) < 1-propanol ($CH_3CH_2CH_2OH$) < 1-butanol ($CH_3CH_2CH_2CH_2OH$).

16. Which gas has a diffusion rate of 25% the rate for hydrogen?

A. helium
B. methane
C. nitrogen
D. oxygen

D. Graham's law of diffusion states:

$$\frac{r_1}{r_2} = \sqrt{\frac{M_2}{M_1}}.$$

Hydrogen (H_2) has molecular weight of 2.0158 u. Using the unknown for material #1 and hydrogen for material #2 in the equation for Graham's law, the ratio of rates is:

$$\frac{r_{unknown}}{r_{hydrogen}} = \sqrt{\frac{2.0158\ u}{M_{unknown}}} = 0.25.$$ Squaring both sides yields $\frac{2.0158\ u}{M_{unknown}} = 0.0625$.

Solving for $M_{unknown}$ gives:

$$M_{unknown} = \frac{2.0158\ u}{0.0625} = 32\ u.$$

The given possibilities are: He (4.0 u), CH_4 (16 u), N_2 (28 u), and O_2 (32 u).

TEACHER CERTIFICATION EXAM

17. 2.00 L of an unknown gas at 1500. mm Hg and a temperature of 25.0 °C weighs 7.52 g. Assuming the ideal gas equation, what is the molecular weight of the gas?

$$760 \text{ mm Hg} = 1 \text{ atm}$$
$$R = 0.08206 \text{ L-atm/(mol-K)}$$

A. 21.6 u
B. 23.3 u
C. 46.6 u
D. 93.2 u

C. Pressure and temperature must be expressed in the proper units. Next the ideal gas law is used to find the number of moles of gas.

$$P = 1500 \text{ mm Hg} \times \frac{1 \text{ atm}}{760 \text{ mm Hg}} = 1.974 \text{ atm and } T = 25.0 + 273.15 = 298.15 \text{ K}$$

$$PV = nRT \implies n = \frac{PV}{RT}$$

$$n = \frac{(1.974 \text{ atm})(2.00 \text{ L})}{\left(0.08206 \frac{\text{L-atm}}{\text{mol-K}}\right)(298.15 \text{ K})} = 0.1613 \text{ mol.}$$

The molecular mass may be found from the mass of one mole.

$$\frac{7.52 \text{ g}}{0.1613 \text{ mol}} = 46.6 \frac{\text{g}}{\text{mol}} \implies 46.6 \text{ u}$$

18. Which substance is most likely to be a gas at STP?

A. SeO_2
B. F_2
C. $CaCl_2$
D. I_2

B. A gas at STP has a normal boiling point under 0 °C. The substance with the lowest boiling point will have the weakest intermolecular attractive forces and will be the most likely gas at STP. F_2 has the lowest molecular weight, is not a salt, metal, or covalent network solid, and is non-polar, indicating the weakest intermolecular attractive forces of the four choices. F_2 actually is a gas at STP, and the other three are solids.

CHEMISTRY

19. What pressure is exerted by a mixture of 2.7 g of H2 and 59 g of Xe at 0 °C on a 50. L container?

   A. 0.69 atm
   B. 0.76 atm
   C. 0.80 atm
   D. 0.97 atm

C. Grams of gas are first converted to moles:

$$2.7 \text{ g H}_2 \times \frac{1 \text{ mol H}_2}{2 \times 1.0079 \text{ g H}_2} = 1.33 \text{ mol H}_2 \quad \text{and} \quad 59 \text{ g Xe} \times \frac{1 \text{ mol H}_2}{131.29 \text{ g H}_2} = 0.449 \text{ mol Xe}$$

Dalton's law of partial pressures for an ideal gas is used to find the pressure of the mixture:

$$P_{total}V = (n_{H_2} + n_{Xe})RT \Rightarrow P_{total} = \frac{(n_{H_2} + n_{Xe})RT}{V}$$

$$P_{total} = \frac{(1.33 \text{ mol} + 0.449 \text{ mol})\left(0.08206 \frac{\text{L-atm}}{\text{mol-K}}\right)(273.15 \text{ K})}{50. \text{ L}} = 0.80 \text{ atm}.$$

20. A few minutes after opening a bottle of perfume, the scent is detected on the other side of the room. What law relates to this phenomenon?

   A. Graham's law
   B. Dalton's law
   C. Boyle's law
   D. Avogadro's law

A. Graham's law describes the rate of diffusion (or effusion) of a gas, in this instance, the rate of diffusion of molecules in perfume vapor.

TEACHER CERTIFICATION EXAM

21. **Which of the following statements are true of vapor pressure at equilibrium?**

    A. Solids have no vapor pressure.
    B. Dissolving a solute in a liquid increases its vapor pressure.
    C. The vapor pressure of a pure substance is characteristic of that substance and its temperature.
    D. All of the above

C. Only temperature and the identity of the substance determine vapor pressure. Solids have a vapor pressure, and solutes decrease vapor pressure.

22. **Find the partial pressure of N_2 in a container holding H_2O and N_2 at 150. kPa and 50 °C. The vapor pressure of H_2O at 50 °C is 12 kPa.**

    A. 12 kPa
    B. 138 kPa
    C. 162 kPa
    D. The value cannot be determined.

B. The partial pressure of H_2O vapor in the container is its vapor pressure. The partial pressure of N_2 may be found by manipulating Dalton's law:
$$P_{total} = P_{H_2O} + P_{N_2} \Rightarrow P_{N_2} = P_{total} - P_{H_2O}$$
$$P_{N_2} = P_{total} - P_{H_2O} = 150.\ \text{kPa} - 12\ \text{kPa} = 138\ \text{kPa}$$

23. **The normal boiling point of water on the Kelvin scale is closest to:**

    A. 112 K
    B. 212 K
    C. 273 K
    D. 373 K

D. Temperature in Kelvin are equal to Celsius temperatures plus 273.15. Since the normal boiling point of water is 100 °C, it will boil at 373.15 K, corresponding to answer D.

24. Which phase may be present at the triple point of a substance?

   I. Gas
   II. Liquid
   III. Solid
   IV. Supercritical fluid

   A. I, II, and III
   B. I, II, and IV
   C. II, III, and IV
   D. I, II, III, and IV

A. Gas, liquid and solid may exist together at the triple point.

25. In the following phase diagram, _____ occurs as P is decreased from A to B at constant T and _____ occurs as T is increased from C to D at constant P.

   A. deposition, melting
   B. sublimation, melting
   C. deposition, vaporization
   D. sublimation, vaporization

D. Point A is located in the solid phase, point C is located in the liquid phase. Points B and D are located in the gas phase. The transition from solid to gas is sublimation and the transition from liquid to gas is vaporization.

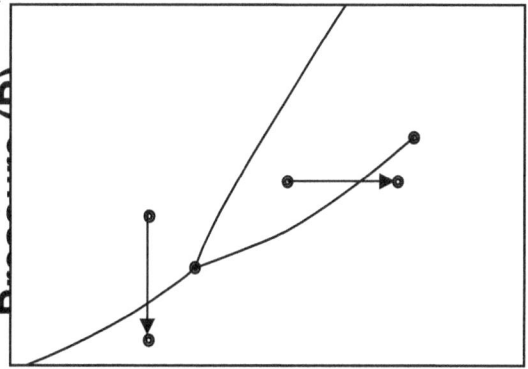

Temperature (T)

26. Heat is added to a pure solid at its melting point until it all becomes liquid at its freezing point. Which of the following occur?

   A. Intermolecular attractions are weakened.
   B. The kinetic energy of the molecules does not change.
   C. The freedom of the molecules to move about increases.
   D. All of the above

D. Intermolecular attractions are lessened during melting. This permits molecules to move about more freely, but there is no change in the kinetic energy of the molecules because the temperature has remained the same.

TEACHER CERTIFICATION EXAM

27. Which of the following occur when NaCl dissolves in water?

    A. Heat is required to break bonds in the NaCl crystal lattice.
    B. Heat is released when hydrogen bonds in water are broken.
    C. Heat is required to form bonds of hydration.
    D. The oxygen end of the water molecule is attracted to the Cl^- ion.

A. The lattice does break apart, H-bonds in water are broken, and bonds of hydration are formed, but the first and second process require heat while the third process releases heat. The oxygen end of the water molecule has a partial negative charge and is attracted to the Na^+ ion.

28. The solubility of $CoCl_2$ is 54 g per 100 g of ethanol. Three flasks each contain 100 g of ethanol. Flask #1 also contains 40 g $CoCl_2$ in solution. Flask #2 contains 56 g $CoCl_2$ in solution. Flask #3 contains 5 g of solid $CoCl_2$ in equilibrium with 54 g $CoCl_2$ in solution. Which of the following describe the solutions present in the liquid phase of the flasks?

    A. #1-saturated, #2-supersaturated, #3-unsaturated.
    B. #1-unsaturated, #2-miscible, #3-saturated.
    C. #1-unsaturated, #2-supersaturated, #3-saturated.
    D. #1-unsaturated, #2-not at equilibrium, #3-miscible.

C. Flask #1 contains less solute than the solubility limit, and is unsaturated. Flask #2 contains more solute than the solubility limit, and is supersaturated and also not at equilibrium. Flask #3 contains the solubility limit and is a saturated solution. The term "miscible" applies only to liquids that mix together in all proportions.

29. The solubility at 1.0 atm of pure CO_2 in water at 25 °C is 0.034 M. According to Henry's law, what is the solubility at 4.0 atm of pure CO_2 in water at 25 °C? Assume no chemical reaction occurs between CO_2 and H_2O.

    A. 0.0085 M
    B. 0.034 M
    C. 0.14 M
    D. 0.25 M

C. Henry's law states that CO_2 solubility in M (mol/L) will be proportional to the partial pressure of the gas. A four-fold increase in pressure from 1.0 atm to 4.0 atm will increase solubility four-fold from 0.034 M to 0.14 M.

30. Carbonated water is bottled at 25 °C under pure CO_2 at 4.0 atm. Later the bottle is opened at 4 °C under air at 1.0 atm that has a partial pressure of 3×10^{-4} atm CO_2. Why do CO_2 bubbles form when the bottle is opened?

   A. CO_2 leaves the solution due to a drop in solubility at the lower total pressure.
   B. CO_2 leaves the solution due to a drop in solubility at the lower CO_2 pressure.
   C. CO_2 leaves the solution due to a drop in solubility at the lower temperature.
   D. CO_2 is formed by the decomposition of carbonic acid.

B. A is incorrect because if the water were bottled under a different gas at a high pressure, it would not be carbonated. CO_2 partial pressure is the important factor in solubility. C is incorrect because a decrease in temperature will increase solubility, and the chance from 298 K to 277 K is relatively small. D may occur, but this represents a small fraction of the gas released.

31. When KNO_3 dissolves in water, the water grows slightly colder. An increase in temperature will _____ the solubility of KNO_3.

   A. increase
   B. decrease
   C. have no effect on
   D. have an unknown effect with the information given on

A. The decline in water temperature indicates that the net solution process is endothermic (requiring heat). A temperature increase supplying more heat will favor the solution and increase solubility according to Le Chatelier's principle.

32. An experiment requires 100. mL of a 0.500 M solution of $MgBr_2$. How many grams of $MgBr_2$ will be present in this solution?

   A. 9.21 g
   B. 11.7 g
   C. 12.4 g
   D. 15.6 g

A.

$$0.100 \text{ L solution} \times \frac{0.500 \text{ mol MgBr}_2}{\text{L}} \times \frac{(24.305 + 2 \times 79.904) \text{ g MgBr}_2}{\text{mol MgBr}_2} = 9.21 \text{ g MgBr}_2$$

TEACHER CERTIFICATION EXAM

33. 500. mg of RbOH are added to 500. g of ethanol (C_2H_6O) resulting in 395 mL of solution. Determine the molarity and molality of RbOH.

A. 0.0124 M, 0.00488 m
B. 0.0124 M, 0.00976 m
C. 0.0223 M, 0.00488 m
D. 0.0223 M, 0.00976 m

B. First we determine the moles of solute present:

$$0.500 \text{ g RbOH} \times \frac{1 \text{ mol RbOH}}{(85.468 + 15.999 + 1.0079) \text{ g RbOH}} = 0.004879 \text{ mol RbOH}.$$

This value is used to calculate molarity and molality:

$$\frac{0.04879 \text{ mol RbOH}}{0.395 \text{ L solution}} = 0.0124 \text{ M RbOH}$$

and

$$\frac{0.04879 \text{ mol RbOH}}{0.500 \text{ kg ethanol}} = 0.00976 \ m \text{ RbOH}.$$

34. 20.0 g H₃PO₄ in 1.5 L of solution are intended to react with KOH according to the following reaction: $H_3PO_4 + 3KOH \rightarrow K_3PO_4 + 3H_2O$. What is the molarity and normality of the H₃PO₄ solution?

A. 0.41 M, 1.22 N
B. 0.41 M, 0.20 N
C. 0.14 M, 0.045 N
D. 0.14 M, 0.41 N

D. We use two methods to solve this problem. In the first method, we determine the moles of solute present and use it to calculate molarity and normality:

$$20.0 \text{ g } H_3PO_4 \times \frac{1 \text{ mol } H_3PO_4}{(3 \times 1.0079 + 30.974 + 4 \times 15.999) \text{ g } H_3PO_4} = 0.204 \text{ mol } H_3PO_4.$$

$$\frac{0.204 \text{ mol } H_3PO_4}{1.5 \text{ L solution}} = 0.136 \frac{\text{mol } H_3PO_4}{L} = 0.14 \text{ M } H_3PO_4$$

and

$$\frac{0.204 \text{ mol } H_3PO_4}{1.5 \text{ L solution}} \times \frac{3 \text{ reaction equivalents}}{1 \text{ mol } H_3PO_4} = 0.408 \frac{\text{reaction equivalents}}{L} = 0.41 \text{ N } H_3PO_4.$$

Alternatively, molarity may be found in one step and normality may be determined from the molarity:

$$\frac{20.0 \text{ g } H_3PO_4}{1.5 \text{ L}} \times \frac{1 \text{ mol } H_3PO_4}{(3 \times 1.0079 + 30.974 + 4 \times 15.999) \text{ g } H_3PO_4} = 0.136 \frac{\text{mol } H_3PO_4}{L} = 0.14 \text{ M } H_3PO_4$$

and

$$0.136 \frac{\text{mol } H_3PO_4}{L} \times \frac{3 \text{ reaction equivalents}}{1 \text{ mol } H_3PO_4} = 0.408 \frac{\text{reaction equivalents}}{L} = 0.41 \text{ N}.$$

TEACHER CERTIFICATION EXAM

35. Aluminum sulfate is a strong electrolyte. What is the concentration of all species in a 0.2 M solution of aluminum sulfate?

  A. 0.2 M Al^{3+}, 0.2 M SO_4^{2-}
  B. 0.4 M Al^{3+}, 0.6 M SO_4^{2-}
  C. 0.6 M Al^{3+}, 0.4 M SO_4^{2-}
  D. 0.2 M $Al_2(SO_4)_3$

B. A strong electrolyte will completely ionize into its cation and anion. Aluminum sulfate is $Al_2(SO_4)_3$. Each mole of aluminum sulfate ionizes into 2 moles of Al^{3+} and 3 moles of SO_4^{2-}:

$$0.2 \frac{\text{mol } Al_2(SO_4)_3}{L} \times \frac{2 \text{ mol } Al^{3+}}{\text{mol } Al_2(SO_4)_3} = 0.4 \frac{\text{mol } Al^{3+}}{L} \text{ and}$$

$$0.2 \frac{\text{mol } Al_2(SO_4)_3}{L} \times \frac{3 \text{ mol } SO_4^{2-}}{\text{mol } Al_2(SO_4)_3} = 0.6 \frac{\text{mol } SO_4^{2-}}{L}.$$

36. 15 g of formaldehyde (CH_2O) are dissolved in 100. g of water. Calculate the weight percentage and mole fraction of formaldehyde in the solution.

  A. 13%, 0.090
  B. 15%, 0.090
  C. 13%, 0.083
  D. 15%, 0.083

C. Remember to use the total amounts in the denominator.

For weight percentage: $\dfrac{15 \text{ g } CH_2O}{(15+100) \text{ g total}} = 0.13 = 13\%$.

For mole fraction, first convert grams of each substance to moles:

$$15 \text{ g } CH_2O \times \frac{\text{mol } CH_2O}{(12.011 + 2 \times 1.0079 + 15.999) \text{ g } CH_2O} = 0.4996 \text{ mol } CH_2O$$

$$100 \text{ g } H_2O \times \frac{\text{mol } H_2O}{(2 \times 1.0079 + 15.999) \text{ g } H_2O} = 5.551 \text{ mol } H_2O.$$

Again use the total amount in the denominator $\dfrac{0.4996 \text{ mol } CH_2O}{(0.4996 + 5.551) \text{ mol total}} = 0.083$.

CHEMISTRY

37. Which of the following would make the best solvent for Br_2?

   A. H_2O
   B. CS_2
   C. NH_3
   D. molten NaCl

B. The best solvents for a solute have intermolecular bonds of similar strength to the solute ("like dissolves like"). Bromine is a non-polar molecule with intermolecular attractions due to weak London dispersion forces. The relatively strong hydrogen bonding in H_2O and NH_3 and the very strong electrostatic attractions in molten NaCl would make each of them a poor solvent for Br_2 because these molecules would prefer to remain attracted to one another. CS_2 is a fairly small non-polar molecule.

38. Which of the following is most likely to dissolve in water?

   A. H_2
   B. CCl_4
   C. $(SiO_2)_n$
   D. CH_3OH

D. The best solutes for a solvent have intermolecular bonds of similar strength to the solvent. H_2O molecules are connected by fairly strong hydrogen bonds. H_2 and CCl_4 are molecules with intermolecular attractions due to weak London dispersion forces. $(SiO_2)_n$ is a covalent network solid and is essentially one large molecule with bonds that much stronger than hydrogen bonds. CH_3OH (methanol) is miscible with water because it contains hydrogen bonds between molecules.

39. Which of the following is not a colligative property?

   A. Viscosity lowering
   B. Freezing point lowering
   C. Boiling point elevation
   D. Vapor pressure lowering

A. Vapor pressure lowering, boiling point elevation, and freezing point lowering may all be visualized as a result of solute particles interfering with the interface between phases in a consistent way. This is not the case for viscosity.

40. $BaCl_2(aq) + Na_2SO_4(aq) \rightarrow BaSO_4(s) + 2NaCl(aq)$ is an example of a _____ reaction.

A. acid-base
B. precipitation
C. redox
D. nuclear

B. $BaSO_4$ falls out of the solution as a precipitate, but the charges on Ba^{2+} and SO_4^{2-} remain unchanged, so this is not a redox reaction. Neither $BaCl_2$ nor Na_2SO_4 are acids or bases, and the nuclei involved also remain unaltered

41. List the following aqueous solutions in order of increasing boiling point.

   I.   0.050 m $AlCl_3$
   II. 0.080 m $Ba(NO_3)_2$
   III. 0.090 m NaCl
   IV. 0.12 m ethylene glycol ($C_2H_6O_2$)

A. I < II < III < IV
B. I < III < IV < II
C. IV < III < I < II
D. IV < III < II < I

C. Particles in solution determine colligative properties. The first three materials are strong electrolyte salts, and $C_2H_6O_2$ is a non-electrolyte.

$AlCl_3(aq)$ is $Al^{3+} + 3\,Cl^-$. So $0.050 \dfrac{\text{mol } AlCl_3}{\text{kg } H_2O} \times \dfrac{4 \text{ mol particles}}{\text{mol } AlCl_3} = 0.200\ m$ particles

$Ba(NO_3)_2(aq)$ is $Ba^{2+} + 2\,NO_3^-$. So $0.080 \dfrac{\text{mol } Ba(NO_3)_2}{\text{kg } H_2O} \times \dfrac{3 \text{ mol particles}}{\text{mol } Ba(NO_3)_2} = 0.240\ m$ particles

$NaCl(aq)$ is $Na^+ + Cl^-$. So $0.090 \dfrac{\text{mol NaCl}}{\text{kg } H_2O} \times \dfrac{2 \text{ mol particles}}{\text{mol NaCl}} = 0.180\ m$ particles

$C_2H_6O_2(aq)$ is not an electrolyte. So $0.12 \dfrac{\text{mol } C_2H_6O_2}{\text{kg } H_2O} \times \dfrac{1 \text{ mol particles}}{\text{mol } C_2H_6O_2} = 0.12\ m$ particles

The greater the number of dissolved particles, the greater the boiling point elevation.

42. Osmotic pressure is the pressure required to prevent _____ flowing from low to high _____ concentration across a semipermeable membrane.

   A. solute, solute
   B. solute, solvent
   C. solvent, solute
   D. solvent, solvent

C. Osmotic pressure is the pressure required to prevent osmosis, which is the flow of solvent across the membrane from low to high solute concentration. This is also the direction from high to low solvent concentration.

43. A solution of NaCl in water is heated on a mountain in an open container until it boils at 100. °C. The air pressure on the mountain is 0.92 atm. According to Raoult's law, what mole fraction of Na$^+$ and Cl$^-$ are present in the solution?

   A. 0.04 Na$^+$, 0.04 Cl$^-$
   B. 0.08 Na$^+$, 0.08 Cl$^-$
   C. 0.46 Na$^+$, 0.46 Cl$^-$
   D. 0.92 Na$^+$, 0.92 Cl$^-$

A. The vapor pressure of H$_2$O at 100. °C is exactly 1 atm. Boiling point decreases with external pressure, so the boiling point of pure H$_2$O at 0.9 atm will be less than 100. °C. Adding salt raises the boiling point at 0.92 atm to 100. °C by decreasing vapor pressure to 0.92 atm. According to Raoult's law:

$$P^{vapor}_{solution} = P^{vapor}_{pure\ solvent}(\text{mole fraction})_{solvent} \Rightarrow (\text{mole fraction})_{solvent} = \frac{P^{vapor}_{solution}}{P^{vapor}_{pure\ solvent}}.$$

Therefore, $(\text{mole fraction})_{H_2O} = \dfrac{0.92 \text{ atm at } 100.\ °C}{1.0 \text{ atm at } 100.\ °C} = 0.92 \dfrac{\text{mol H}_2\text{O}}{\text{mol total}}$.

The remaining 0.08 mole fraction of solute is evenly divided between the two ions:

$(\text{mole fraction})_{solute} = 1 - (\text{mole fraction})_{H_2O} = 1 - 0.92 = 0.08 \dfrac{\text{mol solute particles}}{\text{mol total}}$

$(\text{mole fraction})_{Na^+} = 0.08 \dfrac{\text{mol solute particles}}{\text{mol total}} \times \dfrac{1 \text{ mol Na}^+}{2 \text{ mol solute particles}} = 0.04 \dfrac{\text{mol Na}^+}{\text{mol total}}$

$(\text{mole fraction})_{Cl^-} = 0.08 \dfrac{\text{mol solute particles}}{\text{mol total}} \times \dfrac{1 \text{ mol Cl}^-}{2 \text{ mol solute particles}} = 0.04 \dfrac{\text{mol Cl}^-}{\text{mol total}}.$

TEACHER CERTIFICATION EXAM

44. Write a balanced nuclear equation for the emission of an alpha particle by polonium-209.

A. $^{209}_{84}Po \rightarrow \, ^{205}_{81}Pb + \, ^{4}_{2}He$

B. $^{209}_{84}Po \rightarrow \, ^{205}_{82}Bi + \, ^{4}_{2}He$

C. $^{209}_{84}Po \rightarrow \, ^{209}_{85}At + \, ^{0}_{-1}e$

D. $^{209}_{84}Po \rightarrow \, ^{205}_{82}Pb + \, ^{4}_{2}He$

D. The periodic table before skill 1.1 shows that polonium has an atomic number of 84. The emission of an alpha particle, $^{4}_{2}He$ (eliminating choice C), will leave an atom with an atomic number of 82 and a mass number of 205 (eliminating choice A). The periodic table identifies this element as lead, $^{205}_{82}Pb$, not bismuth (eliminating choice B).

45. Write a balanced nuclear equation for the decay of calcium-45 to scandium-45.

A. $^{45}_{20}Ca \rightarrow \, ^{41}_{18}Sc + \, ^{4}_{2}He$

B. $^{45}_{20}Ca + \, ^{0}_{1}e \rightarrow \, ^{45}_{21}Sc$

C. $^{45}_{20}Ca \rightarrow \, ^{45}_{21}Sc + \, ^{0}_{-1}e$

D. $^{45}_{20}Ca + \, ^{0}_{1}p \rightarrow \, ^{45}_{21}Sc$

C. All four choices are balanced mathematically. "A" leaves scandium-41 as a decay product, not scandium-45. "B" and "D" require the addition of particles not normally present in the atom. If these reactions do occur, they are not decay reactions because they are not spontaneous. "C" involves the common decay mechanism of beta emission.

46. $^{3}_{1}H$ decays with a half-life of 12 years. 3.0 g of pure $^{3}_{1}H$ were placed in a sealed container 24 years ago. How many grams of $^{3}_{1}H$ remain?

A. 0.38 g
B. 0.75 g
C. 1.5 g
D. 3.0 g

B. Every 12 years, the amount remaining is cut in half. After 12 years, 1.5 g will remain. After another 12 years, 0.75 g will remain.

CHEMISTRY

47. Oxygen-15 has a half-life of 122 seconds. What percentage of a sample of oxygen-15 has decayed after 300. seconds?

   A. 18.2%
   B. 21.3%
   C. 78.7%
   D. 81.8%

D. We may assume a convenient number (like 100.0 g) for a sample size. The amount remaining may be found from:

$$A_{remaining} = A_{initially} \left(\frac{1}{2}\right)^{\frac{t}{t_{halflife}}}$$

$$= 100.0 \text{ g } ^{15}O \left(\frac{1}{2}\right)^{\frac{300. \text{ seconds}}{122 \text{ seconds}}} = 18.2 \text{ g } ^{15}O$$

We are asked to determine the percentage that has decayed. This will be 100.0 g – 18.2 g = 81.8 g or 81.8% of the initial sample.

48. Which of the following isotopes is commonly used for medical imaging in the diagnose of diseases?

   A. cobalt-60
   B. technetium-99m
   C. tin-117m
   D. plutonium-238

B. The other three isotopes have limited medical applications (tin-117m has been used for the relief of bone cancer pain), but only Tc-99m is used routinely for imaging.

49. Carbon-14 dating would be useful in obtaining the age of which object?

   A. a 20th century Picasso painting
   B. a mummy from ancient Egypt
   C. a dinosaur fossil
   D. all of the above

B. C-14 is used in archeology because its half-life is 5730 years. Too little C-14 would have decayed from the painting and nearly all of the C-14 would have decayed from the fossil. In both cases, an estimate of age would be impossible with this isotope.

50. Which of the following isotopes can create a chain reaction of nuclear fission?

    A. uranium-235
    B. uranium-238
    C. plutonium-238
    D. all of the above

A. Uranium-235 and plutonium-239 are the two fissile isotopes used for nuclear power. ^{238}U is the most common uranium isotope. ^{238}Pu is used as a heat source for energy in space probes and some pacemakers.

51. List the following scientists in chronological order from earliest to most recent with respect to their most significant contribution to atomic theory:

    I. John Dalton
    II. Niels Bohr
    III. J. J. Thomson
    IV. Ernest Rutherford

    A. I, III, II, IV
    B. I, III, IV, II
    C. I, IV, III, II
    D. III, I, II, IV

B. Dalton founded modern atomic theory. J.J. Thomson determined that the electron is a subatomic particle but he placed it in the center of the atom. Rutherford discovered that electrons surround a small dense nucleus. Bohr determined that electrons may only occupy discrete positions around the nucleus.

52. Match the theory with the scientist who first proposed it:

   I. Electrons, atoms, and all objects with momentum also exist as waves.
   II. Electron density may be accurately described by a single mathematical equation.
   III. There is an inherent indeterminacy in the position and momentum of particles.
   IV. Radiant energy is transferred between particles in exact multiples of a discrete unit.

   A. I-de Broglie, II-Planck, III-Schrödinger, IV-Thomson
   B. I-Dalton, II-Bohr, III-Planck, IV-de Broglie
   C. I-Henry, II-Bohr, III-Heisenberg, IV-Schrödinger
   D. I-de Broglie, II-Schrödinger, III-Heisenberg, IV-Planck

D. Henry's law relates gas partial pressure to liquid solubility.

53. How many neutrons are in $^{60}_{27}Co$?

   A. 27
   B. 33
   C. 60
   D. 87

B. The number of neutrons is found by subtracting the atomic number (27) from the mass number (60).

54. The terrestrial composition of an element is: 50.7% as an isotope with an atomic mass of 78.9 u and 49.3% as an isotope with an atomic mass of 80.9 u. Both isotopes are stable. Calculate the atomic mass of the element.

   A. 79.0 u
   B. 79.8 u
   C. 79.9 u
   D. 80.8 u

C.

Atomic mass of element = (Fraction as 1st isotope) (Atomic mass of 1st isotope)
+
(Fraction as 2nd isotope) (Atomic mass of 2nd isotope)
= (0.507) (78.9 u) + (0.493) (80.9 u) = 79.89 u = 79.9 u

TEACHER CERTIFICATION EXAM

55. Which of the following is a correct electron arrangement for oxygen?

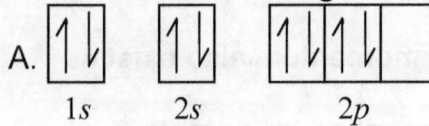

B. $1s^2 1p^2 2s^2 2p^2$
C. 2, 2, 4
D. none of the above

D. Choice A violates Hund's rule. The two electrons on the far right should occupy the final two orbitals. B should be $1s^2 2s^2 2p^4$. There is no 1p subshell. C should be 2, 6. Number lists indicate electrons in shells.

56. Which of the following statements about radiant energy is **not** true?

A. The energy change of an electron transition is directly proportional to the wavelength of the emitted or absorbed photon.
B. The energy of an electron in a hydrogen atom depends only on the principle quantum number.
C. The frequency of photons striking a metal determines whether the photoelectric effect will occur.
D. The frequency of a wave of electromagnetic radiation is inversely proportional to its wavelength.

A. The energy change (ΔE) is <u>inversely</u> proportional to the wavelength (λ) of the photon according the equations:

$$\Delta E = \frac{hc}{\lambda}.$$

where h is Planck's constant and c is the speed of light.

Choice B is true for hydrogen. Atoms with more than one electron are more complex. The frequency of individual photons, not the number of photons determines whether the photoelectric effect occurs, so choice C is true. Choice D is true. The proportionality constant is the speed of light according to the equation:

$$\nu = \frac{c}{\lambda}.$$

TEACHER CERTIFICATION EXAM

57. **Match the orbital diagram for the ground state of carbon with the rule/principle it violates:**

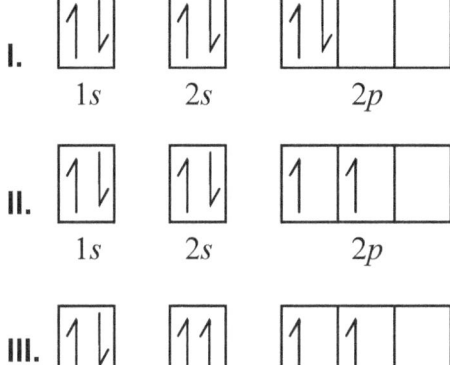

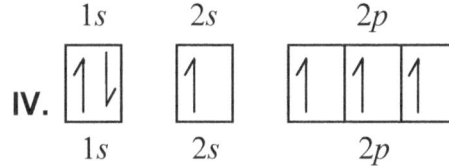

A. I-Pauli exclusion, II-Aufbau, III-no violation, IV-Hund's
B. I-Aufbau, II-Pauli exclusion, III-no violation, IV-Hund's
C. I-Hund's, II-no violation, III-Pauli exclusion, IV-Aufbau
D. I-Hund's, II-no violation, III-Aufbau, IV-Pauli exclusion

C. Diagram I violates Hund's rule because a second electron is added to a degenerate orbital before all orbitals in the subshell have one electron. Diagram III violates the Pauli exclusion principle because both electrons in the 2s orbital have the same spin. They would have the same 4 quantum numbers. Diagram IV violates the Aufbau principle because an electron occupies the higher energy 2p orbital before 2s orbital has been filled; this configuration is not at the ground state.

58. **Select the list of atoms that are arranged in order of increasing size.**

A. Mg, Na, Si, Cl
B. Si, Cl, Mg, Na
C. Cl, Si, Mg, Na
D. Na, Mg, Si, Cl

C. These atoms are all in the same row of the periodic table. Size increases further to the left for atoms in the same row.

TEACHER CERTIFICATION EXAM

59. Based on trends in the periodic table, which of the following properties would you expect to be greater for Rb than for K?

I. Density
II. Melting point
III. Ionization energy
IV. Oxidation number in a compound with chlorine

A. I only
B. I, II, and III
C. II and III
D. I, II, III, and IV

A. Rb is underneath K in the alkali metal column (group 1) of the periodic table. There is a general trend for density to increase lower on the table for elements in the same row, so we select choice I. Rb and K experience metallic bonds for intermolecular forces and the strength of metallic bonds decreases for larger atoms further down the periodic table resulting in a lower melting point for Rb, so we do not choose II. Ionization energy decreases for larger atoms further down the periodic table, so we do not choose III. Both Rb and K would be expected to have a charge of +1 and therefore an oxidation number of +1 in a compound with chlorine, so we do not choose IV.

60. Which oxide forms the strongest acid in water?

A. Al_2O_3
B. Cl_2O_7
C. As_2O_5
D. CO_2

B. The strength of acids formed from oxides increases with electronegativity and with oxidation state. We know Cl has a greater electronegativity than Al, As, and C because it is closer to the top right of the periodic table. The oxidation numbers of our choices are +3 for Al, +7 for Cl, +5 for As, and +4 for C. Both its electronegativity and its oxidation state indicate Cl_2O_7 will form the strongest acid.

CHEMISTRY

61. Rank the following bonds from least to most polar:

C-H, C-Cl, H-H, C-F

A. C-H < H-H < C-F < C-Cl
B. H-H < C-H < C-F < C-Cl
C. C-F < C-Cl < C-H < H-H
D. H-H < C-H < C-Cl < C-F

D. Bonds between atoms of the same element are completely non-polar, so H-H is the least polar bond in the list, eliminating choices A and C. The C-H bond is considered to be non-polar even though the electrons of the bond are slightly unequally shared. C-Cl and C-F are both polar covalent bonds, but C-F is more strongly polar because F has a greater electronegativity.

62. At room temperature, $CaBr_2$ is expected to be:

A. a ductile solid
B. a brittle solid
C. a soft solid
D. a gas

B. Ca is a metal because it is on the left of the periodic table, and Br is a non-metal because it is on the right. The compound they form together will be an ionic salt, and ionic salts are brittle solids (choice B) at room temperature. NaCl is another example.

63. Which of the following is a proper Lewis dot structure of CHClO?

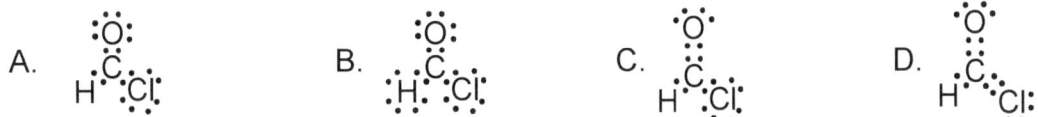

C. C has 4 valence shell electrons, H has 1, Cl has 7, and O has 6. The molecule has a total of 18 valence shell electrons. This eliminates choice B which has 24. Choice B is also incorrect because has an octet around a hydrogen atom instead of 2 electrons and because there are only six electrons surrounding the central carbon. A single bond connecting all atoms would give choice A. This is incorrect because there are only 6 electrons surrounding the central carbon. A double bond between C and O gives the correct answer, C. A double bond between C and O and also between C and Cl would give choice D. This is incorrect because there are 10 electrons surrounding the central carbon.

64. In C_2H_2, each carbon atom contains the following valence orbitals:

A. *p* only
B. *p* and *sp* hybrids
C. *p* and sp^2 hybrids
D. sp^3 hybrids only

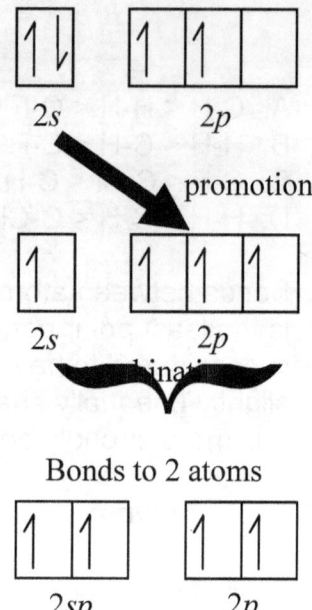

B. An isolated C has the valence electron configuration $2s^2 2p^2$. Before bonding, one *s* electron is promoted to an empty *p* orbital. In C_2H_2, each C atom bonds to 2 other atoms. Bonding to two other atoms is achieved by combination into two *p* orbitals and two *sp* hybrids.

65. Which statement about molecular structures is false?

A. [structure of H₂C=CH–CH=CH₂] is a conjugated molecule.

B. A bonding σ orbital connects two atoms by the straight line between them.
C. A bonding π orbital connects two atoms in a separate region from the straight line between them.
D. The anion with resonance forms will always exist in one form or the other.

D. A conjugated molecule is a molecule with double bonds on adjacent atoms such as the molecule shown in A. Choice B and C give the definition of sigma and pi molecular orbitals. D is false because a resonance form is one of multiple equivalent Lewis structures, but these structures do not describe the actual state of the molecule. The anion will exist in a state between the two forms.

66. **What is the shape of the PH₃ molecule? Use the VSEPR model.**

   A. Trigonal pyramidal
   B. Trigonal bipyramidal
   C. Trigonal planar
   D. Tetrahedral

A. The Lewis structure for PH₃ is given to the right. This structure contains 4 electron pairs around the central atom, so the geometral arrangement is tetrahedral. However, the shape of 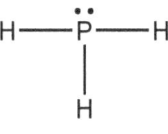 a molecule is given by its atom locations, and there are only three atoms so choice D is not correct. Four electrons pairs with one unshared pair (3 bonds and one lone pair) give a 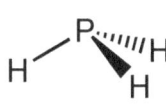 trigonal pyramidal shape as shown to the left.

TEACHER CERTIFICATION EXAM

67. What is the chemical composition of magnesium nitrate?

A. 11.1% Mg, 22.2% N, 66.7% O
B. 16.4% Mg, 18.9% N, 64.7% O
C. 20.9% Mg, 24.1% N, 55.0% O
D. 28.2% Mg, 16.2% N, 55.7% O

B. First find the formula for magnesium nitrate. Mg is an alkali earth metal (**Skill 3.1**) and will always have a 2+ charge. The nitrate ion is NO_3^- (**Skill 5.2**). Two nitrate ions are required for each Mg^{2+} ion. Therefore the formula is $Mg(NO_3)_2$

Skill 5.1 describes determination chemical composition.
  1) Determine the number of atoms for elemen in $Mg(NO_3)_2$: 1 Mg, 2 N, 6 O.
  2) Multiply by the molecular weight of the elements to determine the grams of each in one mole of the formula.

$$\frac{1 \text{ mol Mg}}{\text{mol Mg(NO}_3)_2} \times \frac{24.3 \text{ g Mg}}{\text{mol Mg}} = 24.3 \text{ g Mg/mol Mg(NO}_3)_2$$

$$2(14.0) = 28.0 \text{ g N/mol Mg(NO}_3)_2$$

$$6(16.0) = 96.0 \text{ g O/mol Mg(NO}_3)_2$$

  3) Determine formula mass $\quad$ 148.3 g $Mg(NO_3)_2$/mol $Mg(NO_3)_2$
  4) Divide to determine % composition

$$\%Mg = \frac{24.3 \text{ g Mg/mol Mg(NO}_3)_2}{148.3 \text{ g Mg(NO}_3)_2/\text{mol Mg(NO}_3)_2} = 0.164 \text{ g Mg/g Mg(NO}_3)_2 \times 100\% = 16.4\%$$

$$\%N = \frac{28.0}{148.3} \times 100\% = 18.9\% \qquad \%O = \frac{96.0}{148.3} \times 100\% = 64.7\%$$

Answer A is the fractional representation of the presence of each atom in the formula. Composition is based on mass percentage. Answer C is the chemical composition of $Mg(NO_2)_2$, magnesium nitrite. Answer D is the chemical composition of "$MgNO_3$", a formula that results from not balancing charges.

TEACHER CERTIFICATION EXAM

68. The IUPAC name for Cu_2SO_3 is:

   A. Dicopper sulfur trioxide
   B. Copper (II) sulfate
   C. Copper (I) sulfite
   D. Copper (II) sulfite

C. Cu_2SO_3 is an ionic compound containing copper cation and the SO_3 anion. Choice A is wrong because it uses the naming system for molecular compounds. The SO_3 anion is 2– and is named sulfite. It takes two copper cations in to neutralize this charge, so Cu has a charge of 1+, and the name is copper (I) sulfite.

69. Which name or formula is not represented properly?

   A. Cl_4S
   B. $KClO_3$
   C. Calcium dihydrogen phosphate
   D. Sulfurous acid

A A is the answer because the atoms in the sulfur tetrachloride molecule are placed in order of increasing electronegativity. This formla is properly written as SCl_4. B is a proper formula for potassium chlorate. Calcium dihydrogen phosphate is $Ca(H_2PO_4)_2$. It derives its name from the Ca^{2+} cation in combination with an anion composed of a phosphate anion (PO_4^{3-}) that is doubly protonated to give a $H_2PO_4^-$ ion. Sulfurous acid is $H_2SO_3(aq)$.

70. Household "chlorine bleach" is sodium hypochlorite. Which of the following best represent the production of sodium hypochlorite, sodium chloride, and water by bubbling chlorine gas through aqueous sodium hydroxide?

   A. $4Cl(g) + 4NaOH(aq) \rightarrow NaClO_2(aq) + 3NaCl(aq) + 2H_2O(l)$
   B. $2Cl_2(g) + 4NaOH(aq) \rightarrow NaClO_2(aq) + 3NaCl(aq) + 2H_2O(l)$
   C. $2Cl(g) + 2NaOH(aq) \rightarrow NaClO(aq) + NaCl(aq) + H_2O(l)$
   D. $Cl_2(g) + 2NaOH(aq) \rightarrow NaClO(aq) + NaCl(aq) + H_2O(l)$

D. Chlorine gas is a diatomic molecule, eliminating choices A and C. The hypochlorite ion is ClO^- eliminating choices A and B. All of the equations are properly balanced.

CHEMISTRY

TEACHER CERTIFICATION EXAM

71. Balance the equation for the neutralization reaction between phosphoric acid and calcium hydroxide by filling in the blank stoichiometric coefficients.

$$\_\_H_3PO_4 + \_\_Ca(OH)_2 \rightarrow \_\_Ca_3(PO_4)_2 + \_\_H_2O$$

A. 4, 3, 1, 4
B. 2, 3, 1, 8
C. 2, 3, 1, 6
D. 2, 1, 1, 2

C. We are given the unbalanced equation (**step 1**).

Next we determine the number of atoms on each side (**step 2**). For reactants (left of the arrow): 5H, 1P, 6O, and 1Ca. For products: 2H, 2P, 9O, and 3Ca.

We assume that the molecule with the most atoms—i.e. $Ca_3(PO_4)_2$—has a coefficient of one, and find the other coefficients required to have the same number of atoms on each side of the equation (**step 3**). Assuming $Ca_3(PO_4)_2$ has a coefficient of one means that there will be 3 Ca and 2 P on the right because H_2O has no Ca or P. A balanced equation would also have 3 Ca and 2 P on the left. This is achieved with a coefficient of 2 for H_3PO_4 and 3 for $Ca(OH)_2$. Now we have:

$$2H_3PO_4 + 3Ca(OH)_2 \rightarrow Ca_3(PO_4)_2 + ?H_2O$$

The coefficient for H_2O is found by a balance on H or on O. Whichever one is chosen, the other atom should be checked to confirm that a balance actually occurs. For H, there are 6 H from $2H_3PO_4$ and 6 from $3Ca(OH)_2$ for a total of 12 H on the left. There must be 12 H on the right for balance. None are accounted for by $Ca_3(PO_4)_2$, so all 12 H must occur on H_2O. It has a coefficient of 6.

$$2H_3PO_4 + 3Ca(OH)_2 \rightarrow Ca_3(PO_4)_2 + 6H_2O$$

This is choice C, but if time is available, it is best to check that the remaining atom is balanced. There are 8 O from $2H_3PO_4$ and 6 from $3Ca(OH)_2$ for a total of 14 on the left, and 8 O from $Ca_3(PO_4)_2$ and 6 from $6H_2O$ for a total of 14 on the right. The equation is balanced.

Mulitplication by a whole number (**step 4**) is not required because the stoichiometric coefficients from step 3 already are whole numbers.

An alternative method would be to try the coefficients given for answer A, answer B, etc. until we recognize a properly balanced equation.

72. **Write an equation showing the reaction between calcium nitrate and lithium sulfate in aqueous solution. Include all products.**

   A. $CaNO_3(aq) + Li_2SO_4(aq) \rightarrow CaSO_4(s) + Li_2NO_3(aq)$
   B. $Ca(NO_3)_2(aq) + Li_2SO_4(aq) \rightarrow CaSO_4(s) + 2LiNO_3(aq)$
   C. $Ca(NO_3)_2(aq) + Li_2SO_4(aq) \rightarrow 2LiNO_3(s) + CaSO_4(aq)$
   D. $Ca(NO_3)_2(aq) + Li_2SO_4(aq) + 2H_2O(l) \rightarrow 2LiNO_3(aq) + Ca(OH)_2(aq) + H_2SO_4(aq)$

B. When two ionic compounds are in solution, a precipitation reaction should be considered. We can determine from their names that the two reactants are the ionic compounds $Ca(NO_3)_2$ and Li_2SO_4. The compounds are present in aqueous solution as their four component ions Ca^{2+}, NO_3^-, Li^+, and SO_4^{2-}. Solubility rules indicate that nitrates are always soluble but sulfate will form a solid precipitate with Ca^{2+} forming $CaSO_4(s)$. Choice A results from assuming that the nitrate anion has a 2– charge instead of its 1– charge. B is correct. C assumes lithium nitrate is the precipitate. Choice D includes the reverse of a neutralization reaction. Water would not decompose due to the addition of these salts.

73. **Find the mass of CO_2 produced by the combustion of 15 kg of isopropyl alcohol in the reaction:**

$$2C_3H_7OH + 9O_2 \rightarrow 6CO_2 + 8H_2O$$

   A. 33 kg
   B. 44 kg
   C. 50 kg
   D. 60 kg

A Remember "grams to moles to moles to grams." Step 1 converts mass to moles for the known value. In this case, kg and kmol are used. Step 2 relates moles of the known value to moles of the unknown value by their stoichiometry coefficients. Step 3 converts moles off the unknown value to a mass.

$$15 \times 10^3 \text{ g } C_4H_8O \times \underbrace{\frac{1 \text{ mol } C_4H_8O}{60 \text{ g } C_4H_8O}}_{\text{step 1}} \times \underbrace{\frac{6 \text{ mol } CO_2}{2 \text{ mol } C_4H_8O}}_{\text{step 2}} \times \underbrace{\frac{44 \text{ g } CO_2}{1 \text{ mol } CO_2}}_{\text{step 3}} = 33 \times 10^3 \text{ g } CO_2$$

$$= 33 \text{ kg } CO_2$$

TEACHER CERTIFICATION EXAM

74. What is the density of nitrogen gas at STP? Assume an ideal gas and a value of 0.08206 L-atm/(mol-K) for the gas constant.

   A. 0.62 g/L
   B. 1.14 g/L
   C. 1.25 g/L
   D. 2.03 g/L

C The molecular mass M of N_2 is 28.0 g/mol.

$$d = \frac{nM}{V} = \frac{PM}{RT} = \frac{(1\,\text{atm})\left(28.0\,\frac{g}{mol}\right)}{\left(0.08206\,\frac{L\cdot atm}{mol\cdot K}\right)(273.15\,K)} = 1.25\,\frac{g}{L}$$

Choice A results from forgetting that nitrogen is a diatomic gas. Choice B results from using a value of 25 °C for standard temperature. This is the thermodynamic standard temperature, but not STP.

A faster method is to recall that one mole of an ideal gas at STP occupies 22.4 L.

$$d\,(\text{in}\,\tfrac{g}{L}) = \frac{M\,(\text{in}\,\tfrac{g}{mol})}{22.4\,\tfrac{L}{mol}} = \frac{28.0\,\tfrac{g}{mol}}{22.4\,\tfrac{L}{mol}} = 1.25\,\tfrac{g}{L}.$$

75. Find the volume of methane that will produce 12 m³ of hydrogen in the reaction: $CH_4(g) + H_2O(g) \rightarrow CO(g) + 3H_2(g)$. Assume temperature and pressure remain constant.

   A. 4.0 m³
   B. 32 m³
   C. 36 m³
   D. 64 m³

A Stoichiometric coefficients may be used directly for ideal gas volumes at constant T and P because of Avogadro's Law.

$$12\,m^3\,H_2 \times \frac{1\,m^3\,CH_4}{3\,m^3\,H_2} = 4.0\,m^3\,CH_4$$

12 g of H_2 will be produced from 32 g of CH_4 (incorrect choice B).

CHEMISTRY

76. A 100. L vessel of pure O_2 at 500. kPa and 20. °C is used for the combustion of butane:

$$2C_4H_{10} + 13O_2 \rightarrow 8CO_2 + 10H_2O.$$

Find the mass of butane to consume all the O_2 in the vessel. Assume O_2 is an ideal gas and use a value of $R = 8.314$ J/(mol•K).

A. 183 g
B. 467 g
C. 1.83 kg
D. 7.75 kg

A We are given a volume and asked for a mass. The steps will be "volume to moles to moles to mass."

"Volume to moles…" requires the ideal gas law, but first several units must be altered.
  Units of joules are identical to $m^3 \cdot Pa$.
  500 kPa is 500×10^3 Pa.
  100 L is 0.100 m^3.
  20 °C is 293.15 K.
$PV = nRT$ is rearranged to give:

$$n = \frac{PV}{RT} = \frac{(500 \times 10^3 \text{ Pa})(0.100 \text{ m}^3 \text{ O}_2)}{\left(8.314 \, \frac{\text{m}^3 \cdot \text{Pa}}{\text{mol} \cdot \text{K}}\right)(293.15 \text{ K})} = 20.51 \text{ mol O}_2$$

"…to moles to mass" utilizes stoichiometry. The molecular weight of butane is 58.1 u.

$$20.51 \text{ mol O}_2 \times \frac{2 \text{ mol C}_4\text{H}_{10}}{13 \text{ mol O}_2} \times \frac{58.1 \text{ g C}_4\text{H}_{10}}{1 \text{ mol C}_4\text{H}_{10}} = 183 \text{ g C}_4\text{H}_{10}$$

77. Consider the reaction between iron and hydrogen chloride gas:
$$Fe(s) + 2HCl(g) \rightarrow FeCl_2(s) + H_2(g).$$

7 moles of iron and 10 moles of HCl react until the limiting reagent is consumed. Which statements are true?

I. HCl is the excess reagent
II. HCl is the limiting reagent
III. 7 moles of H_2 are produced
IV. 2 moles of the excess reagent remain

A. I and III
B. I and IV
C. II and III
D. II and IV

D The limiting reagent is found by dividing the number of moles of each reactant by its stoichiometric coefficient. The lowest result is the limiting reagent.

$$7 \text{ mol Fe} \times \frac{1 \text{ mol reaction}}{1 \text{ mol Fe}} = 7 \text{ mol reaction if Fe is limiting}$$

$$10 \text{ mol HCl} \times \frac{1 \text{ mol reaction}}{2 \text{ mol HCl}} = 5 \text{ mol reaction if HCl is limiting.}$$

Therefore, HCl is the limiting reagent (II is true) and Fe is the excess reagent.

5 moles of the reaction take place, so 5 moles of H_2 are produced, and of the 7 moles of Fe supplied, 5 are consumed, leaving 2 moles of the excess reagent (IV is true).

TEACHER CERTIFICATION EXAM

78. 32.0 g of hydrogen and 32.0 grams of oxygen react to form water until the limiting reagent is consumed. What is present in the vessel after the reaction is complete?

A. 16.0 g O_2 and 48.0 g H_2O
B. 24.0 g H_2 and 40.0 g H_2O
C. 28.0 g H_2 and 36.0 g H_2O
D. 28.0 g H_2 and 34.0 g H_2O

C First the equation must be constructed:
$$2H_2 + O_2 \rightarrow 2H_2O$$

A fast and intuitive solution would be to recognize that:
1) One mole of H_2 is about 2.0 g, so about 16 moles of H_2 are present.
2) One mole of O_2 is 32.0 g, so one mole of is O_2 is present
3) Imagine the 16 moles of H_2 reacting with one mole of O_2. 2 moles of H_2 will be consumed before the one mole of O_2 is gone. O_2 is limiting. (Eliminate choice A.)
4) 16 moles less 2 leaves 14 moles of H_2 or about 28 g. (Eliminate choice B.)
5) The reaction began with 64.0 g total. Conservation of mass for chemical reactions forces the total final mass to be 64.0 g also. (Eliminate choice D.)

A more standard solution is presented next. First, mass is converted to moles:

$$32.0 \text{ g } H_2 \times \frac{1 \text{ mol } H_2}{2.016 \text{ g } H_2} = 15.87 \text{ mol } H_2 \quad \text{and} \quad 32.0 \text{ g } O_2 \times \frac{1 \text{ mol } O_2}{32.00 \text{ g } O_2} = 1.000 \text{ mol } O_2$$

Dividing by stoichiometric coefficients give

$$15.87 \text{ mol } H_2 \times \frac{1 \text{ mol reaction}}{2 \text{ mol } H_2} = 7.935 \text{ mol reaction if } H_2 \text{ is limiting}$$

$$1.000 \text{ mol } O_2 \times \frac{1 \text{ mol reaction}}{1 \text{ mol } O_2} = 1.000 \text{ mol reaction if } O_2 \text{ is limiting.}$$

O_2 is the limiting reagent, so no O_2 will remain in the vessel.

$$1.000 \text{ mol } O_2 \text{ consumed} \times \frac{2 \text{ mol } H_2O \text{ produced}}{1 \text{ mol } O_2} \times \frac{18.016 \text{ g } H_2O}{1 \text{ mol } H_2O} = 36.0 \text{ g } H_2O \text{ produced}$$

$$1.000 \text{ mol } O_2 \text{ consumed} \times \frac{2 \text{ mol } H_2 \text{ consumed}}{1 \text{ mol } O_2} \times \frac{2.016 \text{ g } H_2}{1 \text{ mol } H_2} = 4.03 \text{ g } H_2 \text{ consumed}$$

Remaining H_2 is found from:
32.0 g H_2 initially − 4.03 g H_2 consumed = 28.0 g H_2 remain.

79. Three experiments were performed at the same initial temperature and pressure to determine the rate of the reaction
$$2ClO_2(g) + F_2(g) \rightarrow 2ClO_2F(g).$$
Results are shown in the table below. Concentrations are given in millimoles per liter (mM).

Exp.	Initial [ClO$_2$] (mM)	Initial [F$_2$] (mM)	Initial rate of [ClO$_2$F] increase (mM/sec)
1	5.0	5.0	0.63
2	5.0	20	2.5
3	10	10	2.5

What is the rate law for this reaction?

A. Rate = $k[F_2]$

B. Rate = $k[ClO_2][F_2]$

C. Rate = $k[ClO_2]^2[F_2]$

D. Rate = $k[ClO_2][F_2]^2$

B A four-fold increase in [F$_2$] at constant [ClO$_2$] between experiment one and two caused a four-fold increase in rate. Rate is therefore proportional to [F$_2$] at constant [ClO$_2$], eliminating choice D (Choice D predicts rate to increase by a factor of 16).

Between experiment 1 and 3, [F$_2$] and [ClO$_2$] both double in value. Once again, there is a four-fold increase in rate. If rate were only dependent on [F$_2$] (choice A), there would be a two-fold increase. The correct answer, B, attributes a two-fold increase in rate to the doubling of [F$_2$] and a two-fold increase to the doubling of [ClO$_2$], resulting in a net four-fold increase. Choice C predicts a rate increase by a factor of 8.

If this were an elementary reaction describing a collision event between three molecules, choice C would be expected, but stoichiometry cannot be used to predict a rate law.

80. The reaction
$$(CH_3)_3CBr(aq) + OH^-(aq) \rightarrow (CH_3)_3COH(aq) + Br^-(aq)$$
occurs in three elementary steps:
$$(CH_3)_3CBr \rightarrow (CH_3)_3C^+ + Br^- \text{ is slow}$$
$$(CH_3)_3C^+ + H_2O \rightarrow (CH_3)_3COH_2^+ \text{ is fast}$$
$$(CH_3)_3COH_2^+ + OH^- \rightarrow (CH_3)_3COH + H_2O \text{ is fast}$$
What is the rate law for this reaction?

A. Rate = $k[(CH_3)_3CBr]$
B. Rate = $k[OH^-]$
C. Rate = $k[(CH_3)_3CBr][OH^-]$
D. Rate = $k[(CH_3)_3CBr]^2$

A The first step will be rate-limiting. It will determine the rate for the entire reaction because it is slower than the other steps. This step is a unimolecular process with the rate given by answer A. Choice C would be correct if the reaction as a whole were one elementary step instead of three, but the stoichiometry of a reaction composed of multiple elementary steps cannot be used to predict a rate law.

81. Which statement about equilibrium is <u>not</u> true?

A. Equilibrium shifts to minimize the impact of changes.
B. Forward and reverse reactions have equal rates at equilibrium.
C. A closed container of air and water is at a vapor-liquid equilibrium if the humidity is constant.
D. The equilibrium between solid and dissolved forms is maintained when salt is added to an unsaturated solution.

D Choice A is a restatement of Le Chatelier's Principle. B is a definition of equilibrium. A constant humidity (Choice C) occurs if the rate of vaporization and condensation are equal, indicating equilibrium. No solid is present in an **un**saturated solution. If solid is added, all of it dissolves indicating a lack of equilibrium. D would be true for a saturated soution.

TEACHER CERTIFICATION EXAM

82. Which statements about reaction rates are true?

   I. A catalyst will shift an equilibrium to favor product formation.
   II. Catalysts increase the rate of forward and reverse reactions.
   III. A greater temperature increases the chance that a molecular collision will overcome a reaction's activation energy.
   IV. A catalytic converter contains a homogeneous catalyst.

   A. I and II
   B. II and III
   C. II, III and IV
   D. I, III, and IV

B Catalysts provide an alternate mechanism in both directions, but do not alter equilibrium (I is false, II is true). The kinetic energy of molecules increases with temperature, so the energy of their collisions increases also (III is true). Catalytic converters contain a heterogeneous catalyst (IV is false).

83. Write the equilibrium expression K_{eq} for the reaction
   $CO_2(g) + H_2(g) \rightleftharpoons CO(g) + H_2O(l)$

   A. $\dfrac{[CO][H_2O]}{[CO_2][H_2]^2}$

   B. $\dfrac{[CO_2][H_2]}{[CO][H_2O]}$

   C. $\dfrac{[CO][H_2O]}{[CO_2][H_2]}$

   D. $\dfrac{[CO]}{[CO_2][H_2]}$

D Product concentrations are multiplied together in the numerator and reactant concentrations in the denominator, eliminating choice B. The stoichiometric coefficient of H_2 is one, eliminating choice A. For heterogeneous reactions, concentrations of pure liquids or solids are absent from the expression because they are constant, eliminating choice C. D is correct.

84. What could cause this change in the energy diagram of a reaction?

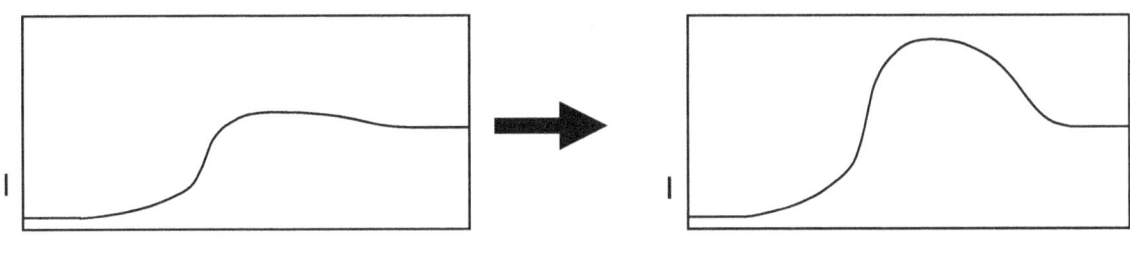

A. Adding catalyst to an endothermic reaction
B. Removing catalyst from an endothermic reaction
C. Adding catalyst to an exothermic reaction
D. Removing catalyst from an exothermic reaction

B The products at the end of the reaction pathway are at a greater energy than the reactants, so the reaction is endothermic (narrowing down the answer to A or B). The maximum height on the diagram corresponds to activation energy. An increase in activation energy could be caused by removing a heterogeneous catalyst.

85. $BaSO_4$ (K_{sp} = 1×10^{-10}) is added to pure H_2O. How much is dissolved in 1 L of saturated solution?

A. 2 mg
B. 10 µg
C. 2 µg
D. 100 pg

A $BaSO_4(s) \rightleftharpoons Ba^{2+}(aq) + SO_4^{2-}(aq)$, therefore: $K_{sp} = [Ba^{2+}][SO_4^{2-}]$.

In a saturated solution: $[Ba^{2+}] = [SO_4^{2-}] = \sqrt{1 \times 10^{-10}} = 1 \times 10^{-5}$ M.

The mass in one liter is found from the molarity:

$$1 \times 10^{-5} \frac{\text{mol } Ba^{2+} \text{ or } SO_4^{2-}}{L} \times \frac{1 \text{ mol dissolved } BaSO_4}{1 \text{ mol } Ba^{2+} \text{ or } SO_4^{2-}} \times \frac{(137 + 32 + 4 \times 16) \text{g } BaSO_4}{1 \text{ mol } BaSO_4}$$

$$= 0.002 \frac{g}{L} BaSO_4 \times 1 \text{ L solution} \times \frac{1000 \text{ mg}}{g} = 2 \text{ mg } BaSO_4$$

TEACHER CERTIFICATION EXAM

86. The exothermic reaction $2NO(g) + Br_2(g) \rightleftharpoons 2NOBr(g)$ is at equilibrium. According to LeChatelier's principle:

   A. Adding Br_2 will increase [NO].
   B. An increase in container volume (with T constant) will increase [NOBr].
   C. An increase in pressure (with T constant) will increase [NOBr].
   D. An increase in temperature (with P constant) will increase [NOBr].

C LeChatelier's principle predicts that equilibrium will shift to partially offset any change. Adding Br_2 will be partially offset by reducing $[Br_2]$ and [NO] via a shift to the right (not choice A). For the remaining possibilities, we may write the reaction as: 3 moles $\rightleftharpoons$ 2 moles + heat. An increase in container volume will decrease pressure. This change will be partially offset by increasing the number of moles present, shifting the reaction to the left (not choice B). An increase in pressure will be offset by a decrease the number of moles present, shifting the reaction to the right (choice C, correct). Raising the temperature by adding heat will shift the reaction to the left (not choice D).

87. At a certain temperature, T, the equilibrium constant for the reaction $2NO(g) \rightleftharpoons N_2(g) + O_2(g)$ is $K_{eq} = 2 \times 10^3$. If a 1.0 L container at this temperature contains 90 mM N_2, 20 mM O_2, and 5 mM NO, what will occur?

   A. The reaction will make more N_2 and O_2.
   B. The reaction is at equilibrium.
   C. The reaction will make more NO.
   D. The temperature, T, is required to solve this problem.

A Calculate the reaction quotient at the actual conditions:
$$Q = \frac{[N_2][O_2]}{[NO]^2} = \frac{(0.090 \text{ M})(0.020 \text{ M})}{(0.005 \text{ M})^2} = 72$$

This value is less than K_{eq}: $72 < 2 \times 10^3$, therefore $Q < K_{eq}$. To achieve equilibrium, the numerator of Q must be larger relative to the denominator. This occurs when products turn into reactants. Therefore NO will react to make more N_2 and O_2.

88. Which statement about acids and bases is not true?

   A. All strong acids ionize in water.
   B. All Lewis acids accept an electron pair.
   C. All Brønsted bases use OH⁻ as a proton acceptor.
   D. All Arrhenius acids form H⁺ ions in water.

C   Choice A is the definition of a strong acid, choice B is the definition of a Lewis acid, and choice D is the definition of an Arrhenius acid. By definition, all Arrhenius bases form OH⁻ ions in water, and all Brønsted bases are proton acceptors. But not all Brønsted bases use OH⁻ as a proton acceptor. NH₃ is a Brønsted base for example.

89. Which of the following are listed from weakest to strongest acid?

   A. H_2SO_3, H_2SeO_3, H_2TeO_3
   B. $HBrO$, $HBrO_2$, $HBrO_3$, $HBrO_4$
   C. HI, HBr, HCl, HF
   D. H_3PO_4, $H_2PO_4^-$, HPO_4^{2-}

B   The electronegativity of the central atom decreases from S to Se to Te as period number increases in the same periodic table group. The acidity of the oxide also decreases. Choice B is correct because acid strength increases with the oxidation state of the central atom. C is wrong because HI, HBr, and HCl are all strong acids but HF is a weak acid. D is wrong because acid strength is greater for polyprotic acids.

CHEMISTRY

90. NH₄F is dissolved in water. Which of the following are conjugate acid/base pairs present in the solution?

I. NH_4^+/NH_4OH
II. HF/F^-
III. H_3O^+/H_2O
IV. H_2O/OH^-

A. I, II, and III
B. I, III, and IV
C. II and IV
D. II, III, and IV

D NH₄F is soluble in water and completely dissociates to NH_4^+ and F^-. F^- is a weak base with HF as its conjugate acid (II). NH_4^+ is a weak acid with NH_3 as its conjugate base. A conjugate acid/base pair must have the form HX/X (where X is one lower charge than HX). NH_4^+/NH_4OH (I) is not a conjugate acid/base pair, eliminating choice A and B. H_3O^+/H_2O and H_2O/OH^- (III and IV) are always present in water and in all aqueous solutions as conjugate acid/base pairs. All of the following equilibrium reactions occur in NH₄F(aq):

$$NH_4^+(aq) + OH^-(aq) \rightleftharpoons NH_3(aq) + H_2O(l)$$
$$F^-(aq) + H_3O^+(aq) \rightleftharpoons HF(aq) + H_2O(l)$$
$$2H_2O(l) \rightleftharpoons H_3O^+(aq) + OH^-(aq)$$

91. What are the pH and the pOH of 0.010 M HNO₃(aq)?

A. pH = 1.0, pOH = 9.0
B. pH = 2.0, pOH = 12.0
C. pH = 2.0, pOH = 8.0
D. pH = 8.0, pOH = 6.0

B HNO₃ is a strong acid, so it completely dissociates:
$$[H^+] = 0.010 \text{ M} = 1.0 \times 10^{-2} \text{ M}.$$
$$pH = -\log_{10}[H^+] = -\log_{10}(1.0 \times 10^{-2}) = 2.0 \text{ (choices B or C)}.$$
From pH + pOH = 14: pOH = 12.0 (choice B).

92. What is the pH of a buffer made of 0.128 M sodium formate (HCOONa) and 0.072 M formic acid (HCOOH)? The pK_a of formic acid is 3.75.

A. 2.0
B. 3.0
C. 4.0
D. 5.0

C From the pK_a, we may find the K_a of formic acid:
$$K_a = 10^{-pK_a} = 10^{-3.75} = 1.78 \times 10^{-4}$$
This is the equilibrium constant:
$$K_a = \frac{[H^+][HCOO^-]}{[HCOOH]} = 1.78 \times 10^{-4} \text{ for the dissociation:}$$
$$HCOOH \rightleftharpoons H^+ + HCOO^-.$$
The pH is found by solving for the H^+ concentration:
$$[H^+] = K_a \frac{[HCOOH]}{[HCOO^-]} = (1.78 \times 10^{-4}) \frac{0.072}{0.128} = 1.0 \times 10^{-4} \text{ M}$$
$$pH = -\log_{10}[H^+] = -\log_{10}(1.0 \times 10^{-4}) = 4.0 \text{ (choice C)}$$

93. A sample of 50.0 ml KOH is titrated with 0.100 M HClO$_4$. The initial buret reading is 1.6 ml and the reading at the endpoint is 22.4 ml. What is [KOH]?

A. 0.0416 M
B. 0.0481 M
C. 0.0832 M
D. 0.0962 M

A HClO$_4$ and KOH are both strong electrolytes. If you are good at memorizing formulas, solve the problem this way:
$$C_{unknown} = \frac{C_{known}(V_{final} - V_{initial})}{V_{unknown}} = \frac{0.100 \text{ M } (22.4 \text{ ml} - 1.6 \text{ ml})}{50.0 \text{ ml}} = 0.0416 \text{ M}.$$
The problem may also be solved by finding the moles of known substance:
$$0.100 \frac{\text{mol}}{\text{L}} \times \frac{1 \text{ L}}{1000 \text{ mL}} \times (22.4 \text{ mL} - 1.6 \text{ mL}) = 0.00208 \text{ mol HClO}_4$$
This will neutralize 0.00208 mol KOH, and $\frac{0.00208 \text{ mol}}{0.0500 \text{ L}} = 0.0416 \text{ M}$

CHEMISTRY

94. Rank the following from lowest to highest pH. Assume a small volume for the added component:

I. 0.01 mol HCl added to 1 L H_2O
II. 0.01 mol HI added to 1 L of an acetic acid/sodium acetate solution at pH 4.0
III. 0.01 mol NH_3 added to 1 L H_2O
IV. 0.1 mol HNO_3 added to 1 L of a 0.1 M $Ca(OH)_2$ solution

A. I < II < III < IV
B. I < II < IV < III
C. II < I < III < IV
D. II < I < IV < III

A HCl is a strong acid. Therefore solution I has a <u>pH of 2</u> because $pH = -\log_{10}[H^+] = -\log_{10}(0.01) = 2$.

HI is also a strong acid and would have a pH of 2 at this concentration in water, but the buffer will prevent pH from dropping this low. Solution II will have a pH <u>above 2</u> and below 4, eliminating choices C and D.

If a strong base were in solution III, its pOH would be 2. Using the equation pH + pOH = 14, its pH would be 12. Because NH_3 is a weak base, the pH of solution III will be greater than 7 and <u>less than 12</u>.

A neutralization reaction occurs in solution IV between 0.1 mol of H^+ from the strong acid HNO_3 and <u>0.2 mol of OH^-</u> from the strong base $Ca(OH)_2$. Each mole of $Ca(OH)_2$ contributes two base equivalents for the neutralization reaction. The base is the excess reagent, and 0.1 mol of OH^- remain after the reaction. This resulting solution will have a pOH of 1 and a <u>pH of 13</u>.

A is correct because: 2 < between 2 and 4 < betweeen 7 and 12 < 13

95. The curve below resulted from the titration of a _____ _____ with a _____ _____ titrant.

A. weak acid, strong base
B. weak base, strong acid
C. strong acid, strong base
D. strong base, strong acid

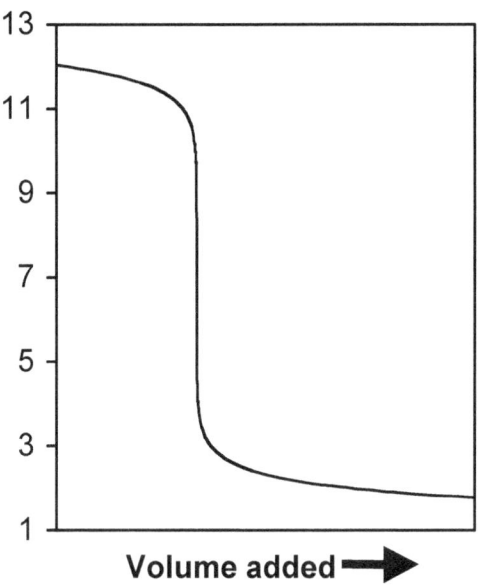

D The pH is above 7 initially and decreases, so an acid titrant is neutralizing a base. This eliminates A and C. The maximum slope (equivalence point) at the neutral pH of 7 indicates a strong base titrated with a strong acid, D.

96. Which statement about thermochemistry is true?

A. Particles in a system move about less freely at high entropy
B. Water at 100 °C has the same internal energy as water vapor at 100°C
C. A decrease in the order of a system corresponds to an increase in entropy.
D. At its sublimation temperature, dry ice has a higher entropy than gaseous CO_2

C At high entropy, particles have a large freedom of molecular motion (A is false). Water and water vapor at 100 °C contain the same translational kinetic energy, but water vapor has additional internal energy in the form of resisting the intermolecular attractions between molecules (B is false). We also know water vapor has a higher internal energy because heat must be added to boil water. Entropy may be thought of as the disorder in a system (C is correct). Sublimation is the phase change from solid to gas, and there is less freedom of motion for particles in solids than in gases. Solid CO_2 (dry ice) has a lower entropy than gaseous CO_2 because entropy decreases during a phase change that prevents molecular motion (D is false).

97. What is the heat change of 36.0 g H₂O at atmospheric pressure when its temperature is reduced from 125 °C to 40. °C? Use the following data:

A. −92.0 kJ
B. −10.8 kJ
C. 10.8 kJ
D. 92.0 kJ

Values for water

Heat capacity of solid	37.6 J/mol•°C
Heat capacity of liquid	75.3 J/mol•°C
Heat capacity of gas	33.1 J/mol•°C
Heat of fusion	6.02 kJ/mol
Heat of vaporization	40.67 kJ/mol

A Heat is evolved from the substance as it cools, so the heat change will be negative, eliminating choices C and D. Data in the table are given using moles, so the first step is to convert the mass of water to moles:

$$36.0 \text{ g } H_2O \times \frac{1 \text{ mol } H_2O}{18.02 \text{ g } H_2O} = 2.00 \text{ mol } H_2O$$

There are three contributions to the heat evolved. First, the heat evolved when cooling the vapor from 125 °C to 100 °C is found from the heat capacity of the gas:

$$q_1 = n \times C \times \Delta T = 2.00 \text{ mol } H_2O(g) \times 33.1 \frac{J}{\text{mol °C}} \times (100 \text{ °C} - 125 \text{ °C})$$

$$= -1655 \text{ J to cool vapor}$$

Next, the heat evolved during condensation is found from the heat of vaporization:

$$q_2 = n \times (-\Delta H_{vaporization}) = 2.00 \text{ mol } H_2O \times (-40.67 \frac{kJ}{mol})$$

$$= -81.34 \text{ kJ to condense vapor}$$

Incorrect answer B results from using a heat of vaporization of 40.67 J/mol instead of kJ/mol.

Finally, the heat evolved when cooling the liquid from 100 °C to 40 °C is found from the heat capacity of the liquid:

$$q_3 = n \times C \times \Delta T = 2.00 \text{ mol } H_2O(g) \times 75.3 \frac{J}{\text{mol °C}} \times (40 \text{ °C} - 100 \text{ °C})$$

$$= -9036 \text{ J to cool liquid}$$

The total heat change is the sum of these contributions:

$$q = q_1 + q_2 + q_3 = -1.655 \text{ kJ} + (-81.34 \text{ kJ}) + (-9.036 \text{ kJ}) = -92.03 \text{ kJ}$$

$$= -92.0 \text{ kJ (Choice A)}$$

98. What is the standard heat of combustion of CH₄(g)? Use the following data:

A. −890.3 kJ/mol
B. −604.5 kJ/mol
C. −252.9 kJ/mol
D. −182.5 kJ/mol

Standard heats of formation

CH₄(g)	−74.8 kJ/mol
CO₂(g)	−393.5 kJ/mol
H₂O(l)	−285.8 kJ/mol

A First we must write a balanced equation for the combustion of CH₄. The balanced equation is:

$$CH_4(g) + 2O_2(g) \rightarrow CO_2(g) + 2H_2O(l).$$

The heat of combustion may be found from the sum of the productions minus the sum of the reactants of the heats of formation:

$$\Delta H_{rxn} = H_{product\ 1} + H_{product\ 2} + \ldots - (H_{reactant\ 1} + H_{reactant\ 2} + \ldots)$$

$$= \Delta H_f^\circ(CO_2) + 2\Delta H_f^\circ(H_2O) - (\Delta H_f^\circ(CH_4) + 2\Delta H_f^\circ(O_2))$$

The heat of formation of an element in its most stable form is zero by definition, so $\Delta H_f^\circ(O_2(g)) = 0 \ \frac{kJ}{mol}$, and the remaining values are found from the table:

$$\Delta H_{rxn} = -393.5\ \frac{kJ}{mol} + 2(-285.8\ \frac{kJ}{mol}) - \left(-74.8\ \frac{kJ}{mol} + 2(0)\right) = -890.3\ \frac{kJ}{mol} \text{ (choice A)}$$

99. Which reaction creates products at a lower total entropy than the reactants?

A. Dissolution of table salt: $NaCl(s) \rightarrow Na^+(aq) + Cl^-(aq)$
B. Oxidation of iron: $4Fe(s) + 3O_2(g) \rightarrow 2Fe_2O_3(s)$
C. Dissociation of ozone: $O_3(g) \rightarrow O_2(g) + O(g)$
D. Vaporization of butane: $C_4H_{10}(l) \rightarrow C_4H_{10}(g)$

B Choice A is incorrect because two particles are at a greater entropy than one and because ions in solution have more freedom of motion than a solid. For B (the correct answer), the products are at a lower entropy than the reactants because there are fewer product molecules and they are all in the solid form but one of the reactants is a gas. Reaction B is still spontaneous because it is highly exothermic. For C, there are more product molecules than reactants, and for D, the gas phase is always at a higher entropy than the liquid.

TEACHER CERTIFICATION EXAM

100. Which statement about reactions is true?

A. All spontaneous reactions are both exothermic and cause an increase in entropy.
B. An endothermic reaction that increases the order of the system cannot be spontaneous.
C. A reaction can be non-spontaneous in one direction and also non-spontaneous in the opposite direction.
D. Melting snow is an exothermic process

B All reactions that are both exothermic and cause an increase in entropy will be spontaneous, but the converse (choice A) is not true. Some spontaneous reactions are exothermic but decrease entropy and some are endothermic and increase entropy. Choice B is correct. The reverse reaction of a non-spontaneous reaction (choice C) will be spontaneous. Melting snow (choice D) requires heat. Therefore it is an endothermic process

101. 10. kJ of heat are added to one kilogram of Iron at 10. °C. What is its final temperature? The specific heat of iron is 0.45 J/g•°C.

A. 22 °C
B. 27 °C
C. 32 °C
D. 37 °C

C The expression for heat as a function of temperature change:
$$q = n \times C \times \Delta T$$
may be rearranged to solve for the temperature change:
$$\Delta T = \frac{q}{n \times C}.$$
In this case, n is a mass and C is the specific heat of iron:
$$\Delta T = \frac{10000 \text{ J}}{1000 \text{ g} \times 0.45 \ \frac{\text{J}}{\text{g °C}}} = 22 \text{ °C}.$$
This is not the final temperature (choice A is incorrect). It is the temperature difference between the initial and final temperature.
$$\Delta T = T_{final} - T_{initial} = 22 \text{ °C}$$
Solving for the final temperature gives us:
$$T_{final} = \Delta T + T_{initial} = 22 \text{ °C} + 10 \text{ °C} = 32 \text{ °C (Choice C)}$$

CHEMISTRY

102. Which reaction is not a redox process?

A. Combustion of octane: $2C_8H_{18} + 25O_2 \rightarrow 16CO_2 + 18H_2O$
B. Depletion of a lithium battery: $Li + MnO_2 \rightarrow LiMnO_2$
C. Corrosion of aluminum by acid: $2Al + 6HCl \rightarrow 2AlCl_3 + 3H_2$
D. Taking an antacid for heartburn:
   $CaCO_3 + 2HCl \rightarrow CaCl_2 + H_2CO_3 \rightarrow CaCl_2 + CO_2 + H_2O$

D The oxidation state of atoms is altered in a redox process. During combustion (choice A), the carbon atoms are oxidized from an oxidation number of –4 to +4. Oxygen atoms are reduced from an oxidation number of 0 to –2. All batteries (choice B) generate electricity by forcing electrons from a redox process through a circuit. Li is oxidized from 0 in the metal to +1 in the LiMnO$_2$ salt. Mn is reduced from +4 in manganese(IV) oxide to +3 in lithium manganese(III) oxide salt. Corrosion (choice C) is due to oxidation. Al is oxidized from 0 to +3. H is reduced from +1 to 0. Acid-base neutralization (choice D) transfers a proton (an H atom with an oxidation state of +1) from an acid to a base. The oxidation state of all atoms remains unchanged (Ca at +2, C at +4, O at –2, H at +1, and Cl at –1), so D is correct. Note that choices C and D both involve an acid. The availability of electrons in aluminum metal favors electron transfer but the availability of CO_3^{2-} as a proton acceptor favors proton transfer.

103. Given the following heats of reaction:

$\Delta H = -0.3$ kJ/mol for $\quad$ Fe(s) + CO_2(g) → FeO(s) + CO(g)

$\Delta H = 5.7$ kJ/mol for $\quad$ 2Fe(s) + 3CO_2(g) → Fe_2O_3(s) + 3CO(g)

and $\Delta H = 4.5$ kJ/mol for $\quad$ 3FeO(s) + CO_2(g) → Fe_3O_4(s) + CO(g)

use Hess's Law to determine the heat of reaction for:

$$3Fe_2O_3(s) + CO(g) \rightarrow 2Fe_3O_4(s) + CO_2(g)?$$

A. −10.8 kJ/mol
B. −9.9 kJ/mol
C. −9.0 kJ/mol
D. −8.1 kJ/mol

B We are interested in $3Fe_2O_3$ as a reactant. Only the second reaction contains this molecule, so we will take three times the opposite of the second reaction. We are interested in $2Fe_3O_4$ as a product, so we will take two times the third reaction. An intermediate result is:

$3Fe_2O_3(s) + 9CO(g) \rightarrow 6Fe(s) + 9CO_2(g)$ $\quad\quad \Delta H = -3 \times 5.7$ kJ/mol = −17.1 kJ/mol

$6FeO(s) + 2CO_2(g) \rightarrow 2Fe_3O_4(s) + 2CO(g)$ $\quad\quad \Delta H = 2 \times 4.5$ kJ/mol = 9.0 kJ/mol

---

$3Fe_2O_3(s) + 6FeO(s) + 7CO(g) \rightarrow$
$\quad\quad 2Fe_3O_4(s) + 6Fe(s) + 7CO_2(g)$ $\quad\quad \Delta H = (-17.1 + 9.0)$ kJ/mol = −8.1 kJ/mol

However, D is not the correct answer because it is not ΔH for the reaction of the problem statement. We may use six times the first reaction to eliminate both FeO and Fe from the intermediate result and obtain the reaction of interest:

$3Fe_2O_3(s) + 6FeO(s) + 7CO(g) \rightarrow$
$\quad\quad 2Fe_3O_4(s) + 6Fe(s) + 7CO_2(g)$ $\quad\quad \Delta H = -8.1$ kJ/mol

$6Fe(s) + 6CO_2(g) \rightarrow 6FeO(s) + 6CO(g)$ $\quad\quad \Delta H = 6 \times (-0.3$ kJ/mol$) = -1.8$ kJ/mol

---

$3Fe_2O_3(s) + CO(g) \rightarrow 2Fe_3O_4(s) + CO_2(g)$ $\quad\quad \Delta H = (-8.1 + -1.8)$ kJ/mol
$\quad\quad\quad\quad\quad\quad = -9.9$ kJ/mol (choice B)

TEACHER CERTIFICATION EXAM

104. What is the oxidant in the reaction: $2H_2S + SO_2 \rightarrow 3S + 2H_2O$?

A. H_2S
B. SO_2
C. S
D. H_2O

B The S atom in H_2S has an oxidation number of –2 and is oxidized by SO_2 (the oxidant, choice B) to elemental sulfer (oxidation number = 0). The S atom in SO_2 has an oxidation number of +4 and is reduced. The two half-reactions are:

$$SO_2 + 4e^- + 4H^+ \xrightarrow{\text{reduction}} S + 2H_2O$$

$$2H_2S \xrightarrow{\text{oxidation}} 2S + 4e^- + 4H^+$$

105. Molten NaCl is subjected to electrolysis. What reaction takes place at the cathode?

A. $2Cl^-(l) \rightarrow Cl_2(g) + 2e^-$
B. $Cl_2(g) + 2e^- \rightarrow 2Cl^-(l)$
C. $Na^+(l) + e^- \rightarrow Na(l)$
D. $Na^+(l) \rightarrow Na(l) + e^-$

C Reduction (choices B and C) always occurs at the cathode. Molten NaCl is composed of ions in liquid form before electrolysis (answer C). A and D are oxidation reactions, and D is also not properly balanced because a +1 charge is on the left and a –1 charge is on the right. The two half-reactions are:

$$Na^+(l) + e^- \xrightarrow{\text{reduction at cathode}} Na(l)$$

$$2Cl^-(l) \xrightarrow{\text{oxidation at anode}} Cl_2(g) + 2e^-$$

The net reaction is:

$$2NaCl(l) \rightarrow 2Na(l) + Cl_2(g)$$

106. **What is the purpose of the salt bridge in a voltaic cell?**

   A. To receive electrons from the oxidation half-reaction
   B. To relieve the buildup of positive charge in the anode half-cell
   C. To conduct electron flow
   D. To permit positive ions to flow from the cathode half-cell to the anode half-cell

D The anode receives electrons from the oxidation half-reaction (choice A) and the circuit conducts electron flow (choice C) to the cathode which supplies electrons for the reduction half-reaction. This flow of electrons from the anode to the cathode is relieved by a flow of ions through the salt bridge from the cathode to the anode (answer D). The salt bridge relieves the buildup of positive charge in the cathode half-cell (choice B is incorrect).

107. **Given $E°=-2.37$ V for $Mg^{2+}(aq)+2e^-\to Mg(s)$ and $E°=0.80$ V for $Ag^+(aq)+e^-\to Ag(s)$, what is the standard potential of a voltaic cell composed of a piece of magnesium dipped in a 1 M Ag^+ solution and a piece of silver dipped in 1 M Mg^{2+}?**

   A. 0.77 V
   B. 1.57 V
   C. 3.17 V
   D. 3.97 V

C $Ag^+(aq)+e^-\to Ag(s)$ has a larger value for $E°$ (reduction potential) than $Mg^{2+}(aq)+2e^-\to Mg(s)$. Therefore, in the cell described, reduction will occur at the Ag electrode and it will be the cathode. Using the equation:

$$E^O_{cell} = E^O(\text{cathode}) - E^O(\text{anode}),$$ we obtain:

$$E^O_{cell} = 0.80 \text{ V} - (-2.37 \text{ V}) = 3.17 \text{ V (Answer C)}.$$

Choice D results from the incorrect assumption that electrode potentials depend on the amount of material present. The balanced net reaction for the cell is:

$$Mg(s) \to Mg^{2+}(aq) + 2e^- \qquad E^O_{ox} = 2.37 \text{ V}$$

$$2Ag^+(aq) + 2e^- \to 2Ag(s) \qquad E^O_{red} = 0.80 \text{ V (not 1.60 V)}$$

$$Mg(s) + 2Ag^+(aq) \to 2Ag(s) + Mg^{2+}(aq) \qquad E^O_{cell} = 3.17 \text{ V (not 3.97 V)}$$

108. A proper name for this hydrocarbon is:

A. 4,5-dimethyl-6-hexene
B. 2,3-dimethyl-1-hexene
C. 4,5-dimethyl-6-hexyne
D. 2-methyl-3-propyl-1-butene

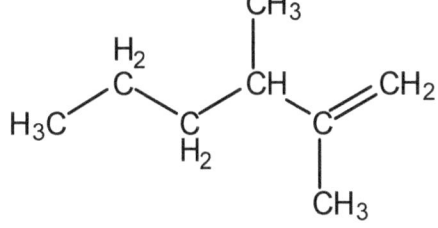

B The hydrocarbon contains a double bond and no triple bonds, so it is an alkene. Choice C describes an alkyne. The longest carbon chain is six carbons long, corresponding to a parent molecule of 1-hexene (circled to the left). Choice D is an improper name because it names the molecule as a substituted butane, using a shorter chain as the parent molecule. Finally, the lowest possible set of locant numbers must be used. Choice A is an improper name because the larger possible set of locant numbers is chosen.

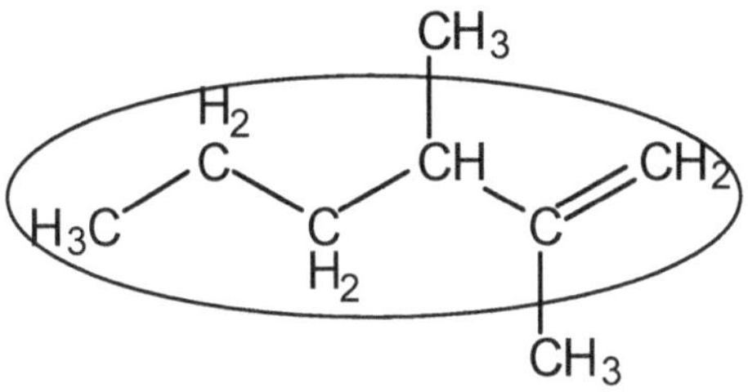

109. An IUPAC approved name for this molecule is:

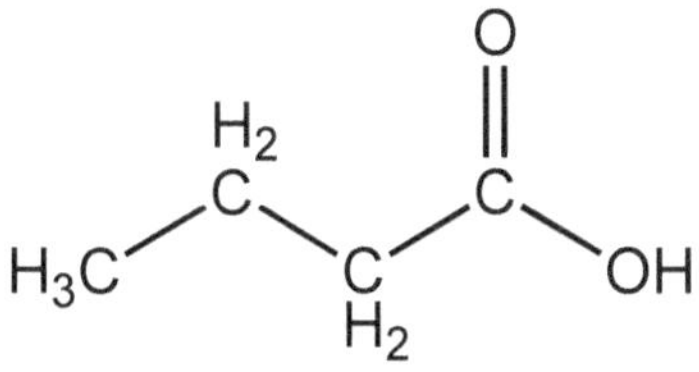

A. butanal
B. propanal
C. butanoic acid
D. propanoic acid

C The COOH group means that the molecule is a carboxylic acid and its name will use the suffix –*oic acid*. The presence of 4 carbon atoms means the prefix *butan*- will be used. An alternate name for the molecule is butyric acid. Choices A and B would be used for aldehydes (CHO group). Choices B and D would be used for 3 carbon atoms:

butanal (also called butyraldehyde):

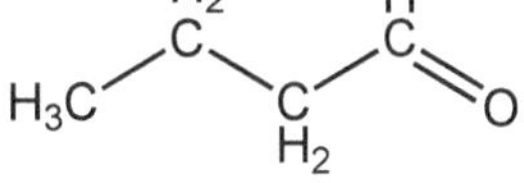

propanal (also called propionaldehyde):

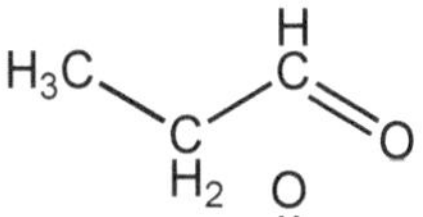

propanoic acid (also called propionic acid):

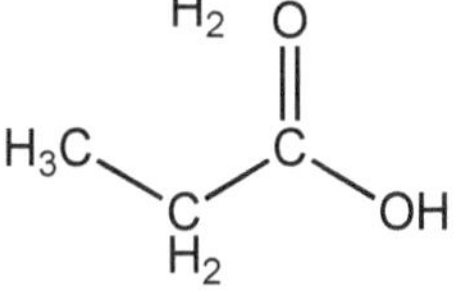

110. Which molecule has a systematic name of methyl ethanoate?

A. 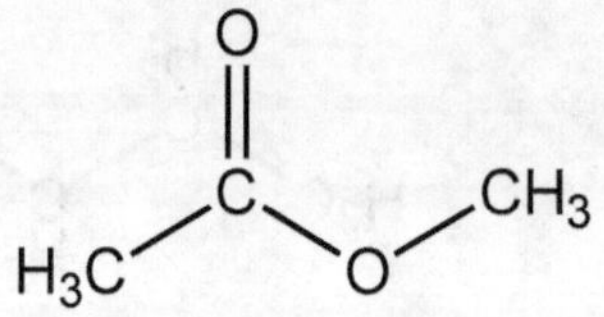 $H_3C-C(=O)-O-CH_3$

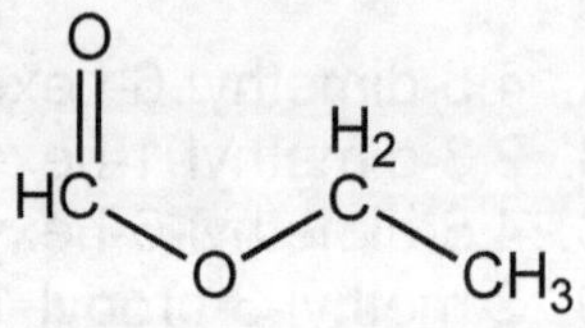

B. $HC(=O)-O-CH_2-CH_3$

C. $H_3C-C(=O)-CH_2-CH_3$

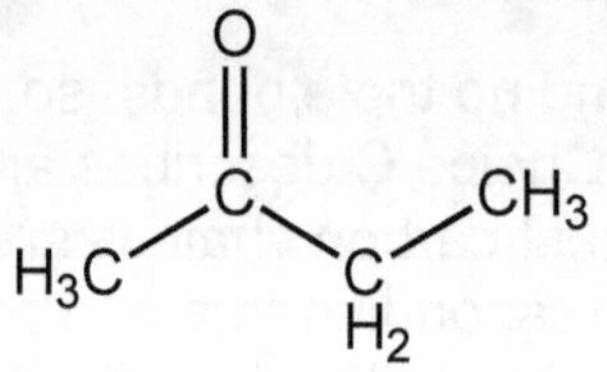

D. 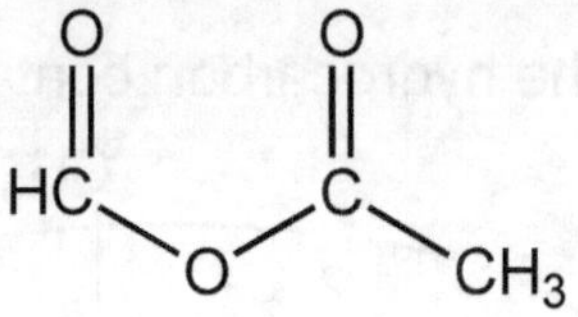 $HC(=O)-O-C(=O)-CH_3$

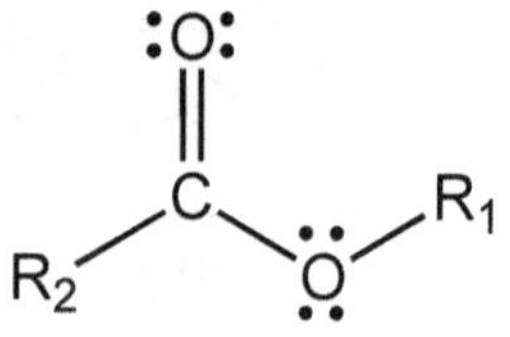

A The suffix –*oate* is used for esters. The ester group is shown to the right. Choice C is a ketone (ethyl methyl ketone or 2-butanone). The ketone group is shown to the left. Choice D is an acid anhydride (ethanoic methanoic anhydride). The acid anhydride group is shown below to the right. A and B are both esters. The hydrocarbon R_2 with the carbonyl group receives the –*oate* suffix and the hydrocarbon R_1 with the -*yl* suffix is attached to the other oxygen. Choice B is ethyl methanoate and A is correct.

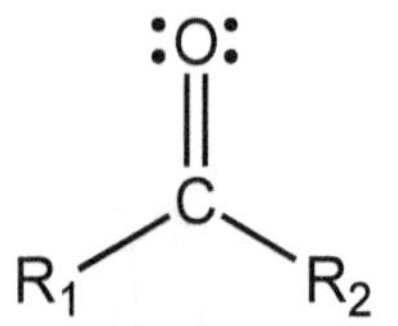

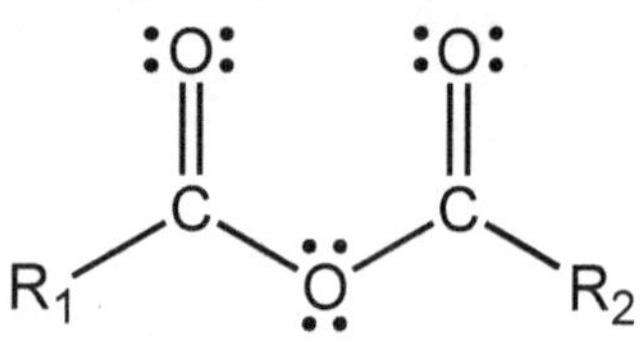

111. **This compound contains an:**

A. alkene, carboxylic acid, ester, and ketone
B. aldehyde, alkyne, ester, and ketone
C. aldehyde, alkene, carboxylic acid, and ester
D. acid anhydride, aldehyde, alkene, and amine

C The derivatives are circled below:

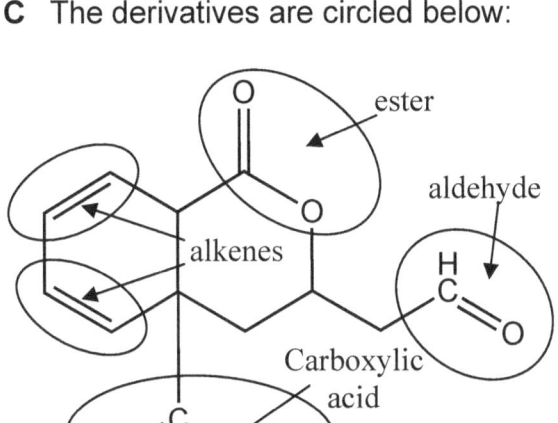

Choice A is wrong because there are no ketones in the molecule. A ketone has a carbonyl group linked to two hydrocarbons as shown to the right. All the carbonyls in the molecule are linked to at least one oxygen atom. Choice B is wrong because there are no ketones and no alkynes in the molecule. An alkyne contains a $C\equiv C$ triple bond. Choice D is wrong because there are no acid anhydrides (shown to the left) and no amines (shown to the right). Amines require at least one N-C bond and there are no nitrogen atoms in the molecule.

112. **Which group of scientists made contributions in the same area of chemistry?**

A. Volta, Kekulé, Faraday, London
B. Hess, Joule, Kelvin, Gibbs
C. Boyle, Charles, Arrhenius, Pauli
D. Davy, Mendeleev, Ramsay, Galvani

B Hess, Joule, Kelvin, and Gibbs all contributed to thermochemistry and have thermodynamic entities named after them. Volta, Faraday, and Galvani (choice D) contributed to electrochemistry, Kekulé to organic chemistry, London to chemical bonding, Boyle and Charles to gas laws, Arrhenius to acid/base chemistry and thermochemstry, Pauli to quantum theory, Davy and Ramsay to element isolation, and Mendeleev to the periodic table.

113. Which of the following pairs are isomers?

I. 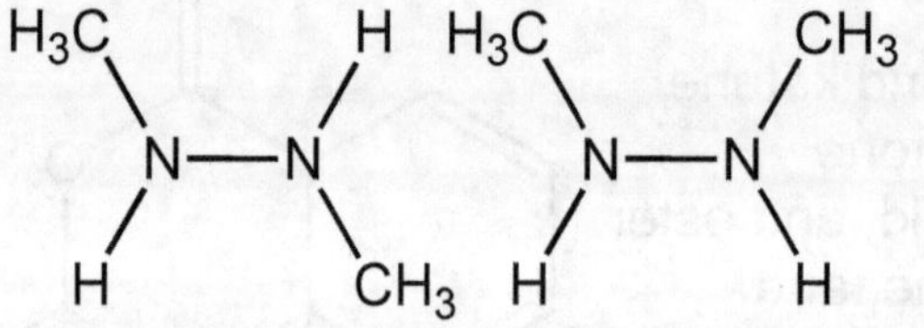 [structure: H3C-N(H)-N(H)-CH3 and H3C-N(CH3)-N(H)-H hydrazine derivatives]

II. pentanal 2-pentanone

III. 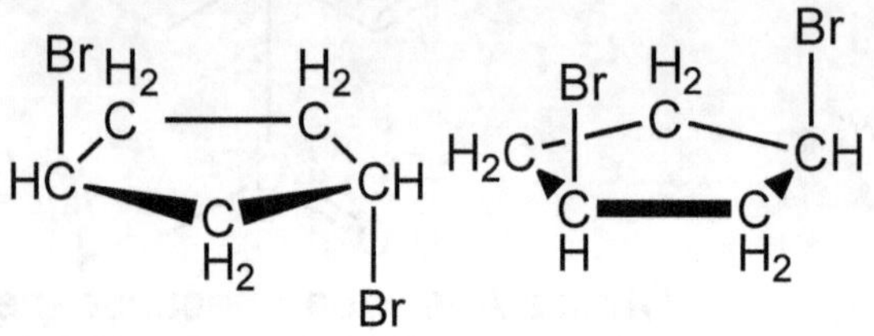 [structure: 1,3-dibromocyclopentane shown in two configurations]

IV. 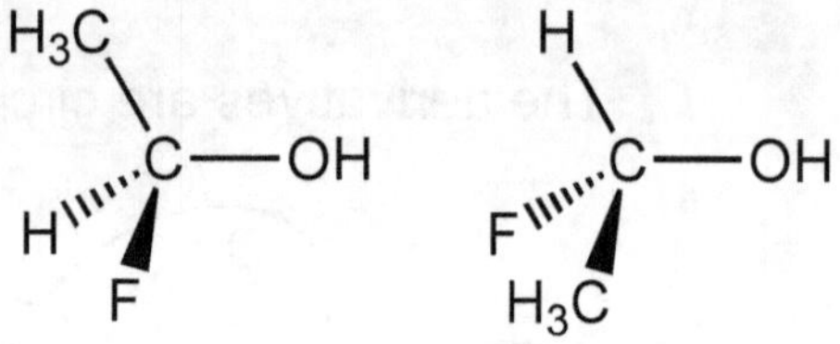 [structure: two 1-fluoroethanol stereochemical drawings with C bonded to H3C, OH, H, F]

A. I and IV
B. II and III
C. I, II, and III
D. I, II, III, and IV

B In pair I, the N—N bond may freely rotate in the molecule because it is not a double bond. The identical molecule is represented twice.

For pair II, pentanal is [structure with O=CH-CH2-CH2-CH2-CH3]

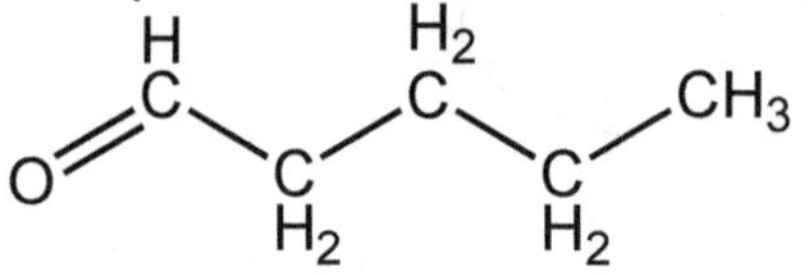

and 2-pentanone is: [structure with H3C-C(=O)-CH2-CH2-CH3]

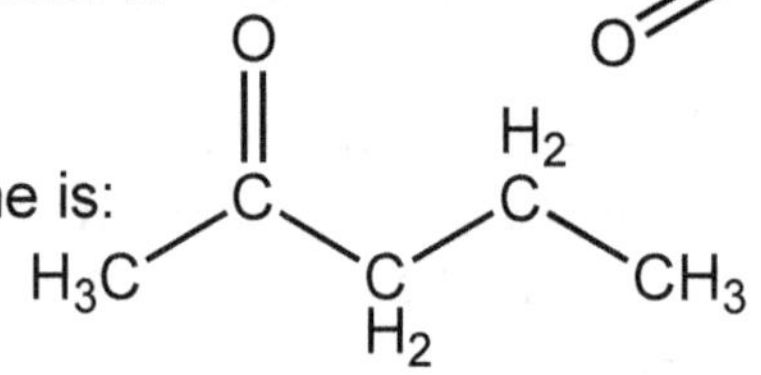

Both molecules are $C_5H_{10}O$, and they are isomers because they have the same formula with a different arrangement of atoms.

In pair III, both molecules are 1,3-dibromocyclopentane, $C_5H_8Br_2$. In the first molecule, the bromines are in a *trans* configuration, and in the second molecule, they are *cis*. The two molecules are also viewed from different perspectives. Unlike pair I, no bond rotation may occur because the intervening atoms are locked into place by the ring, so they are different arrangements and are isomers.

In pair IV (1-fluoroethanol), there is a chiral center, so stereoisomers are possible, but as in pair I, the same molecule is represented twice. Rotating the C-O bond indicates that the two structures are superimposable. This molecule: to the right is a stereoisomer to the molecule represented in IV. The answer is B (pairs II and III).

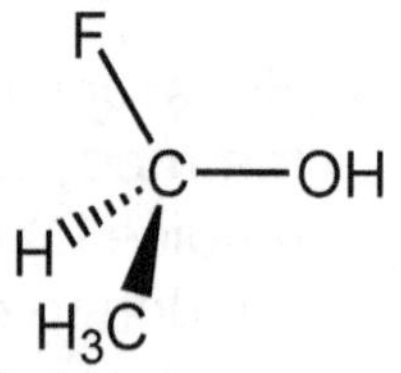

114. Which instrument would be most useful for separating two different proteins from a mixture?

A. UV/Vis spectrophotometer
B. Mass spectrometer
C. Gas chromatograph
D. Liquid chromatograph

D UV/Vis spectrophotometry measures the light at ultraviolet and visible wavelengths that can pass through the mixture, and mass spectrometry determines molecular weights. Both might be used to find the concentration of each protein, but neither is a separation technique. Gas chromatography is used for small molecules in the gas phase. Proteins are too large to exist in the gas phase. Liquid chromatography (answer D) is used to separate large molecules.

115. Classify these biochemicals.

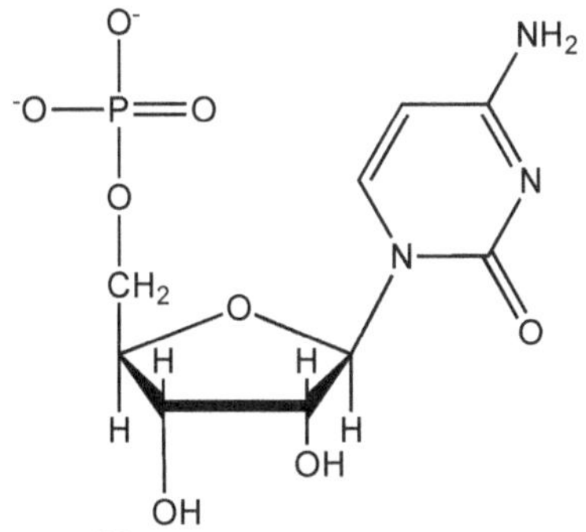

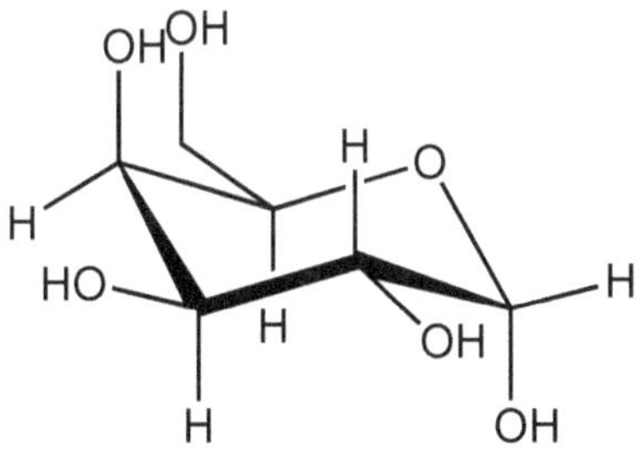

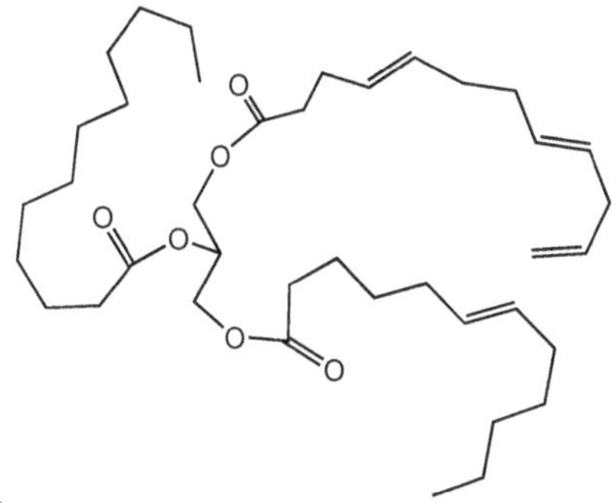

A. I-nucleotide, II-sugar, III-peptide, IV-fat
B. I-disaccharide, II-sugar, III-fatty acid, IV-polypeptide
C. I-disaccharide, II-amino acid, III-fatty acid, IV- polysaccharide
D. I-nucleotide, II-sugar, III-triacylglyceride, and IV-DNA

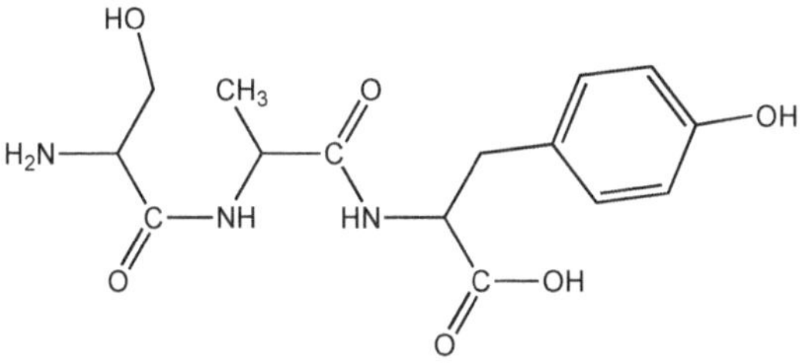

A I is a phosphate (PO_4) linked to a sugar and an amine: a nucleotide. II has the formula $C_nH_{2n}O_n$, indicative of a sugar. III contains three amino acids linked with peptide bonds. It is a tripeptide. IV is a triacylglyceride, a fat molecule.

TEACHER CERTIFICATION EXAM

116. You create a solution of 2.00 µg/ml of a pigment and divide the solution into 12 samples. You give four samples each to three teams of students. They use a spectrophotometer to determine the pigment concentration. Here is their data:

Team	Concentration (µg/ml)			
	sample 1	sample 2	sample 3	sample 4
1	1.98	1.93	1.92	1.88
2	1.70	1.72	1.69	1.70
3	1.78	1.99	2.87	2.20

Which of the following are true?

A. Team 1 has the most precise data
B. Team 3 has the most accurate data in spite of it having low precision
C. The data from team 2 is characteristic of a systematic error
D. The data from team 1 is more characteristic of random error than the data from team 3.

C For choice A, the data from team 2 are closer to the mean for team 2 than the data from team 1 are to its mean. Therefore, team 1's data does not have the most precision.

For choice B, the mean from team 1 is near 1.9 µg/ml (we don't need to calculate exact values). It differs from the actual value by 0.1 µg/ml. The mean from team 2 is near 1.7 µg/ml and is inaccurate by 0.3 µg/ml. The mean from team 3 is not obvious, but it may be calculated as 2.21 µg/ml, differing from the actual value by about 0.2 µg/ml. Team 3's data is less accurate than the data from team 1.

The data from team 2 is clustered close to a central value but this value is wrong. Low accuracy with high precision is indicative of a systematic error. (C is correct).

For choice D, a lack of precision is indicative of random error, and the data from team 1 is more precise than the data from team 3.

117. **Which pair of measurements have an identical meaning?**

   A. 32 micrometers and 0.032 g
   B. 26 nm and 2.60×10^{-8} m
   C. 3.01×10^{-5} m^3 and 30.1 ml
   D. 0.0020 L and 20 cm^3

C For A, the prefix *micro—* indicates 10^{-6}. 32 micrograms is 0.000032 g. For B, the two measurements do not have the same meaning because they differ in the number of significant figures. 26 nm is 2.6×10^{-8} m. The symbol "n" for *nano—* indicates 10^{-9}. For C and D, unit conversions between cubic meters and liters are required.

For C: 3.01×10^{-5} m$^3 \times \dfrac{1000 \text{ L}}{1 \text{ m}^3} \times \dfrac{1000 \text{ ml}}{1 \text{ L}} = 30.1$ ml (C is correct).

For D: $0.0020 \text{ L} \times \dfrac{1 \text{ m}^3}{1000 \text{ L}} \times \dfrac{(100)^3 \text{ cm}^3}{1 \text{ m}^3} = 2.0$ cm^3 (D is incorrect).

118. **Match the instrument with the quantity it measures**

   I. eudiometer
   II. calorimeter
   III. manometer
   IV. hygrometer

   A. I-volume, II-mass, III-radioactivity, IV-humidity
   B. I-volume, II-heat, III-pressure, IV-humidity
   C. I-viscosity, II-mass, III-pressure, IV-surface tension
   D. I-viscosity, II-heat, III-radioactivity, IV-surface tension

B A eudiometer is a straight tube used to measure gas volume by liquid exclusion. A calorimeter is a device used to measure changes in heat. A manometer is a U-shaped tube used to measure pressure. A hygrometer measures humidity (Answer B). Mass is measured with a balance, radioactivity is measured with a Geiger counter or scintillation counter. Viscosity is measured with a viscometer, surface tension is measured by several different techniques.

119. Four nearly identical gems from the same mineral are weighed using different balances. Their masses are:
3.4533 g, 3.459 g, 3.4656 g, 3.464 g.
The four gems are then collected and added to a volumetric cylinder containing 10.00 ml of liquid, and a new volume of 14.97 ml is read. What is the average mass of the four stones and what is the density of the mineral?

A. 3.460 g, and 2.78 g/ml
B. 3.460 g and 2.79 g/ml
C. 3.4605 g and 2.78 g/ml
D. 3.461 g and 2.79 g/ml

B The average mass is the sum of the four readings divided by four:
(3.4533 g + 3.459 g + 3.4656 g + 3.464 g)/4 = 3.460475 g (caculator value)

This value must be rounded off to three significant digits <u>after the decimal point</u> because this is the lowest precision of the added values. The four is an exact number. This means rounding downwards to 3.460 g, eliminating choices C and D. The volume of the collected stones is found from the increase in the level read off the cylinder:
14.97 ml − 10.00 ml = 4.97 ml

The density is found by dividing the sum of the masses by this volume:
$$\frac{3.4533\ g + 3.459\ g + 3.4656\ g + 3.464\ g}{4.97\ ml} = \frac{13.8419\ g}{4.97\ ml} = 2.7850905\ g/ml\ \text{(caculator value)}$$

This value must be rounded off to three <u>total</u> significant digits because this is the lower precision of the numerator and the denominator. The first insignificant digit is a 5. In this case there are additional non-zero digits after the 5, so rounding occurs upwards to 2.79 g/ml (answer B).

120. **Which list includes equipment that would not be used in vacuum filtration.**

   A. Rubber tubing, Florence flask, Büchner funnel
   B. Vacuum pump, Hirsch funnel, rubber stopper with a single hole
   C. Aspirator, filter paper, filter flask
   D. Lab stand, clamp, filter trap

A Florence flasks are round-bottomed and are used for uniform heating. They do not have the hose barb or the thick wall needed to serve as a filter flask during vacuum filtration. Only a designated filter flask should be used during vacuum filtration. Every other piece of equipment could be used in filtration. A spatula is often used to scrape dried product off of filter paper.

121. **Which of the following statements about lab safety is not true?**

   A. Corrosive chemicals should be stored below eye level.
   B. A chemical splash on the eye or skin should be rinsed for 15 minutes in cold water.
   C. MSDS means "Material Safety Data Sheet."
   D. A student should "stop, drop, and roll" if their clothing catches fire in the lab.

D In the lab, the safety shower should be used.

122. **Which of the following lists consists entirely of chemicals that are considered safe enough to be in a high school lab?**

   A. hydrochloric acid, lauric acid, potassium permanganate, calcium hydroxide
   B. ethyl ether, nitric acid, sodium benzoate, methanol
   C. cobalt (II) sulfide, ethylene glycol, benzoyl peroxide, ammonium chloride
   D. picric acid, hydrofluoric acid, cadmium chloride, carbon disulfide.

A Hydrochloric acid (HCl) is a common acid reagent in high school chemistry. Lauric acid is the fatty acid $CH_3(CH_2)_{10}COOH$ also known as dodecanoic acid. Potassium permanganate ($KMnO_4$) is a strong oxidizer. Calcium hydroxide ($Ca(OH)_2$) is a strong base. These chemicals in their pure state are hazardous, but they are considered safe enough to be in high schools. Ethyl ether (Choice B) should not be in high schools because it may form highly explosive organic peroxides over time. Benzoyl peroxide (choice C) at low concentrations in gel form is an acne medication, but the pure compound is highly explosive. Choice D consists entirely of chemicals that are too dangerous for high schools. Picric acid is highly explosive, hydrofluoric acid is very corrosive and very toxic, all cadmium compounds are highly toxic, and carbon disulfide is explosive and toxic.

TEACHER CERTIFICATION EXAM

123. The following procedure was developed to find the specific heat capacity of metals:

1. Place pieces of the metals in an ice-water bath so their initial temperature is 0 °C.
2. Weigh a styrofoam cup.
3. Add water at room temperature to the cup and weigh it again
4. Add a cold metal from the bath to the cup and weigh the cup a third time.
5. Monitor the temperature drop of the water until a final temperature at thermal equilibrium is found.

_____ is also required as additional information in order to obtain heat capacities for the metals. The best control would be to follow the same protocol except to use _____ in step 4 instead of a cold metal.

A. The heat capacity of water / a metal at 100 °C
B. The heat of formation of water / ice from the 0 °C bath
C. The heat of capacity of ice / glass at 0 °C
D. The heat capacity of water / water from the 0 °C bath

D The equation:
$$q = n \times C \times \Delta T$$
is used to determine what additional information is needed. The specific heat, C, of the metals may be found from the heat added, the amount of material, and the temperature change. The amount of metal is found from the difference in weight between steps 3 and 4, and the temperature change is found from the difference between the final temperature and 0 °C. The additional value required is the heat added, q. This may be found from the heat removed from the water if the amount of water, the heat capacity of water, and the temperature change of water are known. The amount of water is found from the difference in weight between step 2 and 3, and the temperature change is found from the difference between the final temperature and room temperature. The only additional information required is the heat capacity of water, eliminating choices B and C. Heat of formation (choice B) is only used for chemical reactions.

A good control simplifies only the one aspect under study without adding anything new. Metal at 100 °C (choice A) would alter the temperature of the experiment and glass (choice C) would add an additional material to the study. Ice (choice B) would require consideration of the heat of fusion. Choice D is an ideal control because the impact of water at 0 °C on room temperature water is simpler than the impact of metals at 0 °C on room temperature water, and nothing new is added.

124. Which statement about the impact of chemistry on society is __not__ true?

   A. Partial hydrogenation creates *trans* fat.
   B. The Haber Process incorporates nitrogen from the air into molecules for agricultural use.
   C. The CO_2 concentration in the atmosphere has decreased in the last ten years.
   D. The concentration of ozone-destroying chemicals in the stratosphere has decreased in the last ten years.

C CO_2 concentrations in the atmospehere continue to increase (answer C), but the concentration of ozone destroying chemicals has fallen (answer D) due to international agreements.

125. Which statement about everyday applications of chemistry is __true__?

   A. Rainwater found near sources of air pollution will most likely be basic.
   B. Batteries run down more quickly at low temperatures because chemical reactions are proceeding more slowly.
   C. Benzyl alcohol is a detergent used in shampoo.
   D. Adding salt decreases the time required for water to boil.

B Souces of air pollution (choice A) will most likely cause acid rain.

Low temperatures decrease reaction rates, and this is also true of electrochemical reactions in batteries. At low temperature, less current is supplied and the effect will be a short life for applications that demand current. (Answer B is correct).

Benzyl alcohol (choice C) has the formula shown to the right. Like detergents, this molecule has a non-polar region (the benzene ring) and a polar region (the hydroxyl group). But, unlike detergents, the non-polar region for benzyl alcohol is small and short. Detergents have long, "tail-like" non-polar regions that can surround oils and grease. Benzyl alcohol is sometimes included in shampoo to prevent itching and bacterial growth.

Adding salt (choice D) increases the boiling point of water, thus increasing the time required for water to boil. It decreases the time required to cook food once boiling occurs.

TEACHER CERTIFICATION EXAM

Sample Constructed-Response Assignment

Directions: Read the information below and complete the given exercise. Explain your reasoning and show your work.

126. What procedure would you use to isolate or purify an organic compound from an aqueous solution containing inorganic contaminants? Clearly describe the apparatus to be used and the steps required to accomplish this.

Sample Constructed-Response Answer

126. What procedure would you use to isolate or purify an organic compound from an aqueous solution containing inorganic contaminants? Clearly describe the apparatus to be used and the steps required to accomplish this.

A solvent extraction is the procedure that would be used to separate different compounds in solution. This technique takes advantage of solubility differences in order to separate an organic product from impurities. For example, water and ether are immiscible solvents and will form two distinct layers, allowing physical separation utilizing laboratory equipment.

Use a separatory funnel with a stopcock and glass stopper, mounted on a ringstand, to perform the extraction. Pour the solution into the separatory funnel via the opening at the top. Then add an organic solvent such as diethyl ether or methylene chloride; the organic solvent should readily dissolve the organic compound to be purified but should not react with it, or be miscible with water. Insert the glass stopper and shake the mixture a few times. In order to vent the funnel of any gas pressure that might build up, hold the funnel upside down with the stem pointing away from people or objects; then slowly open the stopcock to release any pressure and close it again. Repeat the shaking and venting two or three times, allowing time for solute exchange. The layers will eventually separate, and two distinct layers of liquid will be clearly seen. If there is doubt, adding a bit of water to the funnel will indicate which layer is the aqueous layer and which is the organic, because the aqueous layer will increase in size when the water is added. Open the funnel's stopcock carefully to drain the bottom layer into a beaker, then drain the top layer into a second beaker. Save the purified organic layer and discard the aqueous layer, which contains the impurities.

XAMonline, INC. 21 Orient Ave. Melrose, MA 02176
Toll Free number 800-301-4647
TO ORDER Fax 781-662-9268 OR www.XAMonline.com
CERTIFICATION EXAMINATION FOR OKLAHOMA EDUCATORS - CEOE - 2007

PO#   Store/School:

Address 1:

Address 2 (Ship to other):
City, State Zip

Credit card number_____-_____-_____-_____   expiration_____
EMAIL _____
PHONE   FAX

13# ISBN 2007	TITLE	Qty	Retail	Total
978-1-58197-781-3	CEOE OSAT Advanced Mathematics Field 11			
978-1-58197-775-2	CEOE OSAT Art Sample Test Field 02			
978-1-58197-780-6	CEOE OSAT Biological Sciences Field 10			
978-1-58197-776-9	CEOE OSAT Chemistry Field 04			
978-1-58197-778-3	CEOE OSAT Earth Science Field 08			
978-1-58197-794-3	CEOE OSAT Elementary Education Fields 50-51			
978-1-58197-795-0	CEOE OSAT Elementary Education Sample Questions Fields 50-51			
978-1-58197-777-6	CEOE OSAT English Field 07			
978-1-58197-779-0	CEOE OSAT Family and Consumer Sciences Field 09			
978-1-58197-786-8	CEOE OSAT French Sample Test Field 20			
978-1-58197-792-9	CEOE OSAT Library-Media Specialist Field 38			
978-1-58197-787-5	CEOE OSAT Middle Level English Field 24			
978-1-58197-789-9	CEOE OSAT Middle Level Science Field 26			
978-1-58197-790-5	CEOE OSAT Middle Level Social Studies Field 27			
978-1-58197-788-2	CEOE OSAT Middle Level-Intermediate Mathematics Field 25			
978-1-58197-791-2	CEOE OSAT Mild Moderate Disabilities Field 29			
978-1-58197-797-4	CEOE OSAT Physical Education-Health-Safety Field 12			
978-1-58197-783-7	CEOE OSAT Physics Sample Test Field 14			
978-1-58197-793-6	CEOE OSAT Principal Common Core Field 44			
978-1-58197-796-7	CEOE OPTE Oklahoma Professional Teaching Examination Fields 75-76			
978-1-58197-784-4	CEOE OSAT Reading Specialist Field 15			
978-1-58197-785-1	CEOE OSAT Spanish Field 19			
	FOR PRODUCT PRICES GO TO WWW.XAMONLINE.COM		SUBTOTAL	
			Ship	$8.25
			TOTAL	

www.ingramcontent.com/pod-product-compliance
Lightning Source LLC
Chambersburg PA
CBHW080536300426
44111CB00017B/2757